The European Union and Asian Countries

Contemporary European Studies, 16

The European Union and Asian Countries

Georg Wiessala

SHEFFIELD ACADEMIC PRESS
A Continuum imprint
LONDON • NEW YORK

Copyright © 2002 Sheffield Academic Press
A Continuum imprint

Published by Sheffield Academic Press Ltd
The Tower Building, 11 York Road, London SE1 7NX
370 Lexington Avenue, New York NY 10017-6550

www.SheffieldAcademicPress.com
www.continuumbooks.com

British Library Cataloguing-in-Publication Data

A catalogue record for this book is available from the British Library

Typeset by Sheffield Academic Press
Printed on acid-free paper in Great Britain by MPG Books Ltd, Bodmin, Cornwall

ISBN 0-8264-6090-9 (hardback)
     0-8264-6091-7 (paperback)

For Mim

Once on these wharves was Eastern Treasure piled
Ventured from Venice and from Trebizond
And Alicant and Ormuz and beyond,
Far as the Indian coasts and waters isled.
Blond merchants in furred scarlet gravely smiled
In parley or with narrow reckoning conned
The bales, and as they scrutinized their bond,
From ship to shore the swarthy couriers filed.

Now at the bare wharf barges slowly fill.
Rare footsteps echo, as they loiter past.
Yet there is more than stone that is enduring;
And the dulled water seems to colour still
With fancied pennons on a foreign mast
And ghosts of ships that glide to their old mooring.

(Frank Brangwyn [British], 1867–1956: *Geïllustreerde gedichtenbundel* 'Bruges', [Brangwyncollectie, Arentshuis, Brugge, Inv. 02./150.III]).

Contents

Boxes

Series Foreword

The Contemporary European Studies series was launched in 1998 by the University Association for Contemporary European Studies (UACES) the foremost British organization bringing together academics and practitioners interested in the study of Europe. The objective of the series is to provide authoritative texts dealing with a wide range of important issues of interest to both those studying and teaching about European integration and professionals wishing to keep up with current developments.

This latest book in the series critically examines the European Union's increasingly important relationship with key Asian states together with its attempt to construct a coherent strategy towards the continent as a whole. It provides a valuable addition to the literature on the EU as a global actor by providing a case study on its relations with a group of states that have not so far attracted as much attention from EU scholars as their importance in the world today would seem to merit. It also complements the very popular earlier books by Fraser Cameron on the Common Foreign and Security Policy and Terrence Guay on the United States and the European Union and the recent title on the European Union and the Middle East by Søren Dosenrode and Anders Stubkjær.

I am very grateful to Stephen George who undertook editorial responsibility for the book and provided very valuable guidance on its final production.

Jackie Gower
Series Editor

Foreword

We must know each other to improve each other. To appreciate our differences, to adopt what seems appropriate after having adapted it to our needs and transformed it with our culture. It is a conquest of our times, and a sign of tolerance, to have realized that ideal, perfect, models to which to tend do not exist. To force foreign institutions in a reality that has different historical and cultural roots is seldom successful and it often leads to disaster. Our goal is not, and must not be, that of eliminating the differences that to-day, by creating barriers to our mutual understanding, seem to divide us. Our aim cannot be that of increasingly becoming alike, in a world made every day duller and duller by uniformity. The human adventure has more probabilities of perpetuating itself when its roots are deeply and firmly set in variety. Cultures become more vital when they cherish their strong points and when they do so in comparison with other civilisations. In this respect the expansion of contacts between Europe and Asia may lead to a better mutual understanding'. (Susanna Agnelli, former Italian Minister of Foreign Affairs, at the Asia-Europe Forum on Culture, Values and Technology, Venice, 18–19 January 1996).

Maybe it was the Latin phrase *ex oriente lux* that brought Europeans to Asia. Perhaps it was the civilized Occident that lured many Asians to abandon their ways of thinking and ways of life. These reasons (explanations) carried with them more questions than answers. What light shines from the East and what kinds of civilizations do we want to talk about?

As people in various parts of the world are drawn closer by the less than popular process of globalization, one still cannot stop wondering who is being drawn to whom. And, does it really matter? Perhaps it is even more puzzling to note that, in the not too remote past, people of different cultures and beliefs lived together in harmony through the use of a system, where other humans were respected for their cultural differences—not being forced to live under the same rules. Even though differences were annoying to some, they were never judged.

Inferior rules and culture were non-existent for people of the past. They were just different but never repugnant. Hostility was rampant among tribes but its cause was clear. Competing for resources and territory was natural. Europeans and Asians alike shared a common past experience as human beings. Asians had their conflicts, as did Europeans. Often one took over the other and vice versa.

The image of a 'mysterious' Orient was based on past prevarication of those who did not know Asia well. We can no longer allow ignorance to be the excuse as our world continues to shrink every day.

Apirat Petchsiri, JSD
Director of Interdisciplinary
Department of European Studies
Graduate School of Chulalongkorn University
Bangkok

Acknowledgments

Even a piece of work of this modest length does not come about in the 'ivory tower' of academic seclusion. I have incurred a number of debts in researching this book, in both East and West. My particular thanks go to Professors Apirat Petchsiri, Charit Tingsabadh and Pornsan Watanangura in the International European Studies Centre at Chulalongkorn University in Bangkok, Thailand, for their patience and for providing important input during my research leave there in 2000 and 2001. I would also like to thank Professor Suthiphand Chirativat and the very helpful MAEUS office staff, as well as their colleagues in Chulalongkorn University Library.

I am furthermore indebted to Ms Sirinuj Sutirasakul, Ms Savitree Powviriya and Mr Steve Needham from the Delegation of the European Commission to Cambodia, Laos, Malaysia, Burma/Myanmar and Thailand in Bangkok, who have provided many valuable contributions on EU–Asia relations and access to their files in the excellent EU Information Centre in Kian Gwan House II.

Thanks also to Dr Philomena Murray of the Contemporary European Studies Association of Australia, and to Martin Holland of the European Union Studies Association of New Zealand, for the valuable input on EU–Australia and EU–New Zealand relations. On the European side, my special thanks go to Paul Lim at the European Institute for Asian Affairs in Brussels. In the University of Central Lancashire in Preston, I would like to extend my gratitude to Dr Christopher Williams, Dr Peter Anderson, Paul Gentle and Steve Lowe.

Last, but certainly not least, heartfelt thanks also to my wife Maureen and to Becca and James for supporting me in innumerable ways, throughout the writing of this book.

Most of what may be found helpful and constructive in this book is due to the valuable influence and help of these people, whereas all omissions, flaws and mistakes are solely my own responsibility.

Georg Wiessala

Abbreviations

ACP	African, Caribbean and Pacific countries
ADB	Asian Development Bank
AEBF	Asia-Europe Business Forum
AEETC	Asia Europe Environmental Technology Centre
AEITTP	Asia Europe Information Technology and Telecommunications Programme
AEMM	ASEAN-European Union Ministerial Meeting
AETW	Asia Europe Trade Week
AFTA	ASEAN Free Trade Area
ALA	Asian and Latin American countries
AOCG	Asia-Oceania Council Group
APEC	Asia-Pacific Economic Cooperation
ARF	ASEAN Regional Forum
ASEAN	Association of South-East Asian Nations
ASEAN + 3	ASEAN plus China, Japan and Korea
ASEAN-EU-SOM	ASEAN-European Union Senior Officials' Meeting
ASEAN-EU-JCC	ASEAN-European Union Joint-Cooperation Committee
ASEF	Asia Europe Foundation
ASEM	Asia-Europe Meeting
ASEP	Asia-Europe Parliamentary Partnership
CAEC	Council for Asia-Europe Cooperation
CAP	Common Agricultural Policy
CEE	Central and Eastern Europe
CEPT	Common Effective Preferential Tariff (*ASEAN*)
CFSP	Common Foreign and Security Policy
CIS	Commonwealth of Independent States
COASI	Working Party for Asia and the Pacific (Council of Ministers)
CSCAP	Council for Security Cooperation in the Asia-Pacific
CTBT	Comprehensive Test-Ban Treaty
DIPECHO	European Community Humanitarian Office: Disaster Prevention Programme
DPRK	Democratic People's Republic of Korea
EAEC	East Asian Economic Caucus
EC	European Community

ECHO	European Community Humanitarian Office
EEC	European Economic Community
EIB	European Investment Bank
EP	European Parliament
EPG	Eminent Persons' Group (ASEAN – AEMM)
EU	European Union
EURATOM	European Atomic Energy Community
FDI	foreign direct investment
G7	group of seven most industrialized nations—USA, Japan, Germany, France, UK, Italy and Canada
G8	the G7 plus Russia
GATT	General Agreement on Tariffs and Trade
GNP	gross national product
GSP	generalized system of preferences
HSAR	Hong Kong Special Administrative Region
IGC	intergovernmental conference
IFOR	Implementation Force (former Yugoslavia)
ILO	International Labour Organization
IMF	International Monetary Fund
IPAP	Investment Promotion Action Plan
KEDO	Korean Energy Development Organization
KMT	Kuomintang (China / Taiwan)
LDC, LLDC	least developed countries
MFN	most favoured nation (Status)
MSAR	Macao Special Administrative Region
NAFTA	North American Free Trade Area
NGO	non-governmental organization
NIC	newly industrializing country
NLD	National League for Democracy (Burma)
ODA	Official Development Assistance
OECD	Organization for Economic Cooperation and Development
OHCHR	Office of the High Commissioner for Human Rights (Mary Robinson)
OSCE	Organization for Security and Cooperation in Europe
PAP	People's Action Party (Singapore)
PDR	People's Democratic Republic (Laos)
PfP	Partnership for Peace
PRASAC	Programme de Réhabilitation et d'Appui au Secteur Agricole du Cambodge (Rehabilitation and Support Programme for Cambodia's Agricultural Sector)
R&D	research and development
ROK	Republic of Korea
SAARC	South Asian Association for Regional Co-operation
SAR	Special Administrative Region (Hong Kong and Macao)
SEA	Single European Act

SFOR	Stability Force (former Yugoslavia)
SLORC	State Law and Order Restoration Council (Burma)
SME	small and medium enterprise
SOM	Senior Officials' Meeting
SPDC	State Peace and Development Council (Burma)
TEU	Treaty of European Union
TFAP	Trade Facilitation Action Plan
UDHR	Universal Declaration of Human Rights (1948)
UMESP	University of Malaya European Studies Programme
UMNO	United Malays National Organization
UN	United Nations
UNCTAD	United Nations Conference on Trade and Development
WB	World Bank
WEU	Western European Union
WTO	World Trade Organization

1 |

Introduction: Why Asia Matters

> It has sometimes been suggested that even the term 'Asia' may be a false
> concept, bestowing an artificial homogeneity on the vastly diverse econ-
> omic and political geography of the region. But labels matter less than
> the reality, which they represent, and it is the reality of Asia which is of
> essential importance for the EU (Commission 2001c: point 2.1).

This chapter seeks to set the scene for the investigation in the other
parts of the book. It is concerned with the questions of how 'Asia' can
be defined and understood, and sheds some light on origins and development of the contacts between Asia and Europe. An overview of how
Asia has featured in the construction of Europe, and in the imagination
of Europeans over time, introduces the subjects of cultural awareness,
perceptions, values and prejudice, which will reappear elsewhere in the
book. This is followed by a look at the importance of Asia for contemporary Europe and the European Union (EU).

The Background of Europe–Asia Relations

Something about Europe is undeniably Asian: Europe, the continent
Paul Valéry famously called *ce petit cap d'Asie* ('this small promontory
of the Asian landmass'), owes its very name to a princess from Asia
Minor. For de Bartillat and Roba (2000: 7), Europe represents 'a statu-
esque continent with her matrix in the Orient', 'an essential myth,
which came from Asia nearly thirty centuries ago'. But Europe is also a
continent, as well as an idea. Among these three concepts, however, the
myth forms the most enduring aspect. Like so much else that is constituent of European culture, it originated in Asia: Homer or Ovid knew
Europa as the daughter of King Agenor of Phoenicia. Zeus, in the shape
of a bull, abducted her to Crete, the crossroads of Europe, Africa and
Asia. She had three sons, among them Minos, the legendary king of
Crete. As to early historical insight on Asia and Europe, Herodotus
(c. 490–420 BCE—born only one year after Gautama Buddha's tradi-

tional dying date) stated in his *Histories* (Bk IV: 36, 42) that: 'Asia, the daughter of Prometheus, may have been the origin of that continent's name', but, as for Europe, 'nobody knows where it got its name from, or who gave it, unless we are to say that it came from Europa, the Tyrian woman, and before that was nameless like the rest. This, however, is unlikely, for Europa was an Asian woman and never visited the country which we now call Europe'.

A look at the long history of Asia–Europe contacts provides ample illustration of the way it has been informed by—and often overlaid with—myth and prejudice, leaving open room for mutual blaming and misunderstanding. There are many well-known examples of this: according to St Jerome (346–420), Asia, Africa and Europe were divided among Shem, Ham and Japheth, Noah's sons (Gen. 9), and it was Shem whose progeny populated Asia (Gen. 10). Early maps and early connotations of a Europe–Asia dichotomy can be traced to these sources.

De Bartillat and Roba (2000: 40) have shown how later observers took the bigger, bolder, step towards a wholesale, 'tripartite', organization of humanity into three 'castes': freemen, sons of Shem; soldiers, sons of Japheth; and slaves, sons of Ham. Many of these myths were spiritual in nature; mainly Christian 'wishful thinking', they would later provide convenient justifications for missionary and colonial activity. St Isidore of Seville (d. 636) surmised that the Apostle Thomas had died in India, and had left behind a large number of 'St Thomas Christians', and, furthermore, that the descendants of Japheth would possess all of Europe.

On account of a famous, but forged, letter it was widely believed throughout the Middle Ages that a Christian potentate, Prester John, presided over a large empire in Asia (Corn 1999: xxiii; Larner 2001: 9; Milton 2001: 254-55). The 'three wise men' represented Europe, Africa and Asia, the three contributories to all humanity, as it was then known (Larner 2001: 9). Later, in *The City of God* by St Augustine (354–430), the 'East' occupies one-half of the world, Europe and Africa the other (Bk XVI, chs. 2, 3, 8–11). In the context of biblical Scripture, 'Asia' appears as one of the 'four corners of the world' (Rev. 20.7), the source of spices (Ezek. 27.22), a Roman province or the site of the 'seven churches of Asia' of St Paul's mission (1 Cor. 16.19; Rev. 1.4; Acts 19.22). It figures both as the location of the Garden of Eden (Gen. 2.8) and as the site of the final, cataclysmic battle of Armageddon at the end of time (Rev. 9.13-16; 16.12-16).

Asia as Europe's 'Other': Scope and Framework of this Book

Asia is an immense and heterogeneous political, economic and geographical space (see Box 1.1). Its sheer size and diversity constitute a set of circumstances that makes it difficult to devise any one policy prescription—or description—for the entire region. Historical and colonial legacies add to this dilemma. Pertierra (1998: 118) speculates on the use of the term 'Asia':

> its descriptive use is by now well established and as a consequence we must accept this term, even if we insist that its unity as a region is highly questionable. Moreover, we should note that much of Asia's putative coherence is a result of contrasting it with Europe [Boxes 1.1 and 1.2]. Asia is Europe's other, and just as this contrast obscures Asian differences, it simultaneously affirms Europe's unity.

It is in the tradition of this line of thought that this book deals with the subject of 'Asia'–Europe relations. 'Asia', in the terms of this book, consists of four geographical entities comprising more than 20 countries: (1) *South Asia* includes Afghanistan, Bangladesh, Bhutan, India, the Maldives, Nepal, Pakistan and Sri Lanka; (2) *South-East Asia* comprises Brunei-Darussalam, Cambodia, East Timor, Indonesia, The Lao People's Democratic Republic (PDR), Malaysia, Myanmar (Burma), The Philippines, Singapore, Thailand and Vietnam; (3) the *East Asian* region is defined by China, Hong Kong, Macao, the Democratic People's Republic of Korea (DPRK, North Korea), the Republic of Korea (ROK, South Korea) Tibet and Taiwan; (4) *Japan*, on account of its special relationship with the EU, will be counted separately (Commission 1995e: 2 and 4). Overlap is, of course, unavoidable, and it is useful to bear in mind some of the EU's own working definitions of 'Asia' (e.g. Commission 1997g: 6). What the United Nations (UN) refers to as 'Western Asia', for instance, is often referred to as the Middle East, and is dealt with by the EU in its Mediterranean policy and through its involvement in the Middle East Peace Process, while South/Central Asia, Mongolia and a number of former Soviet Union countries are dealt with, by the EU, within the policy framework for the Commonwealth of Independent States (CIS).[1]

---

1.   See *OJ* L41 (18 February 1993: 45-49). For some aspects of EU–Mongolia relations see http://europa.eu.int/comm/external_relations/Mongolia/intro/index.htm; *Central Asia and the EU*, COM (95) 206.

Box 1.1: A Profile of Asia

Population:	3.3 billion (56 per cent of world total)
GNP:	$7440 billion (26 per cent of world total)
CO_2 emissions:	7.4 billion tonnes (33 per cent of world total)
Per capita incomes:	$260 (Cambodia), $450 (India), $780 (China), $3400 (Malaysia), $8490 (Republic of Korea), $32,230 (Japan)
Number of people living on less than $1 per day:	800 million (66 per cent of the world's poor)
Asia's share of world trade:	25.3 per cent (developed Asia: 14.2 per cent; developing Asia: 11.1 per cent)
Asia's share of EC exports and imports:	21.1 per cent and 31.2 per cent (developed Asia: 10.6 per cent and 13.0 per cent; developing Asia: 10.5 per cent and 18.2 per cent)
EU exports to Asia as percentage of EU GNP:	2.3 per cent

Source: Commission 2001c.

Box 1.2: A Profile of the EU

EU 15

Population:	375 million (6 per cent of world total)
GNP:	$8213 billion (28 per cent of world total)
CO_2 emissions:	3.1 billion tonnes (14 per cent of world total)

Candidate countries

Population:	168 million
GNP:	$556 billion
CO_2 emissions:	1.0 billion tonnes

EU + candidate countries

Population:	544 million (9 per cent of world total)
GNP:	$8769 billion (30 per cent of world total)
CO_2 emissions:	4.1 billion tonnes (18 per cent of world total)
Per capita incomes:	$21,877 (EU15); $3306 (candidate countries)
EU 15 share of world trade:	23.3 per cent (EU internal trade); 14.4 per cent (EU external trade); 37.7 per cent (EU total trade)
EU trade deficit with Asia:	€13.3 billion (1996), €121.5 billion (2000)

Source: Commission 2001c.

On naming conventions, I have preferred, throughout the book, to call the Democratic People's Republic of Korea (DPRK) North Korea and the Republic of Korea (ROK) South Korea. Moreover, although the term Union of Myanmar—the new, post-1989 name for Burma—represents a linguistically and culturally accurate reference to the country's cultural history, matters of modern-day politics and propaganda are more complex. I have therefore preferred the name Burma over Myanmar. For similar reasons, Xizang, throughout this book, appears as Tibet.

A number of boxes have been inserted in the text. This serves two purposes: first, to provide further explanations for a concept, an event or an institution referred to in the main text, which, although not central to its understanding, serve nevertheless to provide background information and enhance its meaning, and, secondly, to present short summaries of the development of relations, EU-funded projects, initiatives, problems or activities relating to an Asian country, region or political body.

The Rationale for Europe–Asia Dialogue

> We must respect each other as we want respect for ourselves, because we are members of the same humanity and of the same society of nations. I was glad to state that such is the prevailing conception of mutual rights and duties amongst the ruling powers of the states which I visited (Thai King Chulalongkorn, on his return from a voyage to Europe in 1897).

On, perhaps, the most meaningful level, Asia matters to Europe because dealing with 'abroad', be it 'far' or 'near', will help to overcome European over-preoccupation with 'matters closer to home'. While this has, no doubt, been achieved in part, through the European Community (EC) and EU and their expanding network of external relations, there appears to be little room for complacency, as the following extract from a recent chapter on 'Asia and the EU' may help to demonstrate:

> I believe that, partly because of the strength it derives from our civilization, Europe can and must be a credible partner and mediator *in these new worlds, which have finally returned to history*. Over the centuries, we have contended with many new realities that appeared from beyond our seas, and we have consistently forged new relationships with peoples and countries who differed from ourselves. The tradition that we have inherited has dominated history for this reason—*this ability to lead and to set an example to other peoples and races*. Without the profound

values of tolerance and respect for human rights, *which found their
highest expression precisely in France, the world would be less civilized*
and Europe would be the poorer and less able to meet the demands of the
future (Prodi 2000: 34; emphasis added).

The disturbing aspect of statements like this one is, arguably, not just
the bluntness of its euro-centredness, but the way in which the familiar,
everyday parlance of European politics is mixed with, and clothed in,
historical myopia, ambiguous stereotyping and condescension. The
more credible attempts to approach the Asian region and its significance for the EU are those which best combine an insight into forces of
global interdependence with a realization of Asia's heterogeneity, its
reliance on long-standing traditions beneath a modern surface of con-
tinuous change, as well as of the misrepresentations to which it
continues to be subjected. These issues count because the EU–Asia
relationship has moved on from being a 'fledgling' or 'emerging' one
(Wiessala 1999: 96). The 'widening' and 'deepening' of the EU's Asia
relations over the last decade has meant that the dialogue now comprises aspects of politics, economy, population, security, culture and
'image'.

The political rationale for Europe–Asia relations derives from the
many contemporary challenges straddling the two continents: immigration, poverty, environmental degradation, terrorism, drugs, nuclear
proliferation, internecine strife, or the situation in Burma, to name just
a few. On the other hand, there are undeniable regional achievements,
such as a limited *rapprochement* between North and South Korea, talks
between the Burmese junta and opposition leader Aung San Suu Kyi, or
the consolidation of the status of East Timor. These developments call
for enhanced promotion of interests between Europe and Asia. Seeking
a theoretical base for these interests, the Council for Asia–Europe
Cooperation (CAEC) has termed this process 'advocacy' and 'diversification' of European foreign policy interests (CAEC 1997: 1, 8, 34-
35). The Commission Delegation to Japan found an additional rationale: 'Through common interest, through the need for cooperation and
through shared responsibility towards global concerns a new basis for a
closer relationship between the EU and Asia has been created' (*Rapid
Database*, SPEECH 02/1999: 1-2).

The sheer heterogeneity of Asia itself is a second reason for a political dimension to the EU–Asia relationship (CAEC 1997). Asia possesses all the diversity suggested by its size, from ultra-modern Singapore

to poverty-ridden areas on the Indian subcontinent or elsewhere. A staggering two billion Asians still live on US$2 a day or less. With regard to political organization, Asian societies can be grouped into 'constrained' democracies, democratizing societies and authoritarian regimes of varying persuasions. Asia's diversity ranges from Indonesia, the world's largest Islamic state, to Vietnam and Laos, remaining strongholds of communist ideology. It includes Burma, ruled by a military dictatorship, the affluent sultanate of Brunei, and Thailand and the Philippines, which are, relatively speaking, the longest established, 'Western-style' democracies in the region. The region contains some of the world's oldest nations and East Timor, one of its youngest. By contrast, political systems in Europe seem much more homogeneous in their organization and democratic ambitions. This gives rise to a number of issues relevant to Asia–Europe cooperation, like human rights and governance, civil-military relations and institutional capacity building.

Furthermore, hypotheses of a 'triangle of relationships' (Phatharodom 1998: 59; Hänggi 1999: 56-80), a 'multipolar' or 'triadic' world view, or a 'missing-link' theory is frequently offered as a foundation for Asia–Europe relations: while Europe is linked to the USA through a network of relations, and recently the 'transatlantic dialogue' and while the USA is connected to East Asia in the context of Asia-Pacific Economic Cooperation (APEC) and other Pacific Rim arrangements, Asia–Europe cooperation, according to this theory, constitutes the hitherto underdeveloped, 'anomalous' link' (Pou-Serradell 1996: 187). G. Wang's observation (2001: 17) points to the practical relevance of the theoretical construct:

> although many Asians have still not forgotten the years when Europe was dominant, the depredations that their countries had experienced are now largely irrelevant. Of greater concern is whether, in the context of the economic and technological dynamism of the United States, younger Asians think of Europe at all.

Perhaps mindful of the implications these phenomena have for the European–Asian dialogue, the CAEC concludes: 'The surprising thing is that a dialogue did not exist before' (CAEC 1997: 9). However, all 'triangular' models and related assumptions need to be approached cautiously, since they suggest a deliberate displacement of foreign policy choices of the EU, which is often difficult to prove and may ignore a tradition of trade and cultural contacts between Asia and

Europe that goes back centuries. As External Relations Commissioner Chris Patten explained: 'Europe does not seek to supplant the US in Japan's, or in Asia's affections. We have our own role in Asia' (*Rapid Database*, SPEECH/00/276). Furthermore, Dent (1999: 103) has pointed out that the thinking along lines of triadic competition has largely been rendered obsolete by processes of globalization.

For most, the economic aspect of the EU–Asia dialogue goes hand in hand with the political one. The economic rationale for EU–Asia relations includes trade and investment, 'presence and profile', market access and membership of the World Trade Organization (WTO), industrial cooperation and infrastructure links. In a 2001 report, the European Parliament's Foreign Affairs Committee summarized weight and impact of economics in the EU–Asia dialogue: 'in the past unbalanced economic relations between EU Member countries and Asian countries have often caused deep social repercussions and hindered a long term development and a genuine partnership' (European Parliament 2001: point B). The economics of recent EU–Asia contacts represents a story of temporarily dented confidence and enhanced interdependence. Preceding the financial downturn across Asia in 1997–98 (called 'Asian flu'), the International Monetary Fund (IMF) found that Asian gross national product (GNP) had grown on average by 44 per cent between 1990 and 1995 and the World Bank estimated half the economic growth by the year 2000 would originate from East and South-East Asia. Even after the currency devaluations at the core of 'Asian flu' in 1997–98, the 'globalized' path to growth which Asian nations followed has not been discredited. It seems that the widely predicted Asian 'bounce-back by the turn of the century' (Chirativat *et al.* 1999: 25; Brittan 1999: 498) has happened. The traditional economic dynamism which once gave rise to the description of some Asian countries as 'Tigers' or 'Tiger Cubs', has not altogether abated; the 'Tiger' economies of Hong Kong, Singapore, South Korea and other Asian countries appear just to have 'changed their stripes' (*The Economist*, 12 February 2000). And many informed forecasts for Asia paint a partly or wholly optimistic picture. Chris Patten, for instance, notes: 'Even while they sharpened their pens to write Asia's economic obituary, it was clear that the fundamentals still held good' (*Rapid Database*, SPEECH/00/278).

Asia and the EU also matter to one another in terms of population, wealth, development, ethnicity, stability and migration. The numbers speak for themselves: Asia holds around 56 per cent of all the people on the planet—and 66 per cent of the world's poor—and accounts for 25 per cent of global production. Dimensions like these impinge on the global distribution of wealth and resources and on the equilibrium of power and security.

With regard to security, in particular, Asia and Europe continue to be more relevant to each other than ever before. The Western European Union's 1992 Petersberg Declaration has been proposed as a model for conflict resolution in Asia, and a recent Commission document (Commission 2000b: 12) pointed out that 'The fringes of the European Continent have their own flashpoints which are of interest to Asia'. Apart from the fact that UN personnel in East Timor also included European soldiers, the strategic presence of EU member states in the region may be small, but NATO's 1994 Partnership for Peace (PfP) initiative now stretches all the way to the Chinese border. Contemporary tensions involving India and Pakistan, the situation in the South China Seas and the Taiwan Straits constitute recurring security flashpoints of pressing concern for both the EU and Asia. In addition to this, there are many 'non-traditional' security issues, such as terrorism, the environment, AIDS, drug-trafficking, peace-making and peacekeeping. Funabashi (1993: 111) has asserted that Asian nations 'have a strong tendency to think of security not simply in military terms but as a synthesis of military, economic, technological and social strengths'. And Bridges (1999: 153-54) adds that 'Europeans have tended to underestimate the linkages between security issues in Europe and Asia, feeling that out of sight means out of mind'. Ravenhill points to the level of around 20 per cent of aggregate arms sales of European countries to Asia and poignantly observes 'Indeed the principal peace dividend seems to be flowing to shareholders in the arms industry' (1998: 12-13). Officially, EU foreign policy representative Javier Solana has been at pains to open security talks with Asia, which included his direct involvement in hostage crises (EIAS 2000: 13-14), nuclear issues, the Comprehensive Test Ban Treaty (CTBT), the Non-Proliferation Treaty (NPT) and security dialogue with the ASEAN Regional Forum (ARF).

Perceptions and Stereotypes in the Europe–Asia Dialogue

Apart from politics, economics and security, a 1994 European Commission-led conference on 'A European Economic Strategy towards Asia' emphasized another, vital point:

The EU lacks a clear profile in Asia. Its low profile leads to misunderstandings and confusion. As a result, negative perceptions take root and
go unchallenged—there are many people in Asia who see Europeans as
inward-looking, disunited, protectionist, or simply not interested in Asia
… European perceptions of Asia must catch up with the reality of
modern Asia as an equal economic and trading partner. Asia is an
opportunity, not a threat (Commission 1994b: 4).

It is impossible to underestimate the significance of these issues of
'representation', 'image' or 'stereotyping' in the Europe–Asia relationship. They have to do with laying to rest many painful historical
memories of humiliation and colonialism (Mason 2000: 1) and a
considerable legacy of mutual (mis-)perceptions (Box 1.3). 'Historical
association between Asia and Europe has not, however, removed
cultural barriers and misunderstandings', the Commission stated as
early as 1995 (Commission 1995e: 8). When today, more often than
not, the 'East' is seen as a world of 'sweatshops', competing unfairly,
especially through dumping and wiping out jobs in Europe, and when,
conversely, European integration is looked at, by Asians, as, at best, an
ambivalent and unclear endeavour,[2] then this points to a history of
Euro–Asian perceptions and projections, which can only be hinted at
here (Box 1.3).

   If one can manage to look past this legacy of stereotypes, a second
concern comes to the surface and forms a picture that closes the circle
and establishes a strong continuity with the spice trade or the silk roads
of earlier ages. This composite picture is about the linkages between
economic developments and their imprints in human minds. It is no
coincidence that the term 'values' once denoted an economic concept,
before it came to encompass moral sentiments or claims. Neither is it
accidental that the European Community, in most official publications
on its Asia policy, will not do without mentioning this past or using the
evocative, 'exotic', historical terminology to establish a link with the
present. In the Europe–Asia context of the 'now', much like the 'then',

---

2.   Vitit Muntharbhorn (1998: 8) refers to research involving the BBC and
entitled *The Image of Europe and the EU in South and East Asia,* which resulted in
some sobering findings: (1) 'Europe' is rarely seen as an entity, except in the
geographical sense; (2) not many Asian leaders appear to know about the EU, its
role or activities in Asia; (3) the top of the 'mind image' of the EU is that of a trade
bloc; and (4) many Asian decision-makers are unaware of the existence of an EU
delegation to their country.

it is still predominantly economic circumstances, developments and conditions that introduce, shape, support and reconfirm West–East perceptions. The 'Asian values' debate of the 1990s and the Asian financial crisis, the lively discourse about human rights in Asia in our day (see, for instance, Christie and Roy 2001), the terminology of 'the Asian century', of 'Asian flu', 'Asian Tigers', 'Tiger Cubs' or 'Asian threat', stimulate the imagination and form evidence of strong bonds between the market place and the perception of the people who are interacting and communicating in it. When underlying economic dynamics change, so do attitudes among the interlocutors in the economic arena.

Box 1.3: Asia in the European Mind

The complex, and often tragic, history of European perceptions of Asia throughout the centuries continues to form a historical ballast, which is hard to remove from the present. For the last 1500 years, concepts of 'Asia', 'the Orient' or 'the East' have frequently been no less than figments of the European imagination, freely mixing history with fantasy and legend, the factual with the fictional. More often that not, 'Asia', as refracted in the European mind, was a land of the 'exotic' (Spence 1998: 157) of charm as well as of cruelty. There had been trade in silk and spices between the Roman Empire and India and St Augustine had reported on the introduction of the 'luxuries of Asia' into Rome (*City of God*, Bk III, chs. 21, 22). Moreover, preceding the sixteenth century, Asia and Europe had been equal in their cultural achievements, a fact often ignored even in today's schoolbooks (Mason 2000: 5).

Notwithstanding this, European projections and mental maps regarding Asia were fed by theological tradition, classical memories and popular imagination (Larner 2001: 8). The geographical and intellectual frontiers of Asia were frequently of a 'mythical' nature (Pagden 2001: 9). The separation of the 'myth' from the 'reality' of Asia attempted first by Alexander III of Macedonia ('the Great', reigned 336–323 BCE), continued by the Polo brothers, Sir John Mandeville, and particularly, the European seafarers of the sixteenth century and through the shifting monopolies of the spice trade (Corn 1999: xxi, xxii), contributed to the 'European Dawn of Asia', an unprecedented increase in European knowledge about Asia from 1500 to 1800, mainly through the three channels of trade, missionary activity and the spread of printed books.

But this also cemented prejudicial views of European superiority and the old Aristotelean antagonism between the 'rule of law' in the West and 'despotism' in the East (Wilson and van der Dussen, 1993: 17, 69; Hay, 1968: 5). Echoes of this thinking would later equate 'civilization' with 'Europe'; arguably, they reverberate still in today's human rights debates between European and Asian countries. According to Osborne (2000: 43), what the European East India companies primarily sought in Asia was national prestige, or 'souls, trade and power'. These sentiments are best encapsulated in the Latin phrase *Ex Oriente lux, Ex Occidente lex* ('From the East comes the light, from the West comes the Law'; Coogan 2001: ix).

The spacial and mental detachment of Europe from Asia, its 'cultural myopia' (Vande Walle, 1998: 166) and anxieties about Islam, helped to colour European perceptions of Asia through the Middle Ages and the Renaissance, although objects and ideas of Asian provenance entered Europe in unprecedented numbers and helped to alter balances of power and cultural awareness. Ironically, it was the borrowing of the more obvious of the Asian 'novelties' by Europe—gunpowder, the compass, moveable-type printing or matches—which ultimately contributed to the pre-eminence Europe developed over the achievements of the Greek or Roman civilizations. These processes, however, the European collections of 'Asiana' and the publication of Asian travel accounts, eventually helped to convey to Europe a much enhanced sense of Asia as a 'real place, inhabited by civilized peoples' (Lach 1994: Vol. I, Bk 1, xvii, 86, 91).

This explosion of knowledge about Asia, however, turned into a double-edged sword during the period of colonialism, when the Europe–Asia relationship was unambiguously constructed on sentiments of superiority and increasingly coloured by euro-centrism. Scholars like Edward W. Said, especially in his 1978 work *Orientalism*, would later investigate these concepts and focus much attention on the figure of the Western 'Orientalist', a figure who 'seeks consciously or unconsciously to strip his subject of power, even of his own identity, by casting him in the rôle of "the Other", and as one who by "exoticizing" what he examines serves to represent it as more feeble, contemptible, and so ripe for domination or conquest' (Larner 2001: 97).

Taking these observations as a starting point, there is reason to believe that at the beginning of the twenty-first century, Europe's attitudes towards Asia are again on the move. One of the reasons for this may be globalization. But there is a more tangible point: both politicians and historians point to a remarkable contemporary fault-line, a discrepancy regarding the Asia–Europe relationship. Chris Patten, the former Governor of Hong Kong and subsequently External Relations Commissioner of the EU, has identified this with unfailing precision:

> In the early decades of the 19th Century … Asia still accounted for about 58 per cent of the world's GDP. By 1920, this figure had been more than halved. Over the following 20 years, Asia's share fell further, to 19 per cent, though Asia was home to 60 per cent of the world's population. Recent growth has now (1992 figures) almost doubled that figure, to 37 per cent. The Asian Development Bank believes that, on what is

described as 'plausible assumptions' (which, I hope, are indeed still 'plausible'), Asia could get back to slightly less than its early-nineteenth-century share of the world's wealth by 2025. It will have been a long journey back to 'Go' (Patten 1998: 130).

This, in connection with the implications of the European Industrial Revolution and the traces of colonialism and orientalism, leaves room for a powerful conglomerate of possible 'modern' attitudes—and misunderstandings—towards the Asian nations, especially if one considers issues of participation and representation. In connection with the latter, Mason (2000: 122) hints at the possible misrepresentations of Asia by the 'contemporary chronicles'; the modern media (see Box 1.5): 'when they concern themselves with Asia at all, [they] almost invariably report on the activities of the élite classes, living in capital cities that might make up, at most, five per cent of the Asian population'. Others are concerned with another form of one-directional historiography called 'Westernization', leading to a possible eclipse of Asia, both in history and now. In order to counterbalance similar concerns regarding the Asia–Europe relationship, it seems useful to bear in mind, with Lach (1994: Vol. I, Bk 1, xii) that 'an eclipse is never permanent, that this one was never total and that there was a period in early modern times, when Asia and Europe were close rivals in the brilliance of their civilizations'.

Contemporary initiatives, such as the Europe–Asia Forum on Culture, Values and Technology in Venice in January 1996, are therefore important in attempting to catch up and 'start a process aimed at dispelling misperceptions in relations between Europe and Asia.' (*Rapid Database*: IP/96/38; Commission 1997g: 6). Follow-up initiatives, cultural, educational and scientific-technical linkages and programmes involving transfer of knowledge, communication or inter-regional institutionalization form a crucial part of the EU–Asia dialogue (see Lassen and Chirativat 1999). Not easily categorized, these links are highly significant for a true meeting of minds between Asians and Europeans. Educational exchanges are a case in point: Lim (2000: 129) has justly called education 'the sustainable and long-term trajectory way to enhance Europe–Asia relations', and has advocated the promotion of more cultural ties and the formation in Asia of 'a mental and psychological attachment to Europe' to balance out the current relationship and the one Asia has with the USA (Lim 2000: 110; see also *The Nation*, 18 October 2000).

Conclusion

Asia as a region is as unrivalled in its diversity and heterogeneity as it is important to the contemporary European Union. The question of why Europe should 'bother' with Asia, or why Asia 'matters' to Europe, specifically the European Union, can be answered with reference to the keywords of 'politics', 'economics', 'security', 'representation', 'values' and 'culture'. These, combined with a long history of Euro-Asian misconceptions—which have at times obscured the reality of Euro-Asian contacts—constitute the frame of reference in the evolving relationship between Asia and Europe, as well as the themes running through this book. The East carries more weight and demands more attention in all these key areas, and the EU has realized that this is a phenomenon that both carries and reflects an increased global political impetus. The EU's day-to-day pronouncements clearly show an inten-sification and concentration of Asia-related reporting since the first 'New Asia Strategy' of 1994, and in this way bear witness of Asia's enhanced position in EU affairs (see Box 1.4). It is an ever more inconceivable course of action for the EU to marginalize Asia while striving to maintain a leading role in the economy of the 'global village'. However, if these factors keep nudging Asia and the EU into a constant reappraisal of their relationship and contribute to moving Eastern issues higher up the EU's agendas, 'Asia-awareness' among decision makers—and political terminology as its outwardly sign—do not seem to have fully caught up with the speed of development. While the terms 'Pacific Rim' or 'Pacific Community', for instance, have become familiar—albeit not uncontested—labels (Buckley 1993; Manning and Stern 1994; Mahbubani 1995) in contemporary political parlance, a comparable jargon to describe the relationship between the EU and Asia is only just developing. Perhaps this is a modern variety of the Europeans' traditional conceptual inability to look behind the façade, the myth and the stereotype of Asia.

Box 1.4: The EU's concern with Asia, 1994–2001, as reflected in *The Week in Europe*, the Commission's weekly news update

ASEAN:	8/94; 25/94; 31/94;
ASEM:	8/94; 25/94; 31/94; 13/98;
Asia General:	7/94, 34/94, 39/94, 7/96, 11/96, 20.5.99;
Burma (Myanmar):	4/97, 7/97; 7.9.00;
China:	8/94, 27/94, 28/94, 38/94, 3/95, 15/95, 26/95, 34/95, 40/96, 01/97, 10/97, 37/97, 2/98, 7/98,12/98,13/98, 14/98; 18.6.98, 2.4.98, 29.10.98, 15.11.98, 6.5.99; 27.1.00; 6.4.00; 2.11.00;
Development aid:	4.5.00; 18.5.00;
East Timor:	12.10.00;
Hong Kong:	32/94, 16,95, 26/97, 14.11.99;
India, Bangladesh and Nepal:	46/93, 33/94, 7.1.95; 28/95, 31/97; 25.01.01; 1.2.01;
Indonesia:	28.5.98; 3.2.00;
Japan:	11/94, 28/94, 34/94, 35/94, 9/95, 13/95, 22,95, 7/96, 25/97, 31/97, 6/98, 14.1.99, 2.4.99; 13.1.00; 20.7.00;
Korea and Korean Peninsula Energy Development Organization (KEDO):	10/95, 34/97, 39/97, 10.12.98, 11.3.99; 3.2.00; 16.11.00;
Landmines:	16.3.00; 20.7.00;
Malaria, HIV/AIDS and tuberculosis:	21.9.00;
The Silk Road:	10.9.98;
Trade:	7/94, 33/94, 34/94;
UK presidency and Asia:	Background Report BR B/1/98, January 1998;
Vietnam:	28/95

Source: *The Week in Europe*: http://www.cec.org.uk

Box 1.5: Asia and the EU: Selected Press Reports, 1995–2000

Alexander, Garth, 'Global Warning', *The Sunday Times*, 16 November 1997

Anonymous, 'Pax Asiatica', *Asia Times*, 30 December 1996

Anonymous, Leading Article, 'Asia and the EU', *Financial Times*, 4 March 1996: 19

Anonymous, 'Who's Winning the "Asian Values" Debate?', *The Asian Wall Street Journal*, 27–28 October 1995

Brooks, Libby, 'Freedom on a Knife Edge', *Guardian*, 31 July 1999: 16-24

Brummer, Alex, 'Tiger Takes a Bear's Mauling', *Guardian*, 30 August 1997

Chuan, Ong Hock, 'ASEAN on Collision Course with EU', *Asia Times,* 17 December 1996

Cornwell, Rupert, 'China Will Not Follow Russia Down the Stony Path of Political Reform, *Independent*, 2 April 1998

Dunphy, Stephen H., 'Is it Over in Asia?', *Seattle Times*, 26 January 1997

Gathani, Batuk, 'EU Set to Move Closer to Asia', *The Hindu*, 18 January 1996: 11

Gittings, John, 'Marching through the Storm', *Guardian* (Obituaries), 20 February 1997

Hawkins, Paula, 'Asia Holds Key to the Strength of Europe's Currency', *The European*, 16–22 November 1998

Higgins, Andrew, 'Tung Che-Hwa: Enter the Friendly Dragon', *Guardian*, 16 June 1997

Islam, Shada, 'EU Launches Drive to Boost Links with Asia…', *European Voice*, 14–20 January 1999

Jacques, Martin, 'Asian Tigers Forge no Bond with Fir-weather Friends', *The European*, 30 March–5 April 1998

Kemp, Arnold, 'Sleepless Death in Burmese Cell', *Observer*, 1 March 1998: 20

Lloyd-Parry, Richard, 'A Happy Heisei 12 to All our Readers', *Independent on Sunday*, 2 January 2000: 13

Ong, Timothy, 'All this Talk of "Asian Values" Sends an Unhelpful Message', *International Herald Tribune*, 20 May 1996: 8

Patten, Sally, 'Europe Tries to Let Realpolitik Guide Human Rights Debate with Asia', *Asia Times*, 17 March 1997

Pitman, Joanna, 'Mother Courage', *The Times,* 2 March 1996: TM/10

Segal, Gerald, 'Overcoming the "ASEMetries" of Asia and Europe', *Asia Times*, 19 November 1996

Sprague, Jonathan, 'As the World Gets Tight', *Asiaweek*, 18 February 2000: 30-37

Ustinov, Peter, 'Wind up Deng Xiaoping and He Will Wave …', *The European*, 5–11 December 1996

Verchère, Ian, ' "Business as Usual" even after 1997', *The European*, 12-18 September 1996

2 |

EU–Asia Relations in Context: Evolution, Globalization and Crisis

> …yet all the efforts to either deepen unification via the Maastricht Treaty
> or widen it by including similar European countries are tantamount to re-
> arranging the living-room furniture while floodwaters are seeping in
> from the rising tides just outside the door. It is puzzling that Europe is
> trying to cut off its neighbours, excluding them from growth and pros-
> perity. By contrast, the impulse in East Asia is to draw societies into the
> region's dynamism, starting with Myanmar and Vietnam and eventually
> including even North Korea (Mahbubani 1995: 105; 1998a: 87).

This chapter attempts to show how the framework inside which EU–
Asia relations evolved was slow in the making, compared to the EU's
relations with other world regions. The chapter outlines the different
approaches the EU chose to take towards different Asian countries, and
the way early relations were built on the two strands of trade and
development aid. Central to this section is an investigation of two main
questions: (1) How does the EU's evolving position as a global foreign
policy actor impinge on the Asian region?; (2) What are the effects and
responses, in Asia and the EU, to the two parallel processes of globalization and regionalization? The chapter closes with a look at the causes
and effects of the 1997–98 Asian financial crisis, for which globalization provided many of the causal conditions.

Early Historical Lines and Trade Patterns

Traditionally, the European Community's early relations with Asia
were much less structured than those with either the African Caribbean
and Pacific (ACP) countries (Brenner 1992: 55), the Central and Eastern European (CEE) countries, or the Mediterranean countries. Notwithstanding colonial ties, it was mainly distance, both geographical
and intellectual, and a perceived communist threat that long prevented

Europe from getting better acquainted with Asia. The focal point of early EC development co-operation was Africa: the Lomé I Convention did not extend into Asia to any degree. Vandenborre (1999: 270, 274) points out that, between 1976 and 1988, Africa received five times more aid from the Community, although South Asia was more than two and a half times larger in population. Asian states were 'pushed aside because of their size' and potential financial burdens. Perceived economic threats also came into the equation, and three different European approaches towards Asia emerged: first, South Asia, poor and economically uninteresting, attracted some commercial cooperation, food aid and compassion, but scant economic cooperation. Secondly, the newly industrializing countries—Taiwan, Singapore, Korea and Hong Kong —were seen as dangerous to the Community and became the objects of protectionist trade measures. And thirdly, when the EU intensified relations with the 'middle-group', of nations, those forming the Association of South-East Asian Nations (ASEAN),[1] the immediate rationale was the war in Vietnam. Later, trade interests and changed attitudes further promoted relations. But at least one observer (Grilli 1993: 271-95) has argued that, in spite of this, EU–Asia relations were becoming more competitive the further up the economic ladder ASEAN nations moved. Moreover, the disbursement of funds to Asia has always been applied selectively, in order to contain Communism. In this context, countries like China, Cambodia, Vietnam or Laos compare unfavourably to Thailand or Indonesia.

By 1976, financial and technical cooperation with Asian and Latin American developing countries was budgeted separately for the first time. The first regional agreements, involving ASEAN and China, followed in 1980. Unlike the Lomé framework, however, this dialogue was not to be governed by multi-annual agreements, but by individual Community decisions. From 1976 to 1984, European approaches were still cautious: the more of a geographical and cultural distance there was perceived to be between European and Asian countries, the more the Community relied on co-funding mechanisms. Between €2.19 million and €2.43 million was contributed to 389 projects in 33 countries between 1976 and 1989, with Asia getting 69 per cent (Commission 1976: 54-69). By the end of 1995, the European Investment Bank had financed projects amounting to a total of €251 million (Commission

---

1. In 2002, ASEAN has ten member states: Brunei, Burma, Cambodia, Indonesia, Laos, Malaysia, the Philippines, Singapore, Thailand and Vietnam.

1994a: 7). But this 'co-financing approach' lost importance in inverse proportion to partners in Europe and Asia overcoming cultural and linguistic divides. Subsequently, the EC increasingly took sole responsibility for projects, in agriculture, social services or disaster management, and a stronger 'Asian' involvement of the Community emerged between 1985 and 1988. Since 1988, trade between Europe and Asia has increased by more than 100 per cent, and Asia now takes a 20 per cent share in EU exports, having overtaken the 18 per cent share of the USA. Despite the Asian crisis, EU investment in Asia continued to grow in 1998, up 13 per cent on 1997. EU imports from ASEAN rose by 80 per cent from 1990 to 1994 and EU exports to the ASEAN states are now roughly equal to the EU's overall export volume to 19 Latin American countries (Commission 1996g). In relation to the 'ASEAN + 3' countries (representing ASEAN plus China, Japan and South Korea), there is an equally dynamic development of higher trade flows. But historical and colonial ties between some member states and ASEAN + 3 still lie behind patterns of trade. Brunei and Malaysia sales, for example, still tend to go through the UK, while The Netherlands functions as a main outlet for Indonesian exports. The advent of the euro has contributed to a further expansion of trade between Europe and Asia, and is expected to play a key role in the future of trade and investment finance.

The External Dimension of the EU and its Impact on Asia

> In any case, like it or not, the Commission has to respond to an active global social conscience. In the past people asked God to deliver them from evil. Today they look to international institutions—and in Europe that means the EU (Patten 2000).

Three main aspects can be said to have fostered a closer EU–Asia relationship: the development of wider external competencies of the EU since the Treaty of Maastricht, including the Common Foreign and Security Policy (CFSP) (Wiessala 1998: 125); the phenomenon of globalization; and the economic ups and downs of Asia. The new external aspirations of the Union, in particular, impinge on Asia; this is, first and foremost, because they exist at all. McCormick (1999: 202) recalls the background: 'The world does not yet quite know what to make of the European Union, in large part because the European Union does not yet quite know what to make of itself'. In foreign affairs, more European citizens now appear to back EU external competencies than are in favour of the euro (see e.g. *Standard Eurobarometer* 51 [Spring 1999]: 57-58). Furthermore, the concept of 'a strong Europe, open to the world' has figured strongly in the 1999, 2000 and 2001 Work Programmes of the Commission. In global matters, the Union has become more than a 'Paper Tiger' (Gasteyger 1997: 94-108), by emerging as an international actor *sui generis*. Additionally, the current reform debate feeds into further reassessment of the EU's external role. In this sense, it seems appropriate to claim a 'Global Europe' (Piening 1997), or talk about the EU's status as an international power in the making (Galtung 1973; Laursen 1991: 747-59). Unity on the world stage has almost unanimously been seen as constituting 'added value' for the Union in foreign relations. But in practice, such harmony has often proved elusive or has occurred with less success than anticipated. The different facets of the model of the 'credibility-expectations gap' continue to be a pertinent description of this situation (Hill 1993: 322; Holland 1995: 570).

The 'global reach' of the new EU (Wiessala 2000: 40-55) may be different from Europe's colonial past, but it has grown out of it in at least three ways: first, while five EU member states have been colonial powers in Asia (UK, Spain, Portugal, France, The Netherlands), the Union as a body, by contrast, seems on the whole 'untainted' by this legacy. Secondly, the EU has been of interest to Asia because it represents a successful and unique process of integration. And thirdly, the actions of the EC as a trader or provider of development aid have always concerned Asia. In spite of these roots, however, as regards the foreign policy capacity of the Union, there can be few other regions except Asia, for which Dinan's metaphor of change ever rang more true: 'like a caterpillar into a butterfly which is colourless and cumbersome and had great difficulty getting off the ground' (Dinan 1999: 508).

It was only from the late 1970s onwards that Community attention to Asia began incrementally to add an external dimension to existing trade relationships. This has been interpreted as 'presence', 'opportunity' and 'capability' (Bretherton and Vogler 1999: 5) and broke unprecedented ground. Commerce and trade were catalysts, independent of but closely linked to political events and crises, such as the North Korean nuclear weapons episode, the Vietnamese invasion of Cambodia or tensions across the Taiwan Straits. With regard to Asia, as elsewhere, the evolution of the EU, as a 'non-state' (Nugent 1999: 446), from civilian orientation to a body with external voice, has been both a function and a reflection of the new world 'dis-order' and more complex global change. In practice, this means that, year upon year, there is mounting evidence of more EU contacts with an ever larger number of countries in Asia on different levels: most visibly, the Community's humanitarian aspect extends to much of Asia when floods, tornadoes or earthquakes strike in Bangladesh, India, Thailand, Japan or elsewhere (see *Rapid Database*, IP/01/1614). Parts of (Pacific) Asia are covered by the new Cotonou Agreement, succeeding Lomé IV (*The Courier*, Nos. 180; 181, 2000). The EU is further linked to Asia through multilateral fora, such as the Group of Seven (G7) or Group of Eight (G8), the UN, the IMF, the ILO, the WTO or, more country-specifically, the Korean Peninsula Energy Development Organization (KEDO).

Internal reform and external matters are two sides of the same coin. The relevance of outward projection, or 'externalization' of internal matters, already evident in the 1987 Single European Act (SEA), is thrown into further relief by current developments with relevance to Asia, for example the strengthening of the Council's Secretariat-General or the inauguration of a 'Standing Group' in the Commission with authority in external matters. The reorganization in the Commission has been an extremely relevant development for EU–Asia relations. The appointments of Chris Patten as Commissioner for External Affairs and of Javier Solana as High Representative for the CFSP may have raised concerns over duplication (e.g. Algieri 1999: 94-95; *European Voice*, 5–11 October 2000). However, Patten's activities already decisively shape EU–Asia relations in at least three ways. First, in terms of Patten being known (at times, infamously) in Asian circles because of his time as Governor of Hong Kong (Dimbleby 1997), the Chinese Government tried to block his earlier nomination for a trade portfolio (*Sunday Times*, 27 June 1999). Secondly, it became clear from Patten's answers during his Parliamentary Hearing on 2 September 1999, that he regards his Eastern experience as a valuable precondition for his new portfolio. And, thirdly, Patten himself has often emphasized the commonalities of running an Asian city and running a European body (*Die Welt*, 11 November 1996; *Rapid Database*, SPEECH/00/276: 278).

The EU, in trying to strengthen its global reach, is also attempting to increase its visibility, to adapt and reform its 'image', in Eastern Europe, Asia and the world. Three examples relevant in this context are the EU's New Asia Strategy and its two substantial blueprints for a

China policy (Commission 1994a; 1995b; 1998a). All of these refer explicitly to 'EU presence and profile' as one of the cornerstones of an Asia policy. Similar formulations can be found in other EU–Asia documents on Hong Kong, Korea, Japan, Cambodia or Indonesia. The underlying need of the EU to reinvent itself in Asia, as a body with more global power, becomes clear beyond the rhetoric of 'historic opportunities' or 'milestones'. This is showing some effect: Asia is now looking at a European Union that possesses much stronger diplomatic clout. In the case of Japan, for example, Gilson (2000: 62) argues that 'an increasingly visible economically and politically active European Union has made Japan aware of the European presence on the international stage'. The Commission has now established more than 123 diplomatic Delegations and Representations, many of them in Asian countries (see Box 2.1). In conjunction with 'Asian' fact-finding operations by the *troika*, for instance to Burma, Nepal or Tibet, these form an important part of EU–Asia relations. They are complemented by the 165 diplomatic and consular Representations, many of them from Asian states, in Brussels.

Box 2.1: Delegations of the European Commission in Asian Countries
(see Appendix 2 and 3 for a selection of contact addresses and Websites)

Location of Delegation	*Accredited to:*
Australia/New Zealand (Canberra)	Australia and New Zealand (Aotearoa)
China (Beijing)	People's Republic of China, Mongolia
Hong Kong SAR	Hong Kong, Macao
India (New Dehli)	India, Bhutan, *Nepal**
Indonesia (Jakarta)	Indonesia, Brunei, *Singapore**
Japan (Tokyo)	Japan
Pakistan (Islamabad)	Pakistan
Philippines (Manila)	Philippines
Republic of Korea (Seoul)	South Korea
Sri Lanka (Colombo)	Sri Lanka, Maldives
Thailand (Bangkok)	Thailand, Burma (Myanmar), *Cambodia*, Laos*, Malaysia**
Vietnam (Ha Noi)	Vietnam

* Locations of some of the new Delegations of the Commission in Asia to be opened up in 2002. The new Delegations in Cambodia and Laos are going to be accredited with a non-resident Head of Delegation in Thailand. The opening of a 'Trade Representation Office' in Taiwan is also planned (see Commission 2001f: point 3.2; *Rapid Database*: IP/01/942).

Whose Globalization Is it Anyway?: The Shrinking Globe and Regional Integration in Asia

> Is Globalization good for Asia? Think of multinational corporations clear-cutting tropical forests, home-grown movies being squeezed out by Hollywood blockbusters, and the Asian Financial Crisis. So is Globalization bad for Asia? Contemplate the millions of families who have gone from subsistence farming to steady jobs in export industries, the students who have enriched themselves and their homelands after studying abroad and the blossoming wonders of the Internet (*Asiaweek*, 25 February 2000: 18).

Globalization, the increasing international interrelatedness of economic, social and political processes and phenomena, is as hard to pin down as it is to ignore. Notwithstanding this, many attempts have been made to define it more clearly. (Guptara 2001: 114-25; Anderson, Wiessala and Williams 2000: 5-16). Bartelson (2000: 180) conceives of globalization as 'transference', 'transformation' and 'transcendence', 'altering the very identities of individuals and states and changing conditions of existence'. It is worth asserting, with Richards and Kirkpatrick (1999: 687) that 'there is little doubt that the debate between proponents of the globalization thesis and their critics has yet to run its full course'.

In terms of international relations, globalization is often seen as a set of interrelated economic, social and political phenomena with the potential to promote trade, a multipolar equilibrium and foster progress and collective security for the whole of humanity. On the other hand, a number of concerns relating to a growing interdependence between economies and societies are being articulated. These are mainly expressed as a fear of instability and a concern that permanent change and global competition will bring down wages and damage both legal rights and the environment. Sewell (1998: 7) points to what is probably the greatest challenge: 'Globalization and all the complicated problems related to it must not be used as excuses to avoid searching for new ways to cooperate in the overall interest of countries and people'. And UN Secretary-General Kofi Annan (2000: 3) has stated: 'the central challenge we face today is to ensure that globalization becomes a positive force for all the world's people, instead of leaving billions of them in squalor'. The sheer interrelatedness of global phenomena therefore contains vital keys, which apply to the Asia–Europe dialogue, as developments in North Korea or China illustrate. Multinational enterprises, the Internet, communications, transport and human rights debates are the tools to put this interrelatedness into practice. Javier Solana states: 'In an interdependent world, nothing can be considered foreign' (*Far Eastern Economic Review*, 20 July 2000: 24) and Nayan Chanda agrees that 'all politics is global' (*Far Eastern Economic Review*, 27 July 2000: 29).

Historically, the end of the Cold War is often cited as an accelerator of globalization. But in the Asia–Europe context, globalization is older than that. Globalization has been a part of life in Asia since the arrival of Hinduism, Buddhism and Islam, the trade in silk, spices and ideologies, and the age of European penetration and colonization. The great temples of Angkor in Cambodia, Borobudur on Java or Pagân in Burma testify to globalization, in the sense that ideas triumph over borders and can be long-lasting. And yet 'the global' often has a different ring in Asia. In spite of global millennial celebrations, for example, the change from 1999 to 2000 had little cultural resonance for a large number of people in Asia, where the Gregorian calendar of 1582 is only one of several competing time systems. However, while cultural exchange and trade date back a long way, the new global movement of people and capital makes globalization an unprecedented experience in Asia. Former 'globalizations' were more limited in scope, speed and effect. It took almost 500 years for Buddha's teachings to reach Indonesia. Now it may take only seconds for a digitized picture of the Buddha to be transmitted from Jakarta to Hong Kong. J.C. Kapur's view (1999: 41) is exemplary: 'the next stage will lead to uncontrollable political and economic disasters, and force nations to pull in their horns and protect their sovereignty and save their nation from sliding into new kinds of neo-colonialism'. And Kim Dae-Jung's statement has already proved prophetic for some parts of Asia: 'The globalization of information must be linked to the globalization of benefits. Otherwise, world peace will suffer, and rampant and indiscriminate development in poor nations will damage the environment' (*Far Eastern Economic Review*, 24 November 2000: 114).

For some Asian leaders, however, globalization is little more than a 'Western smokescreen'. Related unease surrounds issues of Western competitors forcing equal access into Asian markets through the WTO, the linkages between trade, labour and human rights or environmental and social protection. Many countries and regions in Asia find themselves increasingly wedged in between the forces of globalization, nationalism and reform. Severino (1999b: 77) re-states the case for

ASEAN: 'there is simply no alternative to a more "open" form of regionalism, for an ASEAN trying to cope with "globalization", if one conceives of regionalism in Asia as the other side of the coin of globalization'.

'Open Regionalism' versus 'Fortress Europe'?

Pooled sovereignty in selected areas has been the recipe through which the EU has achieved a large measure of stability and peace. But can this experience be translated to Asia? More than ten years ago, Schiavone (1989: 5) pointed to the relative dearth in efforts at regional cooperation in the Asia-Pacific. And during his 2001 visit to India, EU External Affairs Commissioner Chris Patten could still point out that 'sharing our experience of regional integration is therefore perhaps one of the most important international contributions that Europe can make (*Rapid Database*, SPEECH/01/23), and that 'it has been a bit of an uphill struggle to persuade some of these [European] countries that their interests are to work with, rather than against, one another. In Asia it now seems to be happening naturally' (*Rapid Database*, SPEECH/00/ 276). However natural this process is considered, the appeal of region-alism in Asia remains high, and there are a number of explanations for this, ranging from the protectionism of industrial countries in the 1980s and the consequences of EU–Japan ('triadic') linkages, to cultural affi-nities, the presence of Chinese minorities across Asia, or European integration itself, and the way in which it may have inspired or deterred Asian decision-makers.

Patten's view would suggest an amount of convergence between European and Asian forms of regionalism. Comparisons made between the European Union, APEC or ASEAN (e.g. Fukasaku, Kimura and Urata 1998), to identify differences inherent in 'European' and 'Asian' forms of regionalism, often run the risk of being rendered obsolete by globalization and the lack of any credible forms of international gover-nance. However, some basic differentiating aspects seem discernible. Examples of these are the degree of 'firmness' or 'institutionalization' of regionalism ('stronger' in Europe, 'more loosely arranged' in Asia, cf. Pfetsch 2000: 160-61), the presence, or absence, of an 'integrationist vision', 'road-map' or 'blueprint' (Schiavone 2000: 206), the existence of a political and economic homogeneity in the relevant region, the amount of reciprocity contained in the relevant Free Trade Agreements, or the amount of discrimination in trade liberalization. Other observers juxtapose European integration with Asian 'de facto' economic regional integration or 'open regionalism' (e.g. Jongwhan Ko 2000b; Dent 1999: 51). China, in particular, has become interested in an 'open' or 'soft' regionalism, driven by economic forces and expressed in the establishment of what Weixing Hu (1996: 45, 56) has called 'natural economic territories' across national boundaries.[2]

The Asian Tail Wagging the Western Dog?[3]: 'Asian Flu' and Its Repercussions

> There is no 'Asian Virus', just as there was never an 'Asian path to growth', based on culturally specific factors (Prodi 2000: 67).

Globalization in its economic form constituted the underlying condition of the Asian financial crisis in 1997–98 and its repercussions in Russia, Brazil or the EU. Pressures of globalized economies encouraged the volatility in capital flows and pressures from massive capital flows compelled Asian governments to float currencies. This generated a 'vicious circle' of increased interest rates, failure to service debts, lower spending and investment, recession, bankruptcies, mass unemployment and other social implications. At the time of the 1994 Commission conference on 'A New European Economic Strategy for Asia', and during the first Asia-Europe Meeting (ASEM 1) in 1996, forecasts had still been optimistic. Citing the dynamic growth statistics, many proclaimed that Europe had to 'take advantage' of opportunities in Asia, lest it risked 'missing out' on the lucrative Asian markets (Commission 1995e: 5).

But the turmoil in 1997–98 called into doubt the economic health of a region already dogged by environmental disasters, political instability and growing fears that Asia might lose out to Latin America in the race for foreign investors. Never were headline writers as imaginative as then: 'Asian Tigers Lose their Way in the Jungle' (*Independent on Sunday*, 17 August 1997: 15); 'Asia's Coming Explosion' (*The Economist*, 21–27 February 1998); and 'Global Warning' (*The Sunday Times*, 16 November 1997) are but a few examples. There is no shortage of

---

2. See also the related article by Chia Siow Yue 1998: 138-55.
3. Term borrowed from H. McRae, *The Independent on Sunday*, 16 November 1997: 5.

attempts to find reasons for the débacle.[4] A number of observers have
investigated possible lessons from the Mexican crisis in 1994–95 or the
Latin American one in the 1980s and have considered concepts of
unsustainably high growth, 'vulnerability' and 'risk', due to insufficient
institutional development during the 'boom' years and leading to
negative shocks, crisis and collapse (Brittan 1999: 493). Bridges (1999:
189) claims that: 'conspiracy theorists have had a field day'. More
poignantly, Filippini (2000: 9) finds that 'looking at the number of
pages that have been written on this subject one might wonder about
the deep, real factors affecting deforestation and ask whether econo-
mists are friends of nature'. Most explanations concentrated on some
form of 'precariousness' of the system in attaining further 'globalization' of the 'Asian' model of capitalism. Factors identified in this
context included putting too much faith in the 'Asian miracle', foreign
over-borrowing, the 'pegging' of Asian currencies to the US dollar or
the lack of clearer communication. Deterioration of local economic
conditions (Lincoln 1999: 121), corruption or exchange rate misalign-
ments have also been blamed (Hainaut and Kaufmann 1999: 149).

The story was one of miracle to mirage to a kind of recovery. The
miracle turned to mirage in July 1997, when currency traders, taking
advantage of external debt, attacked the Thai baht. Devaluation quickly
spread to other regional Asian currencies and eventually engulfed the
stronger economies of Hong Kong, Taiwan and Singapore. Combined
with social pressures this situation prompted another round in the
debate about values (see the next chapter). 'The West would do well to
learn from the success of East Asia and to some extent "easternize". It
should accept our values, not the other way round', a defiant Mahathir
Mohamad stated (*Independent on Sunday*, 17 August 1997: 15). The
terminology for the evolving crisis was overwhelmingly borrowed from
medicine: the 'Asian flu', 'meltdown', 'virus', 'contagion' or 'syndrome'
had to be 'contained'. It demonstrated to many that 'Asian values'
ultimately could not explain economic patterns, and that normal laws of
economics apply even to 'Tigers'. With the plummeting of the stock
markets, the use of the US dollar as a peg was put under scrutiny.
(Losserre and Schütte 1999: 20). But for Asian leaders, the crisis had a
constructive side too: the mirage turned to 'recovery'. The opening of
economies, improvements in corporate structures, a stronger focus on

---

4.   For a widely noticed book-length treatment, see Jackson 1999.

regional strengths or a greater awareness of globalization have all been identified as positive results. Although many have concluded that Asian growth must now slow down from a gallop to a trot, the majority of assessments of the crisis were positive, and China even emerged as the 'outsider that props up the world' (*The Observer*, 7 February 1999).

In the EU, the crisis was overshadowed by the ongoing preparations for enlargement and the Union's 'preoccupation' with the euro (Rüland 2001: 52). For some time the Union appeared to work on the premise that a problem ignored was a problem solved. This indifference confirmed some of the constraints of EU–Asian relations. However, the preliminary apathy was followed by the all the more sudden realization of the outcomes of the crisis. First came an Asian export boom and fall in foreign direct investment (FDI) in Europe, coupled with a European export slowdown, affecting European trade balances. To these were added problems with outstanding European bank loans, potential dangers for the euro, implications for European industry and implications on jobs, the property market, tourism or educational exchanges. In Europe, speculation ensued, for example, about the role of the euro as a reserve currency in Asia, replacing the US dollar, as a catalyst of the much-desired 'enhanced visibility' for the EU, as well as a kind of 'herald of reform' for Asian states. Was there, perhaps, even some kind of competitive edge the EU could reap from the situation?

The introduction of the euro, in particular, and its potential use as a future invoicing currency, before and after 1 January 2002, caused considerable concern among Asian observers (Chayodom Sabhasri 1999: 37). Anxieties focused on a possible diversion of trade and FDI to the CEE countries, or the stability of the new currency against the US dollar. The EU typically reacted to concerns, by reassuring its Asian interlocutors that the new European currency was a 'vehicle', rather than an 'obstacle' in the Asia–Europe dialogue: it would eventually contribute to a diversification of debt structure and would replace over-reliance on the dollar (Brittan 1999: 493). But the EU failed, to a degree, to reassure the Asians that the single currency would not be manipulated to protect European jobs from cheaper Asian imports coming out of the affected countries.

In the relationship between post-crisis Asia and the EU, Asian 'Tigers' clearly took a bear's mauling. But in spite—perhaps just because—of this, they continue to matter to Europe. Narine (1999: 371) argued that Asian flu urged ASEAN members towards greater cooperation with the EU. Similarly, Mahani Z. Abidin (1999: 58) predicted that: 'the relationship between ASEAN and the EU should be further strengthened as a result of this crisis'. The turmoil therefore functioned as a kind of 'catalyst': it injected the Asia–Europe relationship with new energy and revitalized it. It was shown that, again, the EU cannot afford to miss out, this time on the emerging fruits of recovery (*Far Eastern Economic Review*, 19 March 1998).

Conclusions

Building on trade, humanitarian assistance and development aid, the Asian region was not, traditionally, a priority area for EC external relations, nor did the Community develop a coherent and differentiated policy towards Asian countries, until relatively late. The new global reach of a post-Maastricht European Union, equipped with a CFSP and enhanced ambitions regarding external relations, affected Asia in a number of ways—political, diplomatic and through individual appointments such as External Relations Commissioner Chris Patten. In terms of Asia, EU 'presence' and 'profile' in Asia developed into one of the main ambitions of an externally active EU. Globalization, the increasing international interrelatedness of economic, social and political processes and phenomena, had a different ring for a number of Asian partners of the EU, and Eastern concerns over its course and implications impinge on the EU–Asia dialogue. The Asian financial crisis contained lessons for both Asian and EU partners and has provided the relationship with a further impetus. However, in spite of an Asia officially back on the road to fairly rapid recovery, the East is still 'in the red' (*The Economist*, 19 May 2001: 75). Bad loans still loom large, and by the end of 2001, there were signs of renewed weakness and 'reform fatigue'.[5] The social and political fallout from the 1997 crisis still casts its shadow too, prompting calls to re-visit both the international financial architecture and challenging widespread assumptions about values. Richards and Kirkpatrick (1999: 704) conclude that: 'where it had seemed that interregional dialogue would teach Europe lessons from East Asia, it now appears that it will become a conduit for the imposition of a reformed western orthodoxy to the East'. This

5. Survey in 'Asia: Banking, Finance and Investment', *Financial Times*, 8 May 2001: i-vi.

touches on the overarching issue of the part that values, expectations and attitudes play in the EU–Asia dialogue—a topic to be investigated in the following chapter.

3 |

The Structure and Morality of the EU–Asia Dialogue: The EU's Asia Policy, Value Choices and Human Rights

> Asia knows very little about Europe and Europe even less about Asia. Such was the conclusion that led the European Commission in 1995 to produce a document entitled *Towards a New Strategy for Asia* (Gilson 2000: 83).

The following section introduces some of the key elements of the EU's official Asia policy. It focuses on the 1994 and 2001 'Asia Strategy' papers by the European Commission and on the area of development aid. Moreover, the chapter discusses some of the intergovernmental aspects of the EU's Asia policy and the work of the European Parliament (EP). In another section, it investigates one of the most important aspects of EU–Asia dialogue which is also one of the most overlooked: the question of 'Asian' versus 'Western' values, and, generally, of cultural awareness. The discussion seeks to illustrate how arguments over values, negotiating styles, human rights, democracy or 'good governance' inform every aspect of EU–Asia relations. On the Asian side, this argument is frequently rooted in Buddhist, Confucian or other religious, moral or philosophical thought, while on the side of the EU a new political emphasis on human rights serves to project the EU's quality as a value-based system to the outside world.

A New 'Look-East-Approach': EU Policies towards Asia and Asian Countries

The EU's preoccupation with CEE and Mediterranean countries has been highlighted by several comprehensive policy papers (Commission 1994c; 1995f). By contrast, 'a proactive "look East" policy' (Richards and Kirkpatrick 1999: 690) was long overdue. A comparison with the pre-accession framework for the next Eastern enlargement illustrates this: between 1988 and 1993, the EU concluded almost no new agreements of any significance with Asian countries, compared with about twenty accords with CEE states and the CIS (Piening 1997: ch. 7). And the Commission pointed out in its new 2001 Asia policy that only very few countries in Asia have as yet entered into fully comprehensive ('third-generation') agreements with the EC (Commission 2001c: 3). Officially though, Asia was never forgotten: a 1991 Commission report stated:

> there is no doubt that, whatever the political priorities, the Community's commitment to its partners in Latin America and Asia will be neither hindered nor obstructed by other geographical considerations (Commission 1991: 93).

Similarly, the European Parliament resolved in 1992 that increased assistance to the CEE countries 'should not lead to a reduction in Community aid, either in the case of Asia or in the case of other regions in the world' (*OJ* C 125/274, 10 April 1992). Algieri (1999: 87) has investigated the significance of such 'declaratory' efforts of the Union.

What became the 'New Asia Policy' of the EU works on different levels and is made up of diverse components (see Box 3.1). The Commission's general policy initiatives, in particular those constructed between 1994 and 2002, provided a general framework for a 'New Asia Strategy'. This was supplemented by additional Commission papers on particular countries or bodies (e.g. ASEAN, ASEM, China, India, Indonesia, South Korea) and regarding selected policy areas (e.g. trade, environment, energy, human rights). Furthermore, the Commission's Common Commercial Policy, its reformed policies on development and food security and its course of action towards the least developed countries (LDCs) form an integral and traditional part of EU–Asia relations.

The instruments and activities of the member states in the Council of Ministers, through the CFSP, the working groups and networks for Asia and the Pacific (COASI), the presidency or the *troika* frequently form a more regional, subject-focused or country-specific aspect of the EU's Asia policy. This is supplemented, for example, in the area of EU human rights policy, by the working groups on human rights and the Committee on Foreign Affairs, Human Rights, Common Security and Defence Policy. The relevant *démarches*, Joint Actions or Common Positions shape the Union's stance towards individual Asian regions or countries (Afghanistan, Burma, Cambodia, Indonesia, East Timor,

North Korea, South Asia) or in respect of specific topics, such as arms proliferation and trafficking.

To these branches of EU–Asia policy has to be added the work of the European Parliament in two ways: proactively, in debating, investigating, questioning and criticizing the evolving Asia strategies of the Union; and reactively, in presenting opinions and guidelines in respect of current events determining the development of the Asian region or Asia–Europe relations in general.

Last but not least, some individual member state policies towards Asia, in themselves or through the coordinating role of the Commission, can also be said to form a part of EU Asia policy. The German Asia Policy of 1994 stressed development partnerships, 'personal' contacts, investment, human rights and initiatives to combat poverty, to achieve a 'win–win' situation for all.[1] The Swedish Asia Strategy Project of 1999 contained a comprehensive analysis of both EU–Asia and bilateral Sweden–Asia relations, suggestions for their development and projections and perspectives regarding the future of Asia.[2]

Box 3.1: An Overview of Some of the Constituent Elements of the EU's New Asia Strategy

---

- Council Regulation No 443/92, of 25 February 1992, on Financial and Technical Assistance to, and Economic Cooperation with, the Developing Countries of Asia and Latin America (the 'ALA' Regulation).
- General policies or framework 'strategies' towards Asia as a whole, especially the 'New Asia Strategy' in 1994 and its revised and updated version of September 2001.
- External relations of the European Community towards Asia, in the areas of trade, investment, commercial and development policy.
- The EU's human rights policies in respect to Asia.
- The work of the member states in the Council of Ministers through the CFSP, the presidency, the *troika*, the working groups for Asia and the Pacific (COASI) or the Committee on Foreign Affairs, Human Rights, Common Security and Defence Policy.
- The initiatives and deliberations of the European Parliament and relevant Committees, e.g. on human rights in Asian countries.
- 'Asia policies' of individual EU member states (Sweden, Germany) in their own right and through the managing role of the Commission.

---

1.   Federal Government, 1994 (see also *Far Eastern Economic Review*, 18 November 1999: 58-68).

2.   Swedish Ministry for Foreign Affairs, 1999.

Development Cooperation

> As long as there is destitution and malnutrition, the Community shall
> have to keep improving its development aid policy, under pain of becom-
> ing an island of wealth in an ocean of poverty (Commission 1991: 88).

When, in 1971, the Generalized System of Preferences (GSP) was
extended to all non-associated developing countries, Asian countries
emerged as the main beneficiaries. At the 1972 Paris Conference, the
Community formulated a unified development policy and, two years
later, suggested that aid be expanded to include non-associated countries. A 1981 Council Regulation (EEC 442/81) in its updated version
(EEC 443/1992) established a division into financial, technical and
economic cooperation, and re-emphasized poverty alleviation, food
security and rural development. In addition to this, food and emergency
aid were supplemented by the operations of European and Asian non-
governmental organizations (NGOs) from 1976 onwards. For twenty
years, more than €6.5 billion were committed to Asia, with South Asia
the largest single recipient region (Commission 1997g: 13, 15). This
made the EU the second largest donor to the region, after Japan. Moreover, from 1984 onwards, the 'COMPEX' system equalized losses in
export revenue in agriculture of some Asian states. Similarly, the
'STABEX' earnings stabilization programme for commodity exports,
designed originally in the ACP context, was extended to cover Bangladesh, Nepal and Burma after 1986.

Although, in 1988, entries in the Community's budget for Asia and
Latin America were separated, development aid only became a Community activity under the Maastricht Treaty. Its key foci were enhanced
coordination of EU and member state aid, environmental degradation,
social development, the situation of women and gender awareness,
disaster preparedness and rehabilitation of displaced persons. In connection with the latter in particular, a Commission working paper of
2000 highlighted operations to help displaced people in Asian (and
Latin American) developing countries. The programmes encompassed
mine clearance in Afghanistan and assistance for *Rohyngia* refugees in
Burma, for Burmese refugees in Thailand and for Bhutanese migrants
in Nepal. Initiatives also comprised the improvement of services for
internally displaced persons (IDPs) in Sri Lanka, the provision of health
services to returnees in Bangladesh, Cambodia and Vietnam, and work

in the Karen and Mon refugee camps in Thailand and along the Thai/ Burmese border.[3]

The EU's system of development aid was fundamentally streamlined and reformed in 2000–01 (cf. Commission 2000[1]), resulting in the prioritizing of issues like poverty eradication, sustainable development and integration of developing countries into the world economy. The EU deepened its cooperation with the UN/World Health Organization on these issues and established a new *EuropeAid* Office, which began work on 1 January 2001 and incorporated a Directorate D on Asia. In parallel to this, it was decided to open procurement opportunities on all development aid to Asian and Latin American countries, making them available to tendering from companies in developing countries (*European Voice*, 15–21 February 2001).

As far as the LDCs are concerned, the earlier Regulations EEC 442/81 and 443/1992 had already provided the EU with some groundwork. This was later complemented by the ACP framework; 40 of the 49 LDCs are also ACP member states. In 2001–02, there were 49 LDCs (up from 24 in 1971). They represented around 10.5 per cent of the world's population, with an average per capita GDP of €350. Following similar events in Paris in 1981 and 1990, the UN and UNCTAD convened a third LDC conference in Brussels, from 14–20 May 2001. This was the first time a UN Conference was hosted by the EU. The Union had adopted a position paper on the event on 22 December 2000. The conference was held in the Brussels Headquarters of the European Parliament and agreed an Action Programme for the LDCs for 2001–10 (*The Courier*, No. 186, May–June 2001: 13-41). Out of the group of 49 LDCs, eight were Asian countries (Afghanistan, Bangladesh, Bhutan, Burma, Cambodia, Laos, Nepal and the Maldives).

The Commission, building on a 2000 communication about *Reform of External Assistance*, introduced a plan for unrestricted duty-free and quota-free access for goods from 48 of the world's poorest countries. The proposal covered the Asian, non-ACP LDCs of Laos, Cambodia, Bangladesh, the Maldives, Nepal, Bhutan and Burma. On account of the exclusion of the arms trade, the proposal, which was adopted by the Council on 26–27 February 2001 and amended Regulation 2820/1998/

3. Commission Staff Working Paper: Annexes to the Report from the Commission on the Implementation of Council Regulation (EC) No 443/97 of 3 March 1997 on operations to aid uprooted people in Asian and Latin American developing countries, SEC (2000) 934, 30 May 2000.

EC, became known as the 'Everything But Arms' (EBA) Initiative (Commission Delegation Bangkok: *EU Today* 15 [January 2001]: 9; *European Voice*, 8–14 February 2001). Apart from new initiatives, Commission President Prodi and Development Commissioner Poul Nielson strongly reasserted the need for ongoing poverty reduction in the face of the phenomenon of 'donor-fatigue'.[4]

The Commission's 'New Asia Strategy' of 1994

Against the background of instabilities occasioned by the end of the Cold War, the Commission's general 'New Asia Strategy' (1994a) had a largely consolidating function. Its immediate context was a deteriorating EU–ASEAN dialogue, an accelerating EU CFSP, and competing American and Japanese involvement in Asia. The blueprint was endorsed by the Essen Council and the European Parliament in 1994–95 (*OJ* C 166, 3 July 1995). The initiative was called a 'non-confrontational partnership of equals'. One of the most significant points of reference for EU–Asia relations, it offers the following key objectives:

- poverty alleviation;
- improved control of arms, drugs and organised crime;
- human rights issues;
- more assistance with the transition from Asian 'command' to 'market' economies;
- an enhanced EU presence and profile throughout Asia; and
- more audacious trade and investment strategies.

The issue of FDI, in particular, was still reminiscent of the former, overwhelmingly derivative, nature of the Europe–Asia relationship: with only about 10 per cent of FDI between 1986 and 1992, the EU lagged behind other investors in the region, notably Japan and the US. In 1996, a study (Commission 1996f) concluded that European businesses had underestimated Asia's dynamism and over-favoured more obvious opportunities in CEE countries. According to the report, the Union and private business should extend investment programmes to the whole of Asia. After that, year-on-year rates of investment improved. But the volume of Asian FDI in Europe too is small. According to a study by the UN Conference on Trade and Development

---

4.   *Rapid Database*: IP/01/369; IP/01/558; SPEECH/01/178; *European Voice* 23–30 May 2001: 12.

(UNCTAD) in 1995, the EU—largest host to FDI on a global scale—received only a small proportion of (non-Japanese) Asian FDI, mainly because of an intra-Asian orientation of the region's investment schemes.

The framework that this New Asia Strategy offered to policy-makers and business alike was fleshed out with a speed, intensity and enthusiasm that few could have foreseen in 1994. The very foundations for the EU–Asia dialogue evolved almost beyond recognition from then. One of the ways in which this development took place was a country-specific concentration. On account of the significant political and economic developments in countries such as Indonesia, China, Japan, the Koreas or India, the policy quickly branched out into new areas, often responding to the momentous changes in the region. New individual strategy papers on the above and other Asian countries emerged as evidence for the ever-increasing pace of EU–Asia relations. In many cases the partnership moved beyond political and economic cooperation and sustainable development, the main foci of the 1994 document. The process of Asia–Europe Meetings in particular, begun in Bangkok in 1996, deepened and widened relations, and in the process important priority areas were brought to the fore, defining and fine-tuning the future partnership between the Union and Asian countries. Further political, security and economic cooperation, educational and cultural exchange and consumer dialogue were some of those areas. On the other hand, the EU–ASEAN stalemate over Burma, the Asian financial crisis and Euro–Asian divergencies over values and styles of negotiation showed the limitations of this process of widening and deepening. The New Asia Strategy as a general blueprint for the EU's relations with Asian countries therefore had to undergo substantial reviewing and updating.

Tomorrow's EU Agenda for Asia: Modernizing Relations, Enhancing Presence

The above process resulted in a new strategy document in September 2001, entitled *Europe and Asia: A Strategic Framework for Enhanced Partnership* (Commission 2001c; see also Box 3.2). In the months immediately preceding the new communication, speculation had been rife as to shifts in the Commission's policies and priorities (*The Nation*, 8 July 2000). Some had feared a move away from ASEAN, for the benefit of closer ties with India, China, Japan, Indonesia or the Koreas, a development which appeared to be confirmed by Chris Patten, when he stated in an interview in July 2001 that 'it would be easier to focus on ASEAN if the grouping had a clearer agenda' (*Far Eastern Economic Review*, 12 July 2001: 24; see also Bangkok Delegation, *EU Today*, No. 17, October 2001: 8-9). In a similar vein, the Commission's new strategy warns that 'ASEAN seems to have lost some of its momentum in recent years' (Commission 2001c: 2.1). Overall, however, the new blueprint confirmed the key position of EU–ASEAN dialogue which forms, in the words of the document, 'the major focus' of the EU's 'political and security dialogue with South East Asia' (Commission 2001c: 4.3).

Some observers were quick to dismiss the Commission's new Asia paper as inappropriate, incoherent and evidence of a European Union which had 'lost the plot' in Asia (e.g. Camroux 2001: 3). Upon closer observation, the paper revealed itself as not quite the watershed many had expected, but as a logical and solid successor to the 1994 strategy. The September 2001 paper broadly reasserted the approach mapped out in its predecessor document of 1994. It reacted to changes in the 1994–2000 period and to the heterogeneity of the Asian region by acknowledging that the EU's approach should be 'coherent and comprehensive' and 'should respond to the diversity of Asia' (Commission 2001c: 4.1). The new policy recognized that there was still 'great potential for strengthening relations further' and that 'insufficient mutual awareness' was still a key obstacle to the dialogue. It therefore made the EU's *political and economic presence* in Asia its central objective. Moreover, it encompassed six key fields ('dimensions')[5] and a number of resulting 'action points', regarding the Union's future Asia policy as a whole, as well as towards certain Asian regions and countries (see Box 3.2). Compared to the 1994 strategy paper on Asia and the successive 'country-specific' strategies, this structure represented more than just an extension of earlier policy developments. There are a number of points worth noting in the 2001 paper, which make it more than a mere 'update' of the 1994 policy outline:

5.   See 'Remarks by the Rt Hon. Chris Patten, EU Commissioner for External Relations, at the ASEAN Post-Ministerial Conference, Ha Noi, 26 July 2001' (source: Commission Delegation Bangkok).

1. The 'core-objective of enhanced EU *presence* in Asia carries more weight and forms a 'red thread', running through the document.
2. The emphasis on Asian 'sub-regions', such as South Asia, South-East Asia or North-East Asia, is more pronounced, showing a clearer understanding of the region's diversity and needs.
3. Plans to open new Delegations in the region are a logical consequence of this (see Box 2.1), as is the inclusion, for the first time, of Australia and New Zealand in an EU 'Asia-Strategy'.
4. The new approach is more proactive and looks towards 'upgrading the institutional basis' of the EU's relations with Asian countries, by means of more 'third-generation' cooperation agreements, to be finalized in the future.
5. Following earlier documents and the development of the ASEM process, educational exchanges, particularly in the area of European studies, are confirmed as a priority area for the future.
6. There is a stronger emphasis on human rights, following on from the higher priority the EU gives to this subject in other fields of policy.
7. As far as the future is concerned, the paper announces more Asia-related papers, both of the sub-regional and the country-specific variety. The blueprint states that the 2001 strategy constitutes a prelude to the wider revision, later in 2002, of one of the early legal bases for EU–Asia cooperation, the 1992 Asia and Latin America (ALA) Regulation.[6] Last but not least, the paper envisages a review of its 2001 Asia Strategy in about 5–6 years' time.

This new policy paper seemed more firmly embedded in related EU policies and activities and contained extensive references to other Commission papers, in areas ranging from development aid to de-mining and humanitarian issues. It was, therefore, clearly the result of several years' development in the area of EU–Asia cooperation. At the same time, it became clear that this reassessment of the EU's dialogue with Asian countries was, in many ways, just the beginning of a much more detailed future process, which is more than likely to herald—and formalize—further specialization and 'branching-out' of the EU's approach towards Asian sub-regions and countries.

6. Council Regulation (EEC) No 443/92, of 25 February 1992 on Financial and Technical Assistance to, and Economic Cooperation with, the Developing Countries in Asia and Latin America; cf. Chapter 5.

Box 3.2: *Europe and Asia: A Strategic Framework for Enhanced Partnerships,*
COM (2001) 469 final: Key points of the Commission's 2001 strategy towards Asia

---

I.   The Core Objective

'Strengthening the European Union's political and economic presence across
Asia and raising it to a level commensurate with the growing global weight of
an enlarged European Union' (Commission 2001c: 3, 15, 28).

II. Six Key Proposals	**Twenty-one General 'Action Points' for the Future Euro–Asia Dialogue**
To strengthen EU engagement with Asia in the *political and security* areas and contribute to peace and security in Asia and globally.	• Work on security issues in bilateral and regional relations, through the UN, the ARF or ASEM • Work on conflict prevention and taking preventative action (see also COM [2001] 211, of 11 April 2001) • Cooperate in Justice and Home Affairs matters (asylum, immigration, arms trafficking)
To strengthen *trade and investment* flows between the Union and Asia.	• Intensify bilateral initiatives on e.g. market access and investment • Support private-sector cooperation and contacts between SMEs • Coordinate dialogue on economic and financial policy and regarding the euro • Apply special market-access initiatives targeted at LDCs, such as the GSP system or the EBA initiative • Cooperate in the areas of energy, transport and the environment
To promote *development* and *reduce poverty* in Asia	• Enhance capacity-building and realize linkages between poverty and environmental issues • Strengthen dialogue on Social Policy, e.g. on core labour standards (see also Commission 2001h) • Put into practice the reform of the system of EC External Assistance for Asia

To contribute to the protection of *human rights, democracy, 'good governance' and the rule of law* throughout Asia (see also the related Commission 2001e)	• Continue human rights dialogue (e.g. EU–China) • Devise initiatives involving civil society • Emphasize programmes on governance
To forge *'global partnerships'* and alliances with Asian countries, e.g. in *international fora*	• Cooperate within the UN, e.g. on the CTBT, HIV/AIDS or landmines • Cooperate in the WTO framework (e.g. China) • Integrate environmental issues into all areas of policy-making (e.g. climate change) • Cooperate in fighting the 'dark side of globalization', e.g. terrorism, environmental degradation, the drugs trade, money laundering • Reinforce scientific and technological cooperation
To strengthen further the mutual *awareness* between Europe and Asia and to reduce persisting *stereotypes*	• Reform the system of Commission Delegations in Asian countries (new delegations in Cambodia, Malaysia, Nepal, Laos and Singapore) • Strengthen educational and cultural exchange, research and higher education; build more partnerships, e.g. in the 'underdeveloped field' of *European Studies* (point 4E, see also Commission 2001g)

III. Twenty-two Regional, Sub-regional and Country Specific 'Action Points'

Regarding South Asia
- Help defusing tensions on the Indian subcontinent; devise a future strategy towards South Asia as a whole
- Strengthen bilateral links with India and encourage cooperation between member states of the South Asian Association for Regional Cooperation (SAARC)
- Support broader Asian (i.e. South Asian) membership in ASEM

Regarding South-East Asia and ASEAN
- Ensure that ASEAN (and ARF) remain the major focus of political and security dialogue with Asia and a key priority for the EU in the coming years

- Give enhanced attention to human rights issues, educational, intellectual and cultural links
- Continue to apply existing strategy towards Indonesia (outlined in Commission 2000a)

Regarding North-East Asia
China
- Apply existing Communications regarding China (Commission 1995b; 1998a), to 'engage' China further in the international community
- Concentrate on three issues: (1) the Chinese reform process; (2) sustainable development, scientific and technological cooperation; and (3) 'good governance' and the 'rule of law'
- For Hong Kong and Macao: uphold autonomy within the 'one country–two systems' rule; build on existing communications (Commission 1997c; 1999d)
- For Taiwan ('separate customs territory'): help to conduct 'constructive dialogue' on cross-straits issues, WTO accession and trade

Japan
- Adopt the comprehensive 'EU–Japan Joint Action Plan' (which was initiated at the 2000 EU–Japan summit)
- Streamline the 'EU–Japan Regulatory Reform Dialogue'
- Enhance cooperation within the WTO and regarding the environment (Kyoto Protocol)

Korea (ROK and DPRK)
- Encourage South Korean economic reform and intra-Korean *rapprochement* and reconciliation
- Develop the EU–ROK Framework Agreement (in force since 1 April 2001)
- Cooperate with the ROK in the framework of the WTO
- Develop a course of action towards the DPRK and encourage its opening up to the outside world

Regarding Australasia
- Expand 'traditional' trade and investment, while seeking out new areas for cooperation, e.g. education
- Cooperate in the framework of the WTO and on environmental, global and regional issues

Regarding Regional Bodies and the ASEM Process
- Strengthen dialogue with the SAARC, ASEAN and the ARF(see above)
- Ensure progress in the three 'pillars' of ASEM (political, economic and social, see Commission 2000b)
- Ensure broader participation in ASEM (subcontinent, Australia and New Zealand) and its 'informality'

Intergovernmental Aspects of EU–Asia Relations and the Role of the European Parliament

The 1994 Asia strategy emphasized that, predominantly for historical reasons, the legitimacy of the EU–Asia dialogue is rooted in the work of the European Parliament and the Council of Ministers (Commission 1994a: 10). Therefore, intergovernmentalism, the Committee on Foreign Affairs, Human Rights, Common Security and Defence Policy, working parties and the rotating presidency play an important part in defining, shaping and refining the EU's Asia strategy (see Box 3.3). This can occasionally prove to be a minefield, as is exemplified by the attempt of the 1998 UK presidency to forge a so-called 'ethical foreign policy', including a 'Code of Conduct on Arms Exports' (Hill and Smith 2000: 460, document 4c/37), while at the same time providing the Indonesian army with fighter planes used in East Timor's "Killing Fields". Notwithstanding occasional backfiring, however, each presidency brings a certain 'management culture' to Asia (Box 3.3). National, especially colonial histories, play a part in the choice of region or activity prioritized, and sometimes a country or region moves 'in and out' of the foci of presidencies. Asia in particular, since the currency crisis of 1997–98, is a paradigm for national idiosyncrasies and 'floating' priorities.

Within the Council, the working groups and networks for Asia and the Pacific, such as COASI are also relevant in this context. They prepare issues regarding EU relations with countries in the region and come together about three times per month. One of those meetings would normally revolve around matters of CFSP, while the others are devoted to 'First Pillar Issues', such as trade and investment cooperation and development aid. The working group's brief incorporates the EU–ASEAN dialogue, the ASEM process and synchronization with member states on issues including the new approach to China, India, Vietnam or Japan.

Empowered in conjunction with the Council by the 1994 New Asia Strategy, the European Parliament gained both in power and in confidence over the last decade. Its resolutions on the development of the EU–Asia dialogue in general, or on the political, economic and human rights situation in Asia, accompanied the evolution of the New Asia Strategy and introduced a dimension otherwise lacking in the language of the Council of the Commission, which often appeared shrouded in diplomacy and political formulae. The European Parliament's Delegation for Relations with Member States of ASEAN regularly visited Asian states, for example Thailand in April 2001, and reported on the results of these visits. Forster (2000: 792) noted the link between the growth of the European Parliament's powers and the reversal of the old EU–Asian (ASEAN) priorities of 'trade first, values (and rights) second'. Many examples of relevant resolutions and questions contributed by the European Parliament are, whenever possible, referred to in the more specialized areas of this book. However, Burma, China, Taiwan, Tibet, Indonesia or East Timor constituted particularly intensive 'flashpoints' in the European Parliament's activities. Parliament's debates and answers to questions often brought to the fore a divergence in the assessment of 'rights', 'values', 'democracy' or 'legitimacy' between European and Asian partners. It was the ongoing discourse about this divergence which underpinned and shaped much of the present EU–Asia dialogue.

Box 3.3: EU–Asia Relations and the Work of Recent Presidencies of the Council of Ministers

In 2001, the Swedish and Belgian presidencies placed an early, but half-hearted emphasis on EU–Japan relations. Asia had not been an overriding concern of the French or Portuguese either, in 2000, despite ASEM 3 and the commitment of the Portuguese incumbents to the first EU–India summit. The 1999 German priorities briefly mentioned a 'further boost to EU–ASEAN cooperation'. The Blair Government, during the 1998 term (and ASEM 2), gave Asia enhanced priority. The 1997 Luxembourg presidency worked on the premise that EMU, enlargement and the CFSP would all make the Union a more 'indispensable partner' for Asia. EU–Asian relations did not feature prominently on the Dutch agenda. In 1996, the year of ASEM 1, the Irish emphasized that 'a priority of the EU is to develop relations with Asia', because 'in the growing international climate large and small nations must listen to one another' (*EU–China News*, December 1996). In a similar vein, the Italian presidency, although dogged by domestic upheavals, counted 'a new phase in European–Asian relations' among its top priorities. Earlier French and Spanish presidency initiatives in 1995 had led to the appointment of 'ASEM-facilitators'. The 1994 German presidency, in times of an, as yet, unfettered Asian miracle, stressed that, owing to the 'immense innovative impulses' originating in the East, Asia, and China in particular, had become 'increasingly important partners' and 'attractive markets' (Embassy of the FRG, Press Release No. 65/94, 20 June 1994: 3).

How 'Asian' Are 'Asian Values'?

> The value systems of those with access to power and of those far removed from such access cannot be the same. The viewpoint of the privileged is unlike that of the underprivileged. In the matter of power and privilege the difference between the haves and the have-nots is not merely quantitative, for it has far-reaching psychological and ideological implications. And many 'economic' concerns are seldom just that, since they are tied up with questions of power and privilege (Aung San Suu Kyi 1995: 263).

Arguments about 'Western' versus 'Asian' values strikes at stereotypes about Asia developed over the last two and a half millennia. It has always been a mould in which the Europe–Asia relationship was cast. Hutchings (2000: 38) asserts that it is: 'a late twentieth century version of a much older argument among Chinese officials and intellectuals about the relevance of "national conditions" (*guoqing*)'. Views were, of course, subject to change over time: for Renaissance Europe, China and India constituted 'models' of governance worth emulating in Europe. Theologians and humanists contributed to the emergence of an early cultural relativism. In his *Essays*, Michel de Montaigne (1533–92) criticized contemporary ideas about branding everything alien as 'barbaric', and claimed Europe could learn from Asia about the universality of ethical principles (Lach 1994: Vol. II, Bk 2: 297; Bk 3: 561). And Spence (2000: 33) recognizes that 'in contrast to the fragmented states of post-Reformation Europe … China offered a picture of a vast, unified, well-ordered country, held together by a central controlling orthodoxy, that of Confucianism'. The prevailing trend of those times was to stress positive features in Asia, in order to highlight shortcomings of the West, such as absolutism (Vande Walle 1998: 191). In later centuries, however, a remarkable—and wholesale—reversal of attitudes occurred. The European search for 'souls, trade and power' (Osborne 2000: 43), European concepts of Christianity and civilization, commercial activity and mission, colonialism and divergent ideas about ethics, promoted sentiments of superiority and euro-centrism in the West. In our time, Western influence in Asian countries has 'shaped their perspectives on foreign rule and in many cases their domestic organization' (CAEC 1997: 23).

The term 'values', in the sense of a moral sentiment, rather than an economic concept, was first used by Japan during World War II (Mallet 1999: 28). The conferences at Geneva (May 1954) and Bandung (April

1995) had a long-lasting bearing on the issue. Ever since the Bandung Five Principles of Peaceful Co-existence—'non-interference' among them—were formulated, Asian leaders have used them to deflect criticism of their human rights record. But more generally, *l'Asianisme,* the Asianization of Asia, only really 'acquired a vogue' (Hutchings 2000: 37) in more recent times. Referring to Michel Foucault's findings on the power of discourse, Than-Dam Truong (1998: 48-49) shows how, in the 1990s, the discussion about value systems evolved 'from a critique of development policies, to a defence of the Asian style of governance, democracy and Human Rights practices'. The Enlightenment-coloured view Europe held of Asia—as a 'cruel' and 'unreasonable' place—was suddenly being turned around, by stating that, in early capitalist Europe, for instance, democracy had been restricted too (Zakaria 1994: 117). The World Conference on Human Rights in 1993 and the Asian crisis gave ammunition to either side in the evolving dispute. Pronounced dead after the crisis (Mallet 1999: 54; *Seattle Times* 17 June 1998), the issue obstinately survives. The number of pertinent, recent publications (Cauquelin, Lim and Mayer-König 1998; De Bary 1998a, b; De Bary and Tu 1998; Jacobsen and Bruun 2000; Mason 2000; Sheridan 2000; Gilson 2000: 45-46; Preston and Gilson 2001) testifies to its significance. Most recently, the debate has re-emerged in the context of Euro–Asian differences over an alleged 'Western cultural hegemony' or 'Western interference' in international bodies, in the guise of a debate about globalization and values.

Values and the New European Union Human Rights Policy

'Western' values continue to inform every level of the EU's external relations and especially its Asia dialogue. Bretherton and Vogler (1999: 34) are among the few analysts to investigate this aspect:

> The role of the EU can be conceptualized, in the broadest sense, as contributing to overall 'Western' policy, in terms of maintenance within and extension beyond the West of values and beliefs, which are the product of an essentially European culture, and, more specifically, of the European Enlightenment... The EU, as presence, has contributed significantly to consolidation of these values and principles in Western Europe.

However, if the Union refuses visas to officials from Burma, shows concern for democracy in Hong Kong, East Timor and Cambodia or for the victims of the 1989 Tiananmen Square massacre, it now does so, not only out of respect for its cultural and philosophical heritage, or as a 'value-based organization', but also on the basis of concrete policies, which are informed by an enhanced awareness for human rights (Wiessala 2001: 22-26). The EU promotes these with more confidence, since it has drawn human rights into the EU legal system in a much more permanent and solid way. The following ten documents or events point to an inexorable rise of human rights and concerns about human rights in EU planning and policymaking of the last decade.

1. The *EU Declaration on Human Rights* by the Luxembourg European Council (June 1991).
2. The Maastricht Treaty (Article F), which incorporated the European Convention of Human Rights (ECHR) (4 November 1950) into EU law.
3. The Treaty of Amsterdam, which strengthened EU competencies in the area of human rights.
4. The EU Declaration on the Occasion of the 50th anniversary of the United Nations Declaration of Human Rights (UNDHR) in Vienna (10 December 1998).
5. The EU's own 'Millennium Declaration' of December 1999.
6. The Treaty of Nice, which explicitly calls for the respect for human rights in the area of cooperation of the Community with third countries (Title XXI, Article 181a [1]).
7. Since Lomé IV, human rights have played a part in EU development policy, most recently in the Cotonou Agreement.
8. The new *Charter for Fundamental Rights* proclaimed during the Nice Council in 2000.
9. The new *Human Rights Conclusions* of the Council of 19 March 2001, which contained a particularly strong focus on China (2338th Council meeting).
10. Major European conferences have highlighted specific EU concerns about human rights. Recent examples are the European Conference on the Protection of Human Rights in the 21st Century (Dublin, 3–4 March 2000), the European Conference against Racism (Strasbourg, 11–13 October 2000) or the Conference on the EU and Human Rights in the Framework of Conflict Prevention and Resolution (Brussels, 28–29 May 2001).

Last but not least, the Commission's comprehensive communication on *The EU's Role in Promoting Human Rights and Democratisation in*

Third Countries, of 8 May 2001 (Commission 2001e), furnished and focused much of the theoretical foundations of the current human rights debate within the EU.

On a more global scale, the inclusion of human rights in point V/24-25 of the UN's 'Millennium Summit' from 6–8 September 2000, the Anwar Ibrahim trial and the award of the Nobel peace prize to Asians, such as East Timorese human rights advocate José Ramos Horta,[7] provided the EU with a more complete rationale for a more Asia-specific focus on human rights. This found expression in a number of documents emphasizing human rights, most notably in the Commission's report *On the Implementation of Measures Intended to Promote Observance of Human Rights and Democratic Principles in External Relations for 1996–1999* (Commission 2000e), which was supported and budgeted by the European Initiative for Human Rights and Democracy. In terms of Asia, the three-year report (at pp. 73-74) emphasizes the need for human rights education, but also shows the dearth of human rights-related substance in EU–Asia relations, with the few notable examples of the EU–China human rights dialogue, the Commission's 1996 strategy on ASEAN (Commission 1996d: 11) or the ASEM process, which, however, seems deficient, at the very least, when it comes to human rights. Other recent EU initiatives on human rights and Asia are reflected, more or less strongly, in the Commission's *Communication on Election Assistance and Observation* of 11 April 2000, in the regular *Human Rights Reports* by the Council of Ministers, compiled since 1999, or the Commission's *Monthly Reviews on Human Rights and Democratization*. This monthly mirror of EU concerns in particular, contains a regular digest of Asia-related human rights matters. Recent examples of European apprehensions have included evaluations of the Council's Common Position on Afghanistan (2000/55/CFSP) and of the Taliban edict on Hindus, statements on a future Khmer Rouge Tribunal of Cambodia, the pitfalls of the China–EU human rights dialogue, political violence in Bangladesh or the indictment of former Philippine President Estrada (examples taken from issues 1/2001 onwards).

However, several qualifying points need to be made in this context: the human rights issue, although a 'stubborn' one, is still relatively new

---

7.   Ramos Horta succeeded Xanana Gusmao as head of the East Timorese transitional Parliament in April 2001.

for the EU–Asia dialogue and, apart from a few highly visible exceptions, an often neglected issue at that. Most of the initiatives and documents on human rights in EU–Asia relations outlined above, and other related ones, have undoubtedly propelled the issue back into the limelight, and therein lies their considerable merit. However, the existing provision is still only of a largely embryonic and incomplete nature, as is, indeed, the overall human rights framework in the EU. Many issues are only just evolving and are not entirely uncontested, as will be shown later. On account of their incompleteness, none of these documents on its own can be a suitable blueprint for the state of human rights protection in Asia. Secondly, it is more than surprising that, in connection with human rights, the parallel theme of 'cultural software' has so far received so little attention. Pelkmans has explored this latter point in detail and his criticism is very timely: 'the New Asia Strategy risks to be pursued without a reflection of the very fundamentals of the EU-Asia relationship: a sufficient degree of mutual understanding and appreciation of values' (1996: 162). This is all the more surprising if one realizes that, for the EU, the question of linkages between human rights and 'values' informs at least the following areas and events of the EU's Asia policy.

1. Human rights and trade policies towards Asia. The 1994 and 2001 Asia strategies and the 1996 report by the European Institute for Asian Studies. The 1996 Europe–Asia Forum on Culture, Values and Technology.
2. Trade-offs that arise when the implementation of policies is only attainable at the expense of individual freedoms (cf. Algieri 1999: 84-89).
3. EU responses to the deployment of the 'Asian values' point to justify 'soft' and 'hard' authoritarianism (Singapore, Malaysia, China, Burma); styles of negotiation/conflict-settlement (results-oriented, 'legalistic', 'deductive' versus incremental and 'inductive').
4. The ASEM process and political awareness of the codes that govern societies on both continents (Lim 1999b: 6).
5. The EU–ASEAN relationship and its pitfalls; constitution of an ASEAN Human Rights Body.
6. The 'Asian crisis', 'business practices' (Lincoln 1999: 125); '*guanxi*' (Asian 'patron-client communitarianism', or simply: 'connections' (Low 1998: 27).

7. The work of European NGOs diplomats, politicians or academics in Asia.
8. Environmental disasters (deforestation, forest fires, dams) and related health problems (reluctance by ASEAN to 'interfere').

It is well known that in the areas of values, human rights, and the connections and contradictions between these two areas, the EU and its member states are deeply divided. On the one hand, the EU asserts that it 'will not be able to take for granted automatic acceptance of European values and ways of doing things' (Commission 1994a: 2, 18). On the other, struggles over the co-sponsoring of UN Resolutions against China, evident from 1997 onwards, have exacerbated existing internal cleavages. EU–ASEAN disparities over Burma or Cambodia, although now partly resolved, have exposed further cracks. An EU commissioned report on *Understanding Asian Values,* concluded that, 'the strongest challenge to values in Asia is coming from the West', and that it 'tends to manifest itself most strongly over issues of Human Rights, democracy and the development models being pursued' (EIAS [European Institute for Asian Studies] 1996: ix). One of the most pertinent findings of the report was the following statement:

> In Europe, and perhaps elsewhere, there is an unconscious—certainly unquestioned—assumption that all the Asian countries are gradually becoming 'more like Europe' or 'more Western'. It colours policy statements at all levels, including the new Asia strategy, as well as the behaviour of businessmen, the activities of non-governmental organizations and editorials in the quality newspapers in the EU (EIAS 1996: 1).

Cauquelin *et al.* (1998: 4) have put it more succinctly: 'A Japanese in a Western suit does not mean that his way of thinking has become Western'; and Weggel (1994: 22) warns of the fallacy of seeing Asians as *'Europäer mit asiatischem Gesicht'* (Europeans with Asian faces). Ian Buruma (2000: ix) calls the widespread myth of a 'Westernizing' Asia an itching cliché, as irritating as the one about the 'spiritual East' and the 'materialist West'.

Universalism or Particularism: The Debate about 'Asian Values'

What seems at first like a fundamental East–West split is perhaps best encapsulated in the opposing voices of Chris Patten, EU External Affairs Commissioner, and Kishore Mahbubani, Deputy Secretary in the Singapore Ministry of Foreign Affairs. Patten asserts (1998: 161) that 'no alleged national traditions can make right in one place what is wrong in every place'. By contrast, in his brilliantly provocative work, *Can Asians Think?*, Kishore Mahbubani maintains (1998b: 50): 'In the eyes of many Third World Observers, this pragmatic application of moral values leads to a cynical belief that the West will only advance democracy, when it suits its own interests'.

But how severe are these political and cultural divergencies? In 1993, Samuel Huntington[8] famously argued that future conflicts were more likely to be fought out between cultures, rather than between ideologies or nationalities (1993: 22-49). He also predicted a 'clash' of civilizations and an 'Asian affirmation' (Huntington 1998: 32-33, 107-109). Anwar Ibrahim, the imprisoned but not silenced former Deputy Prime Minister of Malaysia, calls this 'Orientalism in a new garb' and replies:

> If the term Asian values is not to ring hollow, Asians must be prepared to champion ideals which are universal. It is altogether shameful, if ingenious, to cite Asian values as an excuse for autocratic practices and denial of basic rights and civil liberties. To say that freedom is Western or un-Asian is to offend our own traditions… (1996: 28, 40).

And Aung San Suu Kyi adds (1995: 175): 'The proposition that the Burmese are not fit to enjoy as many rights and privileges as the citizens of democratic countries is insulting.' However, the key question may not be Mahbubani's 'Can Asians think?' It may be, 'Do Asians think differently?' In *Ways of Thinking of Eastern Peoples*, an early, pioneering survey on mentalities and identities in East and West, Nakamura and Wiener (1984: 3) have strongly dismissed this:

> There has long been a tendency to think in terms of a dichotomy between East and West, presupposing two mutually opposed cultural sets of values, labeled 'Occidental' and 'Oriental'. Thus, the Oriental way of thinking is represented as 'spiritual', 'introverted', 'synthetic' and 'subjective', while the Occidental is represented as 'materialistic', 'extroverted', 'analytic' and 'objective'. This sort of explanation by paired opposites is now rejected as too simple; the cultures of the 'Orient' and 'Occident' are too diversified and each one is extremely complex.

While it seems true that the complexity of the issue challenges static conceptualizations of indivisibility or universality, there have still been attempts to 'categorize' supposedly 'Asian' values. The prime example

---

8. Cameo portrait in Sakwa and Stevens 2000: 210.

for this is the Asia-Pacific Governmental Declaration for Human Rights, or Bangkok Declaration, produced by Asian participants for the World Conference on Human Rights in Vienna in May 1993 (Marbett 1998: 5; Muntharbhorn 1998: 11; Christie and Roy 2001: 10). Singaporean Tommy Koh's repeated reference to a 'catalogue' of ten 'basic Asian values' is another case in point.

Listings of 'Asian values' (see also Box 3.4) assume acceptance of a clear-cut axiom: the West is

> in moral decay, with the decline of the family, excessive expressions of freedom, high crime rates and drugs problems, and the flagrant contradiction between the proclaimed democracy and Human Rights and the everyday facts of discrimination (EIAS 1996: 2, 6, 7, 71).

Asian values, by contrast, are respect for superiors, acceptance of authority, importance of family, filial loyalty, priority of education, hard work, thrift and emphasis on community, rather than individualism. First Minister Lee Kuan Yew of Singapore has emerged as a vocal spokesman of 'Asian values' (Zakaria 1994: 111; *Asiaweek*, 22 September 2000: 46). Fellow Singaporean Linda Low (1998: 26-27), although attempting to be critical of the concept, articulates a distinctively Singaporean point of view, in stating: 'While democracy and human rights are worthwhile ideas, the objective of good government should prevail', and: 'if economic development is the ultimate goal, discipline and conformity cannot be dismissed too lightly over the preference for individualism and freedom'. Ex-President Suharto of Indonesia, Chinese President Jiang Zemin, the Chief Executives of Hong Kong and Macao (Tung Che Hwa and Edmund Ho Hau-wah), or Prime Minister Mahathir Mohamad of Malaysia have also appeared as what Christie and Roy (2001: 50) termed 'aggressive ideologues' in the Asian values debate. The following (non-exhaustive) list (see Box 3.4) illustrates the main points of departure in the 'European' and 'Asian' modes of thinking of the debate (cf. Weggel 1994: 24; Hernandez 1998: 32-33; Muntharbhorn 1998: 6; Leong 1997: 41–42).[9]

---

9.   See also the listing on the Website of the Asia-Europe Young Leaders' Symposium (AEYLS), http://www.aeyls-ii.bka.gv.at/aews5.html, indicating further links.

Box 3.4: Some Questions Surrounding the Politics of the 'Asian Values' Debate

> - Can particular—and different—sets of values be attributed to Asians and Europeans?
> - Are values universal, based in a 'natural law', or 'relative', i.e. culture-specific? (Vijapur 1998: 22-35; Duve 1998: 45-49)
> - Can 'Western' culture be 'equated' with 'World' culture? (Nakamura and Wiener 1984: 23-24)
> - Do Westerners think in a more 'transcendental', principled and rigid fashion, and Asians in a more 'hermeneutic', 'humane' way?
> - Are 'harmony' and 'consensus' a better means of conflict settlement than 'legalism' and 'confrontation'?
> - Does an emphasis on individual rights over community-focused duties breed social ills?
> - Does inclusion of 'conditional' human rights clauses in trade agreements promote democracy or constitute a new form of 'Western Trade Imperialism'?
> - Do 'Asian values' mask authoritarian practices or promote Asian achievement?
> - Are 'well-ordered' societies superior, in which states are like families, and subsistence, economic well-being, not democracy, sets the pace for human rights? (Zhu Muzhi 1998: 38)
> - Are political and socio-economic rights to be implemented concurrently or sequentially, i.e. the former following the latter? (Christie and Roy 2001: 17)

An Asian Heritage of Freedom?

> All Rights to be deserved and preserved come from a duty well-done (Mahatma Gandhi).

Many of the issues behind the debate have been studied in detail: from a Thai perspective, for example, Apirat Petchsiri offers a critique of development of Western (criminal) law and its transplantation, through colonialism on the one hand, and Asian legal evolution on the other. He infers that 'in the Eastern countries Western criminal law has failed because it is ineffective in dealing with problems indigenous to the locality in direct proportion to the degree in which local concepts of law and morality differ from the West' (1987: 94, 113). To support his findings, Petchsiri points out the diverging influences on criminal law, that is, the Judaeo-Christian tradition, Roman law, the Humanists, industrial revolutions on the 'Western' side and Hinduism, Buddhism, Confucianism, Islam and Colonialism. Meanwhile, Nobel peace prize laureate Kim Dae-Jung, who went from political prisoner to president, has turned the debate on its head, claiming that democratic values are, in fact, deeply rooted in Asian culture, society and history (Dae-Jung 1994: 138-39). Others have pointed out that Eastern traditions of human rights often predate European law or philosophy. This has sparked a lively argument on 'freedom' in Asia and its roots in Asian religious and philosophical systems, particularly in Buddhism and Confucianism (Kelly and Reid 1998; Carnegie Council 1994–98: Vol. 6).

Buddhism, Values, Social Engagement and Human Rights

> I am a frog swimming happily in the clear water of a pond
> And I am the grass-snake that silently feeds itself on the frog.
> I am the child in Uganda, all skin and bone, my legs as thin as Bamboo
>   sticks
> And I am the arms-merchant selling deadly weapons to Uganda.
> I am the twelve-year-old girl, refugee on a small boat,
> Who throws herself into the ocean after being raped by a sea pirate
> And I am the pirate, my heart not yet capable of seeing and loving
> (Thich Nhat Hanh, *Please Call Me By My True Names*, quoted in Queen
>   2000: 48 n. 43).

The possible affinities of human rights and Buddhism have been fre-quently and intensely investigated,[10] not least since the emergence of 'Engaged Buddhism', a new chapter of the tradition that seeks to apply Buddhist teachings to the resolution of social and political problems (Queen 2000: 1), as illustrated in this chapter's epithet. The resistance of Nobel prize laureate Aung San Suu Kyi, the Free Tibet Movement represented by Tenzin Gyatso, the current Dalai Lama, and others, or the peace work of the Cambodian monk Maha Ghosananda, the 'Ghandi of Cambodia', are frequently cited in this context. Other cases are the Vietnamese cleric Thich Nhat Hanh, one of the influences behind Martin Luther King Jr, or, more recently, the adoption of a more visible 'Buddhist human rights activism' by Hollywood celebrities such as Harrison Ford, Steven Seagal and Richard Gere. The Vietnamese form of a more socially involved, 'activist' Buddhism, in particular, was born 'out of the crucible of the years of colonialism and war in Vietnam' (Hunt-Perry and Fine 2000: 35). On a more abstract level,

---

10. A 'Bibliography on Buddhism and Human Rights' is at: http://jbe.la.psu. edu/2/rightbib.html; see also Keown 1995: 3-27; Keown, Prebish and Husted 1998; S. Bell 2000: 397-422.

Hershock (2000: 10-11) has reasserted that it is generally impossible to disassociate the politico-legal contents of a human rights discussion from its more 'metaphysical' level. However, on account of Buddhist karmic laws and the interdependence of all things, he claims human rights should not have the primary function of promoting minimal universal standards. Other analysts have pointed out that public power is restricted by Buddhist ethics (Harris 1999: 3, 7, 8, 19). Harvey (2000: 114-15) finds in Buddhist scripture evidence for a quasi-social-contract model of government: 'this clearly gives a ruler no right to abuse the people he rules, for the very basis of his legitimacy is that he should benefit them' (Harvey 2000: 118). But Buddhists are more likely to discuss human rights in terms of universal 'responsibilities', 'dignity' or 'duties'. On the surface this is because Buddhist teachings on 'impermanence', 'interdependence' and 'identity' are essentially deconstructivist: they do not readily acknowledge an 'Unchanging, Essential Self', which could be the owner of 'inalienable' rights. However, Harvey (2000: 119) demonstrates that this does not exclude rights entitlement, and Keown (1995: 3-27) concludes that human rights concepts flow from human nature and are not alien to Buddhist thought. As further evidence for this train of argument, the Declaration on Buddhism and Human Rights, proclaimed during an online conference in 1995,[11] emphasizes principles of dignity, humane treatment, and equality: 'those who have the good fortune to have a "rare and precious human rebirth", with all its potential for awareness, sensitivity and freedom, have a duty not to abuse the rights of others' (see also Harvey 2000: 121). Buddhism rejects discrimination and advocates the value of life, compassion, tolerance, sovereignty, consensus or the quasi-contractual nature of government (Marbett 1998: 21, 25; Thanh-Dam Truong 1998: 53, 56). It encourages ethical behaviour towards humans, animals and plants, guided by compassion and the moral precepts (Harvey 1990: 196-216). As a result, it seems at least difficult to verify that Buddhism really carries the political notions attributed to it under the 'Asian Values' label.

Confucius Would Surely Approve, Wouldn't He?

> Master You said: 'Few indeed are those who are naturally filial towards their parents and dutiful towards their elder brothers but are fond of

---

11. http://jbe.la.psu.edu/1995conf/closing.html

> opposing their superiors; and it never happens that those who do not like opposing their superiors are fond of creating civil disorder (Confucius, *The Analects*, 1993: 1.2).

Confucius, or Kong-Fu-Tzi (551–479 BCE), is often cited in connection with 'Asian family values' or 'Asian ways of doing things'. John H. and Evelyn Nagai-Berthrong have traced and analysed this way of thinking and the changes it has gone through (2000: 4):

> now, however, Confucianism shows signs of internal renewal and the remarkable contemporary economic success of East Asia is being linked to enduring Confucian values of love of education, respect for family, hard work, and the desire for a social order built on consensus and harmony rather than individual competition.

The situation appears more complex, as some Asian countries with an avowedly Confucian heritage (e.g. Japan, Taiwan and South Korea) have also subscribed to the Universal Declaration of Human Rights. Those who attempt to recruit Confucius for the debate point to the five social relationships of Confucian thought—father and son, husband and wife, master and servants, older and younger brothers and friends of equal status—holding Asian societies together (Lach 1994: Vol. 3, Bk 4, 1652). The social relations within the family are of particular importance as a source of guidance for all (Ebrey 2000: 45). Confucius, it is claimed, advocated hierarchy and discipline, which is good for both state authority and the GDP. However, scholars like Chan (1998: 37) find that the five relationships are compatible with human rights. Confucius's *Analects* contain the rights to free will, self-cultivation and self-improvement, integrity or people's trust in Government (De Bary 1998a: 15, 23-4, 29). Confucius promoted a balance between individual and society, the private and the public, and not assertion of one over the other, 'blind allegiance' or subordination (De Bary 1998b: 53). He recognized the tradition of revolt against an unjust government (Christie and Roy 2001: 220). The legitimacy of the ruler derives from *a priori* moral standards (the 'mandate of heaven'); he is 'subject to a de-anthropomorphized and metaphysicized Heaven ("*t'ien*")' (Gang Xu 1999: 426). Governments rule by a 'moral sense' (*jen*), and a sense of justice is tantamount (Nuyen 1999: 195). 'When the [good] way prevails in the state, speak boldly and act boldly. When the state has lost the way, act boldly and speak boldly', is an often quoted saying in this respect. Henkin (1998: 313) concludes that 'the Human Rights idea is not alien to Confucian values today'.

Towards More Coherence?

> The next century belongs not to Asia, or America, or any other continent,
> but to those values, which best combine decency and a good life (Chris
> Patten 1998: 5).

It has been shown that there is little tangible evidence for any inherent
tensions between Buddhism or Confucianism and human rights. This
means that the 'Asian' values, claimed to be traceable to Buddhism or
Confucianism, can quite easily transmutate into more universal, human-
istic values. The argument, it may be concluded, might in time dissolve
towards a higher degree of convergence. This shows that often enough
religion does not carry the modern political notions attributed to it, and
the values debate can become a victim of selective political exploitation. If the scheme of 'Asian' versus 'Western' values is used deliberately as a smokescreen for regime legitimation, values degenerate and
become, to quote Shakespeare, 'a custom more honoured in the breach
than the observance'.[12] In addition, there is significant convergence
already, by means of rapid economic development. Few can deny the
effect of the onslaught of globalism, 'de-isolationalism', urbanization,
the Internet and modernity in general. It is all too easy to underestimate
the homogenizing effect of technological advancement on value
systems. Christie and Roy (2001: 6) summarize that 'the debate may be
miscast; it is not Asian versus western values, but rather tradition
versus modernity'. All this changes the social fabric of societies, from
family structures and religion to crime, and there is an indissoluble
connection between the ability to modernize and the system of values.
For the EU it is vital to understand these developments and to pursue a
harmonious, multi-layered dialogue, without, as Rüland puts it (1996:
81), making sacrifices on the 'altar of economics'. Last, but not least,
Tan Dun, the prolific Hong Kong composer has provided a fascinating
alternative hint at possible convergence: in his *Symphony 1997*, sub-
titled *Heaven-Earth-Mankind*, he recalls one of the primary visions of
Confucian thought: the cosmic 'resonance and unity between and
among heaven, earth and humanity' (John H. and Evelyn Nagai-
Berthrong 2000: 16). Commissioned for the return of Hong Kong to

---

12. *Hamlet*, Act I, Scene iv, line 14, quoted in Thio Li-Ann 1997: 70; the verse
continues: 'This heavy-handed revel east and west makes us traduced and taxed of
other nations'.

China, the symphony evokes the traditional Chinese organization of all knowledge into these three categories, and the underlying striving for unity. It is, perhaps, not inappropriate that within the movement entitled *Jubilation*, the composer quotes the fourth movement of Beethoven's *Ninth (Choral) Symphony*, the European Union's own anthem.

Conclusion

The 1994 New Asia Strategy and its 2001 successor formed one of the key pillars of the EU's Asia policy. These papers, based on the notion of a 'partnership of equals' between European and Asian partners were supplemented by a number of more specialized, country-specific or regional Asia strategies, by the EU's emerging CFSP, the work of successive Presidencies of the Council of Ministers and the activities of the European Parliament, especially in the area of human rights. The Asian financial crisis of 1997–98 and an increased overall EU emphasis on human rights, democracy and 'good governance' in its external relations have contributed to another round in the debate about 'Asian' and 'Western' values. In spite of radically divergent historical and philosophical origins, and anxieties about a 'clash of civilizations', there are important commonalities between the two sides and processes such as globalization contribute to a certain amount of convergence in the argument.

4 |

The EU and ASEAN: Initiatives of a Revitalized Group-to-Group Dialogue

This section investigates the relationship between the European Union and the ten-member Association of South-East Asian Nations (ASEAN). It looks at the development of group-to-group dialogue between the EU and ASEAN and analyses the problems posed for the partnership by individual problems, such as Burma's accession to ASEAN, and general trends, like the need for ASEAN to 're-engineer' itself, that is, to change and construct a new identity for itself. The chapter closes with an overview of the most important regional cooperation initiatives linking the EU to ASEAN as a whole and to ASEAN member states.

Constructive Engagement or Instructive Derangement?[1] Evolution and Identity of ASEAN

> One needs only to whisper—and not shout—to get things done in ASEAN (Domingo Siazon, quoted in *Financial Times*, 26 July 1996: 4).

The EU maintains that the 'web of EU–ASEAN ties' is the 'cornerstone of its developing dialogue with all Asian countries' (Commission 1998c: 5; McMahon 1998: 238). In the same vein, a number of political analysts have conceived of EU–ASEAN relations as a potential 'pillar of the new international order' (Dosch 2001: 57). A number of strong commonalities do, indeed, link the two regions: the need for regional stability; a more and more global ambition; and efforts to enlarge the respective body of membership. However, ASEAN does not share the EU's legal nature, promotes informality (see Box 4.1) and strives neither to set Copenhagen-like criteria for new members, nor to achieve full monetary union or an ASEAN single currency. ASEAN Secretary-

---

1. This phrase was used by Vitit Muntharbhorn, *Bangkok Post*, 23 September 1993.

General Severino (1999a: 17) has re-emphasized that ASEAN 'is not—and was not meant to be—a supranational entity acting independently of its members'.

ASEAN, with its seat in Jakarta, was established by the Bangkok Declaration of 8 August 1967. It is useful to stress, with Ul Haq (1999: 24), that Indonesia, Malaysia, the Philippines, Singapore and Thailand created ASEAN by an act of political will to overcome Malaysian–Indonesian *konfrontasi*. In other words, the birth of ASEAN was not the 'culmination of a natural process'. Following independence from the UK, Brunei Darussalam joined in 1984. Through the 1995 initiative, *Towards One Southeast Asia*, Vietnam was accepted as ASEAN's seventh—and first communist—member on 28 July 1995, which is remarkable, given the fact that, until 1991, ASEAN had still been concerned with getting Vietnam out of Cambodia. Membership gave a much-needed boost to Vietnam's application for WTO accession. In the 'C-L-M Enlargement', Burma and the Lao PDR joined in 1997, Cambodia, belatedly, in April 1999. ASEAN has thus accomplished its goal of membership of all ten South-East Asian states in ASEAN (the 'ASEAN-10'). Apart from multi-level cooperation, members' commitment to resolve intra-regional differences peacefully, were declared an important objective. The notion of ASEAN as a 'peace process', however, next to a security, 'confidence-building' and diplomatic community, is open to debate (Leifer 1999: 25-27, 38).

Box 4.1: Compromise, not Confrontation: The 'ASEAN Creed'

> ASEAN works on what Indonesians call *musyawarah* and *mufakat*, consensus and accommodation (Christie and Roy 2001: 126; Snitwongse 1996: 14). When consultation cannot create consensus, the ASEAN states traditionally 'agree to disagree' (Leong 1997: 20; Narine 1999: 360; Stubbs 2000: 312). It has been further argued (Busse 1999: 39, 45, 56) that this aspect of Asian international relations reveals a 'collective' ASEAN identity. The Vientiane Declaration of 2000 is the latest document to suggest this. However, Western criticism has sparked Asian counter-accusations of 'moralizing through sanctions'. But ASEAN attitudes are changing (Christie and Roy 2001: 79), to what Thio Li-ann (1997: 64) called an 'ASEAN discipline within'. The future is seen in overcoming decision-making paralysis, which may otherwise threaten the grouping with obsolescence (*Bangkok Post*, 13 August 2000: 3).

The ASEAN grouping has undergone a recent transformation from political necessity to economic prosperity and political dynamism (see Box 4.2). This was motivated by a variety of factors such as the end of the Cold War, the Maastricht Treaty, the emerging CFSP and the EC Single Market. These developments are often seen as 'symbolic' or 'catalytic' from an Asian point of view (Phatharodom 1998: 61). They amount to considerable shifts in the ASEAN identity, which have found expression in new initiatives such as the ASEAN Action Agenda for an ASEAN Vision 2020.

Box 4.2: ASEAN Development

> Following the 1977 Preferential Trading Agreement, ASEAN laid the groundwork, from 1992, for an ASEAN Investment Area (AIA) and an ASEAN Free Trade Area (AFTA). This was facilitated, as Stubbs (2000: 300-303, 315) contends, by the shift to liberal economic policies in formerly protectionist Indonesia, Malaysia, the Philippines and Thailand. Implementation of AFTA, originally planned for 2005 is now to take effect in 2002 (with derogations from Vietnam, Burma Laos and Cambodia). Suggested by former Thai Prime Minister Anant Panyarachun, AFTA aimed to establish an open regional market with a low tariff. It employs a Common Effective Preferential Tariff (CEPT) as its main instrument for tariff reduction and trade liberalization. However, AFTA also constitutes, as Chirativat has argued (1996: 33, 43), a 'GATT-plus' and forms 'the way for ASEAN members to increase their international competitiveness and integration within the world'. As opposed to the EU, which has strict rules governing the Single Market, AFTA is an evolving concept, driven by consensus, not meant to be a customs union, let alone a common market (Commission 1996d: 3). But Bonnet (1999: 255) and Dent (1999: 42) have argued convincingly that AFTA itself was a response to fears concerning the Single Market in Europe. Related anxieties about market access or a loss of geopolitical relevance have resurfaced in connection with the EU's efforts towards CEE enlargement, the financial crisis in 1997–98 or changes to the Structural Funds.

It is in this context that Abad (1996: 239, 250) has spoken of a continual 're-engineering' of the ASEAN outlook into a 'rapid-reaction', intergovernmental organization run by 'Aseanocrats'. The change in identity and search for more unity that ASEAN embarked on after the ASEAN summit in Bangkok in July 2000 meant that it took on new directions, like North Korean participation in the ARF, and became involved in the debates about an ASEAN-*troika* or an ASEAN Human Rights Commission. At the same time, ASEAN's dialogue with China, Japan and South Korea—the so-called 'ASEAN + 3' meetings in 1997 and 1999—paved the way to greater regional integration. A number of new countries, including some EU member states, applied to become ASEAN dialogue partners. However, not everyone shared an optimistic view. For some commentators, the importance and influence of ASEAN are in decline, its prospects 'at best discouraging' (Narine 1999: 375). In general, however, the association is still overwhelmingly being called the most successful regional grouping in the developing world, in the same measure by which the EU is routinely described as the most successful regional grouping in the developed world (Tan and Chia, 1997: 1, 3).

Transcending the 'Donor-Recipient Paradigm'

The EU first engaged in relations with ASEAN against the background of the Vietnam War, when many believed that South-East Asian countries risked falling like dominoes under the sway of communism. A second determining factor was the UK's entry into the EC in 1972, bringing with it the question of how to deal with the loss of the UK's Commonwealth preferences. On other levels too, ASEAN is central to the EU: all ASEAN member states, except Thailand, have been European colonies; the EU is ASEAN's oldest and third most important trading partner, after Japan and the USA; and ASEAN is one of the main beneficiaries of the GSP system. The development of the EU–ASEAN relationship (see Box 4.3) forms part of another major transition that ASEAN is undergoing: the move from international relations dominated by development aid to all-encompassing political partnership, beyond the donor-recipient pattern (McMahon 1998: 238; Bonnet 1999: 257; Pattugalan 1999: 43).

The EU–ASEAN relationship was further influenced by the formation by ASEAN of the ARF in 1993–94. ASEAN Secretary-General Rodolfo C. Severino Jr called this 'a historic event in the Asia-Pacific' (Severino 1999a: 16). Less involved observers have compared the ARF to the Asia-Pacific Economic Cooperation grouping (APEC) (see Box 4.4), or have interpreted it as an Asian equivalent to the Conference for Security and Cooperation in Europe (CSCE). The ARF[2] is arguably ASEAN's most significant by-product. Its preventative diplomacy

---

2.   The participants of the ARF are: Australia, Brunei Darussalam, Burma, Cambodia, Canada, China, the EU, India, Indonesia, Japan, North Korea (DPRK), Laos, Malaysia, Mongolia, New Zealand, Papua New Guinea, the Philippines, the Russian Federation, Singapore, Thailand, the USA and Vietnam.

involves most of Asia, the USA, the EU, China and Russia. It is the only forum in the Asia-Pacific which deals with political and security issues. Although neither the ASEAN Concord of 1976 nor the 1987 Manila Declaration had foreseen security as falling within the ASEAN brief, ASEAN was successful in establishing ARF because members felt comfortable about ASEAN's leadership role. Europe also plays a part in the ARF's Council for Security Cooperation in the Asia-Pacific (CSCAP), which consists of non-governmental think-tanks.

Box 4.3: Inter-Regional 'Group-to-Group' Dialogue: The Development of EU–ASEAN Relations

Early ASEAN–EU relations rested on a first Ministerial Meeting in 1978, the 1980 ASEAN–EU Co-operation Agreement (*OJ* L 144/80, 10 June 1980: 1) and the 1992 Regulation on Financial and Technical Assistance to, and Economic Cooperation with, the developing countries in Asia and Latin America (Council Regulation (EEC) No 443/92, of 25 February 1992), which has formed a wide-ranging legal basis for EC–Asia relations. A 1992 European Parliament Resolution on Economic and Trade Relations between the EU and ASEAN (*OJ* C 125/269-276, 10 April 1992), recognized ASEAN as among the Union's most important economic and political partners and suggested measures to amend the 1980 Agreement. Among them were the strengthening of political dialogue, economic and trade cooperation, protection of human rights and initiatives against child labour, sex tourism, environmental deterioration and drug abuse. 1994 and 1995 saw the New Asia Strategy and the creation of the ASEAN–European Union Senior Officials' Meeting (SOM). Moreover, the 11th ASEAN–EU Ministerial Meeting (AEMM) in Karlsruhe in September 1994 established an Eminent Persons' Group (EPG) to enhance the relationship. An EPG Report placed particular emphasis on cultural issues. The 'Karlsruhe Drive' (Dent 1999: 60) was later also to inform the Commission's New Asia Strategy and the ASEM Process.

On this basis, the Commission drafted a new Communication in 1996, *Creating a New Dynamic in EU–ASEAN Relations* (Commission 1996d). It was subject to discussions and opinions in the Economic and Social Committee (*OJ* C 89, 19 March 1997), the Council and the European Parliament (*OJ* C 325, 27 October 1997) and was launched in February 1997. McMahon (1998: 240, 251) likened it to the way the Barcelona Declaration impinged on the Euro-Mediterranean Partnership. The 1996 paper analyses ASEAN in the context of APEC and AFTA and provides a detailed description of the history, structure and process of EU–ASEAN policies, emphasizing the importance of European presence and enhanced cooperation, with regard to dialogue, liberalization of trade and investment, environment, science and technology. A 1997 Joint Declaration, ASEAN's 1998 Ha Noi Plan of Action, a Council Decision of March 1998 and a 1999 Joint Cooperation Committee (JCC) Work Programme have added to the 1996 Communication in areas ranging from market access issues and standardization to investment and capital flows.

Box 4.4: The ASEAN Regional Forum (ARF) and the Asia-Pacific Economic Cooperation (APEC) Grouping

The ASEAN Regional Forum (ARF) is often seen as 'complementary' to APEC, the multilateral Asia-Pacific Economic Cooperation grouping formed in Canberra in 1989 (*Rapid Database*: IP/95/1110). APEC members include: Australia, Brunei Darussalam, Canada, Chile, China, Hong Kong, Indonesia, Japan, South Korea, Malaysia, Mexico, New Zealand, Papua New Guinea, Peru, the Philippines, Russia, Singapore, Taiwan, Thailand, USA and Vietnam. The ASEAN Secretariat is an APEC Observer (cf. Drysdale and Vines 1998).

APEC is unique in comprising, within its membership, more than 44 per cent of global trade and three free trade areas: the North American Free Trade Area (NAFTA), AFTA, and the Australia-New Zealand Closer Economic Relations (CER) Agreement. Low (1996: 93) has characterized APEC as a possible match for the EU and EEA. Pelkmans and Shinkai (1998: 14) have convincingly identified five 'driving factors' behind APEC: (1) a kind of self-appointed leadership in GATT/WTO; (2) the perceived need to underpin market-led integration in East Asia; (3) supporting and strengthening 'do-it-yourself' liberalization; (4) the pre-emption of, or alternative for, East Asian 'go-it-alone'; and (5) a constructive response to the end of the Cold War via an emerging Asia-Pacific 'architecture', while formally avoiding the routes of security or foreign policy.

APEC thus appears as an alternative process; it is a 'paradigm of open regionalism in a region with little history of transnational institutionalization' (Beeson and Jayasuriya 1998: 329). But it is more than a loose community and is valued more as a confidence-building process than as a results-oriented forum (Ravenhill 2000: 331). Individual ASEAN countries' membership in APEC and the 'observer' status of ASEAN as a whole can arguably be seen as a vital, if not an exclusive, motive underpinning ASEAN relations of the EU, which in this way aspires to the keys to the Pacific (Bonnet 1999: 256).

The summits in Seattle (1993), Bogor (1994), Osaka (1995) and Manila (1996) have been landmark meetings in the formalization and institutionalization of APEC, but dynamism has been restrained and observers like Ravenhill (2000: 319-27) have identified lack of consensus and of an institutional engine and failure to engage with civil society as the main obstacles to the further development of the forum (see http://www.apec-china.org.cn/ and the *Guardian*, 16 October 2001: 17 for the 2001 summit meeting).

'Value-System Friction' Revisited: Current and Future Political Issues in the Dialogue between the EU and ASEAN

There is considerable argument surrounding what Dent (1999: 51, 61, 71) termed 'value-system friction' between the EU and ASEAN, an area that other observers termed 'the dark side of ASEAN–EU relations' (Dosch 2001: 64). It concerns a number of issues, notably different concepts, speeds, levels and targets of integration; the effects of trade on the Asian environment; and the requirement that new EU member states must fall in line with the *acquis communautaire*, which can result in new import restrictions being imposed on that country's trade with Asian partners. But it is the subject of human rights which continues to have the strongest impact on the development of the EU–Asia dialogue. Lim (1999a: 9) has shown that human rights appeared first in the EEC–ASEAN dialogue in the context of a meeting in Luxembourg in 1991. The EU admits that over the last 28 years, the two regions have disagreed, both in private and in public, over this point and others, like trade, and that the partners: 'may never completely see eye-to-eye on this issue' (Commission 1998c: 8, 23). The danger is that this may be what Thio Li-ann (1997: 70) aptly termed the 'paralysing effect of relativism' in regional blocs' views on human rights. Therefore, EU–ASEAN contacts leave room for 'enhanced co-operation and greater commitment', as Pattugalan (1999: 62) diplomatically puts it. More directly, Bonnet (1999: 265) concludes that 'obviously, Europe has not yet solved the dichotomy of "cooperation versus competition" regarding its relations with ASEAN, and continues to give with one hand and take away with the other'. Daquila (1997: 131) identifies other obstacles such as trade policy and economic structure. On the political side, Burma in particular (see Box 4.5), has proved to be a major bone of contention over the ASEAN principles of non-interference and 'situational uniqueness' (Christie and Roy 2001: 75). Differences over Burma have contributed to the frequently 'dysfunctional' nature (Forster 2000: 791, 794) of the EU–ASEAN relationship (Box 4.5).

Box 4.5: Burma, ASEAN and the EU

When it joined ASEAN in 1997, Burma did not become part of the 1980 EC–ASEAN Cooperation Agreement, and the EU has objected both to the extension of this Agreement to Burma and to Burma's participation in EU–ASEAN Senior Officials' Meetings (SOM). However, ASEAN members are adamant they cannot prevent a member from being fully involved in meetings (Severino 1999b: 71). Former Thai Foreign Secretary Prachuab Chaiyarsan speculated: 'Even a playboy can become a good husband, with the family's help. That's the Asian way'. And analysts like Narine (1999: 368) warn that 'the decision to bring Myanmar into ASEAN has enormous potential to backfire on ASEAN'. The 1996 Commission Strategy on ASEAN therefore represented an effort to revitalize the dialogue, but, due to lack of progress on Burma, a meeting of the Joint Cooperation Committee (JCC) established under the 1980 Agreement, which had been planned for November 1997, was postponed indefinitely and had to be cancelled, for the third time, in 1999. The situation was eased temporarily by the idea that there would be no 'automatic' participation of new ASEAN members in the process of Asia-Europe Meetings (ASEM, see next chapter). The JCC finally met in Bangkok from 26–27 May 2000. However, the Burmese were obliquely referred to as 'a non-signatory of the EC–ASEAN Agreement' and were banned from speaking or flying their flag. (*European Voice*, 2–8 March 2000; 6–12 April 2000; see also Lim 1999a: 23-30; Dosch 2001: 64, 66).

An Overview of Regional Cooperation Programmes

Some 50 per cent of the Union's diverse, complex and often inter-related cooperation programmes targeting Asia as a whole, concern ASEAN. Development aid as a 'traditional' area of cooperation, is now mainly focused on Burma, Cambodia, Laos and Vietnam. The main characteristic of other programmes is that they group together Asian states in certain geographical areas, according to specific needs and targets. The following projects form some examples of these. They cover the areas of humanitarian aid, energy, environment, health, the institutionalization of business strategies, local government, higher education, information technology cooperation and various related and auxiliary initiatives.[3]

Humanitarian Aid
The European Community Humanitarian Office (ECHO) planned its disaster prevention initiative (DIPECHO) in 1996 (see Box 4.6), to cover disaster-prone areas such as South-East Asia, Central America and the Caribbean. ECHO offices in the region administer a programme that rests on the three pillars of support for human resources, institution building and a firm base in local communities. The programme aims at disaster prevention, preparedness and mitigation in an area regularly plagued by the floodwaters of the Mekong, hurricanes, droughts, earth-quakes or tornadoes.

---

3   See: http://www.asia-invest.com/newhtml/eu-prog-links.html;   or   http://www.pts.ait.ac.th/pts/links.htm

Box 4.6: ECHO's Disaster Prevention Humanitarian Aid Programme (DIPECHO)

In 1999, the DIPECHO funding volume for South-East Asia amounted to €2.4 million. Phase II, initiated on 8 August 2000, has almost doubled the funding available from the Union. It encompasses some 13 individual projects in the Lao PDR, Cambodia, Indonesia, the Philippines and Vietnam, and one (partly) ASEAN-coordinated information exchange component (Commission Delegation Bangkok, Press Release of 9 August 2000).

Energy Cooperation and Environmental Projects

Tingsabadh (1999: 184-85) has stressed the need for mutual EU–ASEAN environmental education and has stated elsewhere (1996: 137), that: 'the other effect of globalization is that environmental issues also become part of international relations'. The Asian Development Bank (ADB) has estimated that the Asia Pacific is expected to replace the OECD countries as the world's biggest sources of greenhouse gas emissions by 2015 (*Financial Times*, 19 June 2001). Against the background of an Asian environment which continues to fall victim, pervasively and unabatedly, to industrialization and urbanization, 'putting energy into EU-Asian relations' (Commission Delegation Bangkok, *EU Today*, No. 5, January–March 1998: 2), has long been the subject of bilateral agreements (see Box 4.7). Previous European initiatives such as 'SYNERGY', 'SAVE', 'ALTENER' or 'JOULE'/'THERMIE', and the work of the European Investment Bank, have paved the way for a more comprehensive EU–Asia Energy cooperation, which has taken its cue from the 1994 New Asia Strategy and the Commission White Paper on *An Energy Policy for the European Union* (Commission 1995d). Energy policy has subsequently been the focus of a more specialized Europe–Asia cooperation strategy for energy (Commission 1996c). The document's rationale is Asian economic growth—still at a peak when the blueprint was drafted—population increase, rapid urbanization and the concomitant rise in demand for energy, and its consequences for the world market in raw materials, the environment and societies. It aims at (1) securing energy supplies in Asia and Europe, (2) increasing European business inroads into Asian energy markets and (3) strengthening environmental protection (Commission 1996c: 3).

Box 4.7: EU–ASEAN Initiatives and 'Green' Energy

A number of energy-related, 'green', projects are located in the EU–ASEAN context, for instance the ASEAN Timber Technology Centre (ATTC), the 1988–99 ASEAN-EC Energy Management and Training Centre (AEEMTRC) in Jakarta/Indonesia (complemented by the ASEM Environment and Techno-logy Research Centre). Related schemes are the 1995–99 EC–ASEAN Cogen programme in biomass energy at the Asian Institute of Technology in Bangkok exploring possible cooperation in energy conversion technologies (Commission 1998c: 38-39). The 1997 ASEAN–EU Roundtables on Energy, an ASEAN-EU Business Forum and an ASEAN–EU Energy Cooperation Conference in Bangkok in June 1998 have all contributed to the sharing of information and the formation of new public-private partnerships in this area. (Commission Delegation Bangkok, *EU Today*, No. 5, January–March 1998: 8).

Environmental degradation in Asia, from water and air pollution, forest fires and excessive dam-building on the Mekong (Osborne 2000: 228) is severe and has far-reaching, global consequences. It is inextricably linked to social and economic issues that the EU cannot ignore. Bilat-eral European–Asian cooperation on the environment has existed for some time (see Box 4.8) and has been further promoted by the ASEM process. The width and breadth of EU–Asia environmental cooperation was further underscored by the Rio Conference in 1992 and the World Environment Summit in Berlin in 1995. A more consolidated framework appeared in 1997, through a Commission communication on *A Europe–Asia Co-operation Strategy in the Field of Environment* (Commission 1997d). The proposal prioritizes urban and industry-related issues and attempts to provide a 'systematic mechanism' to exploit synergies with environment-related member state activities in Asia. It also aims at the protection and sustainable use of natural resources and the attainment of increased awareness through research and development (R&D). It has been the inspiration for a number of EU–Asia programmes in the field of the environment.

Health Initiatives
Malaria and other communicable diseases are among the globe's biggest obstacles to socio-economic development, both in developed and in developing nations. But they are not the only ones. Development Commissioner Poul Nielson stated: 'TB, HIV/AIDS and malaria are all diseases that kill in developing countries—and they are all exacerbated

Box 4.8: EU–Asia Environmental Cooperation Projects

The Regional Institute of Environmental Technology (RIET) in Singapore was founded in July 1993, in order to provide expertise to firms and governments, build up networks and facilitate the exchange of 'green' services and resources. RIET supports integrated approaches towards tackling the downside of Asian economic vibrancy. Its project developments and business promotions aim to support environmentally sound technology and to introduce services which benefit both consumers and (European) investors alike. Phase II (1997–2002) is about to transform RIET gradually into a more permanent RIET Foundation (Commission 1998c: 43).

The Asia-Ecobest (AEB) initiative (1997–2002), funded by €8 million of Community money, is administered through RIET. It provides training and consultation and helps European partners with investment in the Asian market of environmental products and services. Asia-Ecobest emphasizes 'awareness and promotion', 'information and intelligence', 'human resource development', 'diagnostics' and 'matchmaking'. Among its instruments are environmental roundtables and impact assessments (Commission 1997d: 16).

Many individual EU-supported environmental projects are expected to reach self-support status, following a period of funding. Worth mentioning are the Community Participation in Mangrove Forest Management and Rehabilitation project in Southern Thailand, the Wastewater Management at That Luang Marshes project in the Lao PDR or Support Programme to the Environment Sector in Cambodia (SPEC). (Delegation Bangkok, *EU Today*, No. 2, April–June 1997: 5-7).

by poverty' (Commission, *The Courier*, No. 184, January–February 2001: 2). Disease and poverty form a mutually exacerbating, vicious circle. Next to care and prevention of sexually transmitted diseases, the task of fighting malarial infection is a permanent challenge for the EU and other health actors. Following its April 1999 reform initiative, *The European Community's Development Policy* (Commission 2000[l]), the Commission unveiled, in 2000, a new strategy for Accelerated Action targeted at major communicable diseases within the context of poverty reduction (Commission 2000d). Its main objectives were the 'interlocking' of trade, development and research policies and the improvement of the effect of EU policies against HIV/AIDS, malaria and tuberculosis (Commission Delegation Bangkok, *EU Today* No. 15, January 2001: 4; *Week in Europe*, 21 September 2000; *Rapid Database*: IP/00/1031). This policy framework was developed through a more concrete 2001 Programme for Action, covering 2001–06 and focusing on R&D, affordability and specific instruments for action (Commission

2001i: points 3.2-3.4). Regarding Asia in particular, the EU's €29 million Regional Malaria Control Programme, in particular, aims to influence both morbidity and mortality related to the disease. It suspends a net, as it were, over Laos, Cambodia and Vietnam and has a supra-regional component. Moreover, the €25 million Asia-Initiative for Reproductive Health scheme is funded by the Commission, under the auspices of the United Nations Population Fund. The initiative covers Bangladesh, Cambodia, India, Laos, Nepal, Pakistan, Sri Lanka and Vietnam. Among its objectives are the provision of health advice and services relevant to the region, touching on issues ranging from infertility and rape to attitudes towards condoms or commercial sex. This assumes a particular importance in countries with a high percentage of younger people. There is a large number of EC AIDS programmes and sub-initiatives in the region. They aim at controlling the spread of the HIV epidemic and have existed in Thailand (since 1988), Burma (since 1996) and Cambodia and Laos (since 1997). However, there is an equally large number of practical and cultural hurdles. One relevant Commission source, for instance, observes that: 'risk reduction in commercial sex is often not given the importance it deserves due to a sense of fatigue in addressing this issue' (Commission Delegation Bangkok, *EU Today*, No. 6, April–June 1998: 8).

Internationalizing Business Strategies: AsiaInvest, ECIP and EBICs
Many projects under this heading (see also Box 4.9) are complementary to similar initiatives within the ASEM process, such as Asia-Europe Business Fora, the Trade Facilitation Action Plan (TFAP) or the Investment Promotion Action Plan (IPAP). The AsiaInvest initiative, launched by the Commission in 1997, offers financial support, facilitates business cooperation and investment, and promotes contacts. The five-year scheme is worth €45 million and maintains a Secretariat in Brussels. A regular newsletter updates both applicants and the so-called AsiaInvest Antennae, holders of expertise within organizations that represent small and medium-sized enterprises.[4] The key to AsiaInvest is a marketplace monitoring scheme (cf. *AsiaInvest Newsletter* No. 10, March 2000: 6). An additional Technology and Trade Information Promotion System (TIPS) provides specific help for Laotian and Cambodian businesses. Further key elements of AsiaInvest are a

4.   See the case-studies at: http://www.asia-invest.com/newhtml/factsheet.html

Business Priming Fund, including components such as the European Community Investment Partners (ECIP) scheme, the sectoral business meetings called Asia Interprise and Asia-Partenariat, the AsiaInvest Facility on Business Research, as well as technical assistance and language and culture familiarization components.[5]

Box 4.9: Helping Business to 'Bridge the Gap'

European Community Investment Partners (ECIP), launched in 1988, has sub-programmes assisting joint ventures between SMEs in the EU and their partners in Asia. The facilities connected to the scheme offer a mix of start-up grants and interest-free loans. The Commission has approved more than 500 ECIP projects in the ASEAN region (Commission 1998c: 46-47). The European Business Information Centres (EBIC), located throughout South-East Asia, act as gateways, facilitators, databases, EU sales agents and contact providers for these and other schemes. The EU–ASEAN Managers Exchange Programme (JEM) has fostered cultural and business related immersion experiences for young executives since 1996, while the focus of the ASEAN–EC Management Centre in Brunei Darussalam is more on relevant training and applied research (Commission 1998c: 34-35). Last but not least, the EU-ASEAN Industrialists' Roundtable (IRT), the Euro-Partenariats and Asia-Partenariats, a system of company-level meetings held since 1988, round off this group of business-creating initiatives.

Local Government, Higher Education and Information Technology Cooperation and Related Initiatives

In 1995, around 45 per cent of the world's population lived in urban areas, a percentage expected to increase to 59 per cent by 2025 (*Asia Urbs Magazine* No. 1, summer 1999: 3). Osborne (1997: 10-11) points to the contrast between countryside and cities in Asia, and to the unprecedented growth of the latter throughout the twentieth century. Apart from further urban growth, migration from rural areas to the cities will continue to be a powerful feature in Asia, where the links between international movements of commodities and people have only recently become the subject of wider analysis (see, for instance, Lloyd and Williams 1998). Migration to urban centres has numerous implications for ecology, poverty, employment, settlement management or quality of life. Against this background, the philosophy of the Asia-Urbs framework programme, launched in March 1998 is that (1) 'no

5.   For an example of calls for AsiaInvest proposals, see *OJ* C 185/9 et seq. 1 July 1999, 1999/C 185/07, Nos. 1B/AP/338/339/384 and 391.

city is an island', (2) cities can learn from one another across boundaries, and (3) cities must build their own capacities (*Asia Urbs Magazine* No. 1, summer 1999: 9, 15). *Asia Urbs* focuses on building and maintaining capacities, and partnerships at local government level in Asia and Europe. Built on existing experience and information exchange, the programme supports projects regarding urban socio-economic and infrastructural development, urban management and urban environment. It involves local governments, community groups, NGOs or universities in Europe and Asia. On 17 October 2000, the Commission launched the Second Call for Proposals under the Programme, worth over €9 million (*Asia Urbs Magazine* No. 4, winter 2000: 2, 5).

Box 4.10: EU–Asia Academic and Technical Cooperation

Building, in part, on the Commission's new policy paper *Strengthening Cooperation with Third Countries in the Field of Higher Education* (Commission 2001g), the ASEAN-EU University Network Programme (AUNP) was initiated. It is related to the ASEAN University Network (AUN), chartered in 1995, which aims to enhance the sense of 'ASEANness' among its members (*AUN Newsletter* 1.1, November 2000: 4). The 1997 AUNP aims to initiate sustainable relationships between higher education institutions in both regions through the investigation of subjects of common interest and research collaboration. A large number of schemes co-exist. Some examples are the European Studies Centre at Chulalongkorn University, Bangkok, the European Studies Programme in the Philippines, the ASEAN-EC Management Centre in Brunei, the EU-ASEAN Junior Managers' Programme, the Southeast Asia-Europe University Network or the University of Malaya European Studies Programme (UMESP) (Commission 1997h; Website: http://www.aun.chula.ac.th).

In the area of technical cooperation, the 1998 Europe-Asia Cooperation Programme in Information and Communication Technology (IT & C), to which the EU contributed €25 million, seeks to enhance European technology in Asia and to create a more 'involving' IT and 'e-commerce' environment for South and South-East Asia (Guy Franck, *The Asia IT&C Programme*, June 2000: 3-11).

Furthermore, initiatives like the EC–ASEAN Port Management HRD Project and the EU–Asia Civil Aviation Cooperation Project, including the relevant financing agreements signed in 2001 (*Rapid Database*, IP/01/1557), primarily concern transport safety and industry cooperation in the relevant sectors. The Regional EU–South Asia Intellectual Property Rights Programme is a trade and investment facilitation scheme aiming to update IPR systems in Bangladesh, Pakistan and Sri Lanka, while its counterpart, the EC–ASEAN Intellectual Property Programmes (ECAP I and II) covers patents and trademarks, copyrights, geographical indications and industrial designs. The EC–ASEAN Standards, Quality and Conformity Assessment Programmes (ISQAP I and II) have been designed to bring about a more harmonious environment for cooperation in quality management policy.

Conclusion

The EU is linked to ASEAN by a large number of cooperation programmes, ranging from energy and environment to health, business and higher education. These schemes deepen the EU's commitment towards a group of countries that were, traditionally, among the oldest Asian partners of the EU. ASEAN itself went through a number of transitions, its dynamics were of varying degrees, and, at the beginning of the third millennium, the organization was in urgent need to 're-engineer' itself again and find a new identity, commensurate with new geo-political realities and security concerns. The 'ASEAN creed' of non-interference came under renewed pressure, both within ASEAN, and in its relations with the EU. At the end of 2001, EU–ASEAN relations had moved away from a 'donor-recipient pattern' towards a much wider dialogue. However, in the light of recent problems over Burma and/or human rights, and against the background of the emergence of parallel EU–Asian fora, and changing priorities of the EU in Asia, there is a need for the EU–ASEAN relationship to be redefined in the near future.

5 |

Towards a New Summitry: Process and Substance of the Asia–Europe Meetings

> As purely national solutions to problems lose their efficacy and domestic policies are reversed by transnational activities, cooperation or some kind of transnational management seems to be necessary. Although the sovereignty of states remains the foundation for Asia-Europe relations, the initiation of ASEM is an implicit admission of the limits of state power (Manila Forum on Culture, Values and Technology: The Message of Manila, Executive Summary, 1998: 23).

> The EU, which began as a response to the cataclysm of WW II, is now propelled forward by a shared purpose far greater than the original idea simply of promoting peace. In Asia too, nations are coming together for mutual advantage and support. It is the next logical step, having brought ourselves nearer to one another within our continents, that we should reach our hands out across them (from the opening address by Tony Blair, UK Prime Minister, at ASEM 3 in Seoul in October 2000).

This chapter analyses the process of Asia–Europe Meetings (ASEM), one of the most recent of the many channels of EU–Asia contacts. Following an introduction to why and how the ASEM process started, the main section is an investigation of the ambitions for, and the main results of, the three summits which have taken place so far: ASEM 1 in Bangkok in 1996, ASEM 2 in London in 1998, and ASEM 3 in Seoul in 2000. Particular emphasis is put on the debatable claim that ASEM is an 'informal' process, trying to avoid widespread 'institutionalization'. The chapter contrasts these claims with a critical survey of the plethora of initiatives and programmes which have evolved into the political, economic and cultural 'pillars' of ASEM. Economic and political circumstances for all three ASEM gatherings have been very different, so the chapter also shows ASEM as a mirror of wider EU–Asia relations and offers some possible scenarios for the future reform and development of ASEM. Moreover, it seeks to investigate the amount of overlap and competition with other EU–Asia-related organizations. Among the enabling and constraining factors for the ASEM process, questions of values and human rights presented a particular piece of 'unfinished business', as partners prepared for ASEM 4 in Copenhagen in 2002.

Origins and Rationale of an Asia–Europe Meeting

The idea for an 'Asia–Europe Meeting' can claim both European and Asian parentage. It originates in the 1992 ASEAN summit and was formally initiated in 1994—the year of the EU New Asia Strategy—by Singaporean Prime Minister Goh Chok Tong, in conjunction with the French and German Governments.[1] The ASEM concept, interpreted by some as a substitute for the then stalled EU–ASEAN relationship (Forster 2000: 796), received further impetus from post-Cold War uncertainties and the perception of a 'tripolar' world, in which the 'trans-Pacific' and 'trans-Atlantic' links were well served, through APEC and the G7/G8 respectively, but the Asia–Europe leg showed a paucity of networking. Goh Chok Tong stated: 'It is as though we are using radio waves instead of fibre optics for communication'. From a European viewpoint (Forster 1999: 752), the 'common explanation' for ASEM was that: 'Lee Kuan Yew wanted to make Asia less dependent on the US (in APEC) and therefore read too much into the [EU's] new Asia Strategy'. As far as the EU is concerned, the initiative offered a way out of an EU–ASEAN dialogue that had gone nowhere for some time.

The EU endorsed ASEM during the Essen, Cannes and Madrid summits in 1994–95. The Commission, in its communication regarding the ASEM to be held in Bangkok on 1–2 March 1996 on 16 January 1996 (Commission 1996a), set out its preliminary position, on the basis of the 'historical uniqueness' of the event, the diversity of Asia, and the perceived congruity of interests between East and West. Complementing other inter-regional initiatives, such as ASEAN and APEC, ASEM was to be a 'process' and would, at its most fundamental level, 'open a dialogue on the values and codes in both continents' (Commission 1996a: 4; *Rapid Database*: IP/96/173). Bridges (1999: 183) comments on the appropriateness of Bangkok as the location for ASEM 1— Thailand never experienced European colonial rule—but also observes that:

1.   For a detailed analysis of origin and development of the ASEM idea, see Pou-Serradell 1996: 185-86.

the Asian concern with past dependency and exploitation helped to account, for example, for the phraseology adopted in the Chairman's concluding statement ... about strengthening 'dialogue on an equal basis between Asia and Europe' (1999: 18).

The Asian side, mindful that this was not to be yet another bloc-to-bloc gathering, claimed that the Asian 'coming-out-of-age' (Royal Thai Government 1996d: 30) was the main rationale for the meeting. ASEM would thus be based on informality, multi-dimensionality, equality and evolution. It would deal with political, economic, cultural and security topics, in the pursuit of global issues and in recognition of the growing interdependence of the world. Last, but by no means least, it would take place without the Americans.

ASEM 1: A New 'Euro-Asia House'?

'When the Asians come over here, we'll put sleeping pills in their coffee. It's the only solution', said a European diplomat, desperate to slow down Asian policy makers as they charge ahead with plans for European–Asian co-operation. 'What we need is pep-pills in the coffee of most European member states' retorted an official at the European Commission (Pisani 1996).

It could be argued that the first ASEM meeting involved a confusion of the two sets of objectives. Europe was primarily interested in the human rights issue whereas the Asian participants wanted to talk about trading conditions. The result was an agreement to exchange students (McMahon 1998: 250).

Under the slogan 'Towards a New Asia-Europe Partnership for Greater Growth', the inaugural ASEM (Bangkok, 1–2 March 1996) brought together ten Asian states (the then seven ASEAN countries plus China, Japan and South Korea), the fifteen member states of the EU and the Commission President. This composition led to a wide-ranging debate on participation and representation of parts of Asia, in particular with regard to South Asia and the members of the South Asian Association for Regional Cooperation (SAARC) and India. Moreover, this make-up of ASEM echoed, deliberately or not, the earlier East Asian Economic Caucus (EAEC), proposed by Malaysian Prime Minister Mahathir Mohamad in 1990 (McMahon 1998: 241). Compared to ASEM or the ARF, however, the embryonic EAEC lacked political confidence—it was quickly dubbed a 'Caucus without Caucasians', on account of the exclusion of the USA, Canada, Australia and New Zealand (Godement 1997: 282).[2]

The main purpose of ASEM 1 was modest. It would help, in the words of the Thai hosts, to 'get to know one another' (Royal Thai Government 1996c: 3) and to foster understanding between the EU and Asia. Subsidiary motives behind the summit were of a more global nature: the counteracting of perceptions regarding a 'Fortress Europe', the 'engagement' of China, and the creation of an alternative to the powerful American–Japanese axis in Asia. Yeo Lay Hwee (2000: 116) has made an interesting alternative point, reading ASEM as: 'a sort of conduit to the APEC process', from which the EU is, of course, excluded. The removal of stereotypes, informality and 'ignorance reduction' were the keys for the meeting, which, it should not be forgotten, was also a considerable public relations boost for the host, Thailand (Maclay 1996). The event had no fixed agenda, and ex-Commission President Jacques Santer, in his opening address, stated the obvious: 'the EU is keen to know Asia much more'. 'From a governmental perspective, it was as smooth as Thai silk', notes Vitit Muntharbhorn (1998: 25). And Chirativat and Erdmann-Kiefer (1998: 5) point to the fact that, to the Asian side, the process was as important as the outcome. During the meeting, EU representatives showed themselves more concerned about the political aspects of the dialogue, while their Asian interlocutors often put more stress on economics, culture, business, poverty alleviation and the environment (Cacnio 1996: 7-8). This was frequently perceived as a 'dysfunctionality' (e.g. Forster 2000: 799). Participants asserted that through an 'appreciation of each other's values', Europe and Asia needed to be 're-linked' (Royal Thai Government 1996a: 13), for the benefit of the correction of 'distorted impressions' (Royal Thai Government 1996b: 1). A certain 'Euro–Asian divergence' became evident in the EU leaders' difficulties in coping with the enthusiasm and speed with which the Asians determined and extended the agenda. The meeting illustrated that decision-making in the EU is much slower, competencies much more complex, and bureaucratic hurdles more formidable.

Contentious issues such as Burma's human rights record, the 1988 Tiananmen Square killings in Beijing or the pre-referendum violence in East Timor, were deliberately thrust into the margins of the event for

2.   The Fourth Informal ASEAN Summit in November 2000 has taken the 'EAEC idea' further towards implementation.

the benefit of bilateral relations. Only the briefest of references to international human rights instruments figured in point II/7 of the closing statement of host Banharn Silpa-Archa, then Thailand's Prime Minister. The issue was otherwise largely left to the parallel First Asia–Europe NGO conference on the future of Asian–European relations. This neglect was deplorable and widely condemned, but had been predicted by observers such as Vitit Muntharbhorn (1998: 4): 'The economic and political agenda is likely to prevail, while the call for human rights is likely to be diluted for the sake of inter-regional pragmatism'. Some common themes were nevertheless present, however, noticeably economic synergies, trade and investment liberalization, the WTO, SMEs, security, energy and academic exchange.

ASEM 1 (see Box 5.1) has been termed a 'feel-good summit', designed to be the beginning of a long-term process. Despite protestations to the contrary, it institutionalized a sprawling proliferation of activities (from 17 in 1996 to over 50 now) and spawned an 'alphabet-soup' of initiatives. ASEM 1 has therefore had a mainly catalytic and prompting function. If nothing else, it propelled speed and intensity of the rapprochement between the EU and set an agenda for the future. Pou-Serradell (1996: 210) concludes that 'it is safe to say that ASEM has raised expectations for the future relationship between Europe and Asia' and, similarly, Yeo Lay Hwee adds (2000: 122) 'success breeds expectations'. This seems somehow in contrast with ASEM's avowed 'informality'. However, as Chirativat and Erdmann-Kiefer (1998: 8) have pointed out, there were also considerable bilateral gains, such as talks between Portugal and Indonesia about the future degree of autonomy for the East Timor province of Indonesia, a former Portuguese colony.

Bridging ASEM 1 and ASEM 2, the Commission working document 'Perspectives and Priorities for the ASEM Process' (Commission 1997e), surveys the snowballing institutionalization in ASEM, summarizes the EU position and further defines the agenda of the new ASEM institutions on the basis of the new philosophy of 'synergies', and 'equality'. The Commission maintains the goal of ASEM as an informal catalyst for greater awareness of the issues. However, this informality, it has to be noted, also cuts out the European Parliament to a large degree (Forster 2000: 797). At the same time, the EU Executive seeks to outline the EU position for the further course of ASEM. In order to: 'avoid the risk of an exaggerated and uncoordinated proliferation of activities' (Commission 1997e: 2), the Commission proposes a more structured framework for ASEM, incorporating issues ranging from regional security and the environment, to ASEM enlargement, a process in which countries as diverse as Australia, New Zealand, India, Pakistan, Russia, Switzerland, Norway or Turkey have shown an interest. The working document strongly emphasizes personal contacts, the 'human face' (Commission 1997e: 4) of ASEM and stresses the need for enhanced cooperation, consensus and coordination. As far as the Asia-related work of the Council of Ministers is concerned, this has already had an impact on the management of ASEM matters by the relevant Asia-Oceania Working Group. The European Parliament, reacting to the Commission document in a later Resolution (A4-0197/ 1999 of 4 May 1999), pointed to the gaps: it deplored the lack of 'clearer objectives' in ASEM and called for an extension of ASEM membership to South Asia.

More than 'Fair Weather Friends': The Second ASEM

During the inaugural Asia-Europe Foundation Lecture, ex-Commission President Jacques Santer claimed ASEM 1 had been: 'unburdened by precedent and with everything to gain'. It had, however, cast a long shadow to the ASEM 2 in London (3–4 April 1998). The second ASEM had a large, diverse and more politicized agenda. To help manage it, ASEM 2 launched new mechanisms and think-tanks, for instance an Asia-Europe Cooperation Framework or the Asia-Europe Vision Group. However, while the summit continued the mutual learn- ing process on every level, including a considerable fringe programme on 'Asian Arts and Culture',[3] it could not have taken place under more radically different circumstances. In 1995, the Commission had still asserted: 'It would be wrong to describe Asia as a sleeping economic giant' (Commission 1995e: 28). 'Tigers' (and 'Cubs') were riding high, their economic achievements envied by the 'Far West' who desperately wanted a slice of the cake. Now Asia suffered from 'flu', and the EU became entangled in the debates about the financial crisis. ASEM 2 began to mark a profound shift in EU–Asian relations. For the UK presidency, Tony Blair established the memorable 'friends in good times and in bad' theme, and the press, for the most part, was behind him: 'East Asia's troubles cannot be used as a reason to return to the

3. *Asia Meets Europe in Britain*, Visiting Arts, 1998.

isolationist stance that preceded ASEM 1' (*The European*, 30 March–5 April 1998: 32). In this climate, the Council of Ministers debated the symbolism and feasibility of making a special EU effort: appointing a dedicated EU 'Ambassador' for Asia (*OJ* C 196/124; 98/C 196/173; *Question* E-0299/98). The EU and ASEM were also the subject of European Parliament Resolutions of 12 March 1998 (*OJ* C 104, 6 April 1998) and 4 May 1999 (*OJ* C 279, 1 October 1999). The financial crisis and its implications had raised a twofold perspective for the dialogue: both a test of the mettle of which the new partnership was made, and—more visibly to the outside—an opportunity to weld crisis into constructive action and provide the relationship with more impetus. The second ASEM Foreign Ministers' Meeting on 29 March in Berlin (Council 8709/99, point 4) had set the tone by recognizing that: 'these changes can only strengthen … mutual commitment to the ASEM process and to stronger links between Asia and Europe'.

Did ASEM 2 help to overcome the 'ASEM-etries' (G. Segal, *Asia Times*, 19 November 1996) both within Asia and between Asia and Europe? On the surface, there was, again, plenty of activism. Among the many measures agreed were a European Studies Centre at Kuala Lumpur, an Asia-Europe Environment Technology Centre, an Investment Promotion Action Plan and a particular 'anti-Asian flu' vaccination: a €42 million special Trust Fund at the World Bank, towards which the EU contributed €19 million. Beyond these measures, the degree of continuing 'soft' institutionalization, 'which it would be wrong to overestimate but perverse to ignore' (CAEC 1997: 25) stood in remarkable contrast to the general professions of 'informality' and 'the human dimension' in ASEM. Looking at the plethora of programmes, working meetings and other activities (see Box 5.1), Lim (1999b: 5) justifiably asks: 'Is this not institutionalization?' Other critics point to the danger that: 'from all these many meetings, fora and activities, no concrete results have been produced beyond public declarations extolling confidence in ASEM' (Yeo Lay Hwee 2000: 120). However, it should be noted that both world regions did get much more involved with one another, e.g. by way of Japanese and Malaysian involvement in Bosnia and Hercegovina, the EU's assistance in the Cambodian elections, or food aid to North Korea.

But the way in which the issue of human rights was 'deliberately sidelined' (Forster 2000: 800), continued to be a grave matter for concern. Representative of many, Forster (1999: 757) warns that 'pushing the human rights, environmental and employment rights issues into the margins is only a partial solution, since they remain to be tackled'. Furthermore, some specific issues (Burma, East Timor) did not—unlike at ASEM 1—even find their way into the Chairman's Statement. 'In this way the good cameradie atmosphere was kept' observes Lim critically (1999b: 8). This gave rise to cutting comments by the by now established parallel summit, the Asia-Europe People's Forum and also led to numerous questions to the Commission (e.g. *OJ* C 354/110, 98/C 354/175 *Question* P-1531/98). Was this really a gathering with 'Tyrants on Parade' (*The Observer*, 5 April 1998: 18), sacrificing basic liberties for the sake of investment opportunities, or a meeting of world leaders seeking to cooperate in the legitimate pursuit of global issues?

ASEM 3: Towards more 'Disorderly Multiplication'?

In the light of increasing public disapproval, ASEM 3, hosted by Seoul from 19–21 October 2000, had to prove the continued relevance of the new Asia–Europe summitry. The South Koreans themselves publicly sought to investigate the ASEM challenge to maintain momentum: from 29–30 September 2000, the Korean Society for Contemporary European Studies held an interdisciplinary conference to critically evaluate ASEM in year four.[4] Had the process really 'come of age', as Commission President Romano Prodi argued in his opening address, or had what Algieri (2000: 215) calls *Ermüdungserscheinungen* ('forum fatigue') set in? Many, indeed, argued that the importance of ASEM would decline, on account of the EU's preoccupations with internal reform, Agenda 2000, Eastern enlargement and the euro. Official sources, however, such as the 1999 report by the Asia-Europe Vision Group (AEVG), founded its forecasts more on the importance of education, individuals, free trade, IT, the environment and good governance. The report predicted, not surprisingly, that: 'the ASEM process will become more complex, not less', recommended the establishment of a permanent ASEM Secretariat and cautioned against 'disorderly multiplication' of ASEM activities (AEVG 1999). The Commission produced a second significant ASEM-related blueprint called 'Perspectives and Priorities for the ASEM Process (Asia-Europe Meeting) into

4. http://www.EUROPA.co.kr

the new Decade' (Commission 2000b). It built on the 1997 Perspectives and Priorities (see above) by reinforcing old concerns, and identifying new ones in the light of globalization and the need to engage public opinion. Taking its cue from the AEVG report, there was significant emphasis on educational exchange, the environment and social security (Commission 2000b: 7-9, 11; *Rapid Database*: IP/00/398). Among the specific priorities, 'non-traditional' security issues, including 'cyber-warfare' found a place, as did reactions to the Asian crisis, the WTO debate after the Seattle summit, and consumer concerns. Successive high-level gatherings, such as the second ASEM Economics Ministers' Meeting (AEMM) in Berlin in October 1999, had already prepared the ground by emphasizing 'the phasing out of the financial and economic crisis in East Asia' (Chairman's Statement, p. 2, Doc. 11835/99). In addition, the European Parliament, in a Resolution of 4 October 2000, continued to remind the participants of the importance of human rights, good governance social dialogue and 'democracy clauses'. Parliament's Committee on Foreign Affairs, Human Rights, Common Security and Defence Policy accentuated these points in its own report of 31 May 2001, while also advocating an ambition for stronger social, educational and cultural ties in the ASEM process.[5]

ASEM 3 therefore took place against the background of altogether higher expectations and raised stakes. The fact that 'Asian flu' was pronounced all but cured, took some pressure off the agenda. The Chairman's Statement reveals an ASEM which appears more cautious, consolidating, all-encompassing and retrospective than its predecessors, reviewing existing programmes, rather than initiating too many new ones, and even putting the brakes on in some areas (see Box 5.1). Regional issues such as the Pyongyang inter-Korean summit of June 2000, the ASEAN + 3 meetings, China, Japan, Timor or the ARF gave a dominant framework to the summit. This framework included debates about globalization, the EU's role as a 'balancing power' in the global triangle, racism, or weapons proliferation (cf Pfetsch 2000: 165-67). In terms of concrete Asia-Europe cooperation, delegates followed the Asia Vision Group Report and their own 'ASEM 3 Draft Indicative List for Reference'. They gave high priority to educational exchanges (Chairman's Statement, point 15), in order to redress existing imbalances

    5.   EP Resolution of 4 October 2000: minutes of 4 October 2000—Provisional Edition: B5-0768, 0769, 0770, 0773, 0774 and 0775/2000; EP Report of 31 May 2001: A-5-0207/2001, RR\441407EN.doc, PE 294.868.

when compared to Asia–USA exchanges. The new DUO-ASEM Fellowship Programme is a case in point. Furthermore, the 1998 Asia-Europe Cooperation Framework (AECF) was updated. The new 'AECF 2000' is a summary of vision and mechanisms of the ASEM summitry. It is meant to constitute the central medium of the intercontinental collaboration. The meeting also endorsed the extension of the TFAP for 2000–02 and of the ASEM Trust Fund (ATF).

Human rights, again, featured only briefly (Chairman's Statement, points 8, II/5, IV/12). There were other novel initiatives, which French President Jacques Chirac, called 'a first step', for example the 'e-ASEM'-plan, suggested by Thai ex-Prime Minister Chuan Leekpai, or plans for health, migration, globalization and lifelong learning (Chairman's Statement, point 19). Detailed decisions on ASEM enlargement were not taken, but a future 'two-key' approach to it was agreed (point VI/28): a candidate will first have to secure the support of partners within its own region (Asia or Europe) and can then, secondly, be accepted, 'by consensus', among all ASEM partners. Against the background of the ROK's chairmanship of ASEM 3, the award, in mid-October 2000, of the Nobel peace prize to Kim Dae-Jung[6] and the inter-Korean summit on 13–15 June 2000, summit participants also issued a Seoul Declaration for Peace on the Korean Peninsula (cf. *EURASIA Bulletin* 4.10, October 2000: 5). As before, the meeting was accompanied by a 'shadow-summit', the ASEM 2000 People's Forum under the theme of 'People's Action and Solidarity—Challenging Globalization'.

Box 5.1: The ASEM Process: 'Soft Institutionalization' or 'Alphabet Soup'?

ASEM 1 (Bangkok, 1–2 March 1996)

ASEM Process Initiated, Asia-Europe Cooperation Framework, Asia-Europe Business Forum (AEBF) and Asia-Europe Business Conference (AEBC), Asia-Europe Foundation (AEF), Asia-Europe Environmental Technology Centre (AEETC), Asia-Europe University Programme (AEUP), Structure of Inter-summit Meetings (see below), Railway Network Study.

ASEM 2 (London, 3–4 April 1998)

ASEM Trust Fund at the World Bank and European Financial Expertise Network (EFEX), Asia-Europe Vision Group (AEVG), Asia-Europe Co-operation Framework (AECF) adopted, Investment Promotion Action Plan (IPAP), Trade Facilitation Action Plan (TFAP), Investment Experts Group

---

6.   In 2001, Kim Dae-Jung was also honoured with the World Statesman Award (*Rapid Database*: IP/01/12330).

(IEG) adopted, Asia-Europe Environmental Technology Centre (AEETC) launched, Asia-Europe Young Leaders' Symposia (AEYLS) welcomed, 'ASEM-Connect' Electronic Resource Network.

ASEM 3 (Seoul, 20–21 October 2000)
Asia-Europe Cooperation Framework updated and extended, ('AECF 2000'), Seoul Declaration for Peace on the Korean Peninsula, Trade Facilitation Action Plan (TFAP) work programme ('Deliverables and Goals 2000-2002') endorsed, Asian Trust Fund (ATF): extension into a 'phase 2', ASEM Education Hubs (AEH) and Asia-Europe University (AEU) discussed, Trans-Eurasia Information Network, ASEM Roundtable on Globalization, DUO ASEM Fellowship Programme, Initiatives against the Digital Divide.

Inter-Summit Meetings
Foreign Ministers' Meetings (ASEM – FMM)
ASEM – Coordinators' Meetings
Senior Officials' Meetings (ASEM –SOM)
Economic Ministers' Meetings (ASEM – EMM)
EMM Coordinators' Preparatory Meetings
ASEM Senior Officials' Meeting Trade & Investment (SOMTI)
SOMTI Coordinators' Meetings
Finance Ministers' Meetings (ASEM – FinMM)
Working Group Preparatory Meetings for FinMM
Finance Deputies' Meetings
ASEM Customs Director Generals' / Commissioners' Meetings
ASEM Customs 'Enforcement' Working Group
ASEM Customs 'Procedures' Working Group

Economic and Cultural Cooperation, Think-Tanks, Events, Conferences
Asia-Europe Vision Group (AEVG)
Asia-Europe Foundation
Asia-Europe 'Young Leaders' Symposia (e.g. *EURASIA Bulletin* 4.6-7, June-
    July 2000: 46-47)
ASEF Young Parliamentarians' Meeting
Europe-Asia Cultural Forum
Conference on 'Societies in Transition: Asia and Europe at a Moment of
    Change', London, 19–22 March 1998
Seminar on Labour Relations, The Hague, 26–27 October 1998
Investment Promotion Action Plan (IPAP), including Investment Experts
    Group – IEG
Trade Facilitation Action Plan (TFPAP): 'shepherds'' meetings (The 'shep-
    herds' are: the Philippines, the Republic of Korea, the European Commis-
    sion and the Presidency of the Council of Ministers)
'ASEM Connect' Electronic Resource Network
Virtual Information Exchange (VIE) Website on Investment Regulations
    (*http://www.asem.vie.net*)

ASEM Trust Fund (ATF)

European Financial Expertise Network (EFEX)

Symposium on Economic Synergy

Asia-Europe Business Fora

AEBF Joint Standing Committees' Meeting

Business Forum Task Force Meeting on Infrastructure, environment and quality of projects

Symposium on Infrastructure Financing (transport, telecommunications, energy)

Asia-Europe Small and Medium Enterprises (SME) Conference, Naples, 28–30 May 1998

Asia-Europe Business Conference, Jakarta, 8–10 July 1997

ASEM Conference on 'State and Market', Copenhagen, 8–10 March 1999

ASEM Conference on 'Asian Crisis, Democracy and Human Rights', Berlin, 26–28 March 1999

Cooperation in the Areas of the Environment, Technology, Science, Education, the Media and Law

Asia-Europe Environmental Technology Centre (AEETC)

Environment Officials' Technology Transfer Centres

Asia-Europe Expert Meeting on Technological Cooperation

Website on ASEM Science and Technology Cooperation (http://www.cordis. lu/asem/home.html)

ASEM Science and Technology Ministers' Meeting (STMM)

Multimedia Symposium

ASEM Symposium on Human Rights and the Rule of Law, ASEM (Informal) Seminars on Human Rights

Europe-Asia Forum on Culture, Values and Technology, 'Towards a Stronger Mutual Understanding'

ASEM Experts' Meeting on Protection and Promotion of Cultural Heritage, Ha Noi, 20–22 January 1999

Roundtables on Asia-Europe University Relations

Europe-Asia Forum on University Relations, Naples/ Rome, 16–18 January 1997

Asia-Europe University Forum and Fair, Kuala Lumpur, 17–19 March 1998

Asia-Europe Centre, University of Malaya, Kuala Lumpur

European Studies Centre, Chulalongkorn University, Bangkok

ASEM Action on Child Welfare

ASEM Seminar on Traditional and Modern Medicine, Ha Noi, 18–19 March 1999

Railway Network Study, trans-Asian railway network, linked to Mekong-Delta Basin Development

Sources: Lim 1999b: 5-6; Yeo Lay Hwee 2000: 132-43; European Commission: *Matrix of ASEM Activities* (39 pp.); Chairman's Statement at ASEM 3; http://www.asef.org

Conclusions and Outlook: New Dynamism or 'Institutional Overkill'?

What of Asia-Europe contacts, both inside and outside the framework created by ASEM, at the beginning of the twenty-first century? According to Chris Patten, EU External Relations Commissioner, ASEM now: 'transcends the old relationships of 19th Century imperial powers and colonies, aid donors and recipients, and tetchy protagonists in trade disputes' (*Rapid Database*: SPEECH/00/383). In addition, Jong-Hwan Ko (2000a; 2000b: 65-99) and others have argued that even an Asia-Europe Free Trade Agreement might now become more feasible, although it will, no doubt, require more coordination of domestic reform policies particularly among the Asian ASEM members.

In the debates about the future of ASEM, Chong-wha Lee (2000: 51-54) has identified three useful possible future scenarios. The first is a 'status-quo scenario': ASEM would continue to be an inter-regional consultative forum, which facilitates information networks. The second is an 'APEC-type-evolution' scenario: ASEM would evolve to strengthen further the liberalization of the multilateral trading system. The third is a 'hybrid scenario': this would lead to new activities such as cooperation in the area of development aid or economic and technical cooperation, which in turn would have a modest effect both on the support of information networks and informality, and on the reinforcement of 'multilateral openness'. What seems clear in whatever scenario one prefers, is that ASEM, having grown out of the EU–ASEAN group-to-group dialogue (Dent 1999: 59, 71), now needs to surpass its status quo as an 'informal' body and to acquire a purpose beyond that, for example through a free trade agreement (Jonghwan Ko, 2000a, 200b). McMahon's statement (1998: 250) that: 'the lack of a concrete and agreed goal for the dialogue process is an overt sign of its inadequacy' should serve as a warning sign for anyone involved in ASEM.

In addition to this, the 'unintended institutionalization', proliferation and further mushrooming of ASEM concerns and initiatives is already leading to a de facto overlap and multiplication with processes in other relevant fora. Questions of competition or complementarity in regard to ASEAN or APEC need to be addressed, particularly in response to signs of declining interest in ASEM at a political level. However, as O'Brian points out (2001: 26) the political 'pillar' of ASEM is 'precisely where the greatest challenge lies today'. Moreover, if ASEM is not increasingly to mimic, or take over from related bodies, it needs to redefine its brief and identity more clearly. A more 'streamlined' image will benefit the ASEM summitry overall, an aspect the ASEM foreign ministers seem to have taken on board since their meeting in Beijing on 24–25 May 2001. With the necessary processes of familiarization and 'getting-to-know-one-another' now accomplished, ASEM will need to focus on a 'less-is-more' maxim. The process will have to continue working towards more tangible results. This may, eventually, counterbalance growing perceptions of ASEM as a grouping that is 'all process without product'.[7]

One possible way of doing this is to strengthen what is exchangeably termed the 'human', 'inter-personal' or 'sociological' dimension of ASEM. By placing a strong emphasis on exchange and education between Asian and European partners, an important beginning has already been made (*The Nation*, 18 October 2000). But there is plenty of leeway for more culturally sensitive manoeuvre in the areas of common values, governance and human rights. The latter area, in particular, appears to be consistently shied away from. It is fast becoming an ASEM liability. McMahon's conclusion (1998: 245) that 'the ASEM dialogue process will suffer from the same impotence with respect to human rights that afflicts the EU–ASEAN dialogue process', again, appears to the point. Neglecting human rights will also impinge on other, as yet unresolved, ASEM areas such as enlargement, compatibility of ASEM/ASEAN memberships, Burma, or access to justice. Strengthening the 'human aspect' of ASEM would not only be in line with the ASEM founding philosophy and overall thrust of the process; it would also go a long way towards countering allegations increasingly made against ASEM, of being too 'top-down', 'heavy' and not for the benefit of the people or civil society as a whole. The European Union, itself struggling with a considerable 'democratic deficit' on several levels, has an important contribution to make in this respect and can pass on experience with its own current process of re-invention and reform. Above all, it must not allow its engagement in ASEM to be overshadowed by its own priorities 'closer to home', its difficulties in forming a CFSP or its attempts to find a counterbalance to US unilateralism in Asia.

---

7. For a useful 'mid-term review' of the ASEM process, see Pelkmans and Shinkai 1997 (EIAS)

6 |

Beyond Distant Neighbours: The European Union and China

> Does China matter? No, it's not a silly question—merely one that is not asked often enough. Odd as it may seem, the country that is home to a fifth of humankind is overrated as a market, a power, and a source of ideas (Gerald Segal, *Foreign Affairs*, September/October 1999: 24).

This chapter offers a comprehensive critique of the EU's relations with the People's Republic of China (PRC). In terms of EU–China dialogue, there is an emphasis on the European Commission's three relevant strategy papers on China of 1995, 1998 and 2000, and on the numerous wide-ranging EU–China cooperation programmes which have been a hallmark of the partnership. Other topics under investigation are the recent accession of China to the WTO, the function of the euro in the EU–Chinese relationship, and the position of human rights in the EU's approach to China.

The chapter also includes an investigation of the EU's relations with Taiwan (the Republic of China, ROC), and a brief look at the Tibet question and the way that religion can be instrumentalized for political ends. Hong Kong and Macao, the two territories which reverted to mainland China in 1997 and 1999 respectively, are assessed separately, with the emphasis on the territories' relations with the EU following their return to China as 'Special Administrative Regions' (SARs), and on their future democratic and economic prospects.

The Legacy of China–Europe Relations and Modern China

Since before the times of Marco Polo, the responses to Europeans in China (for an example see Box 6.1) have vacillated between acceptance and xenophobia, mistrust and admiration, suspicion and empowerment. Trade, war, missionary activity, European imperial ambitions or Chinese territorial leases are just a few ingredients of the Sino-European relationship over time.

Box 6.1: Europeans in China

> Few other examples are more symbolic of the changeable Chinese-European relationship today than the historical figure of the Jesuit missionary and astronomer Johann Adam Schall von Bell of Cologne (T'ang Jo-wang, 1591–1666): successively elevated to highest honours and influence in the Chinese civil service and put on trial in 1665 for high treason, he witnessed the fall of the Ming Dynasty (1368–1644) and embodied the zenith of an early European influence in China. (more in Lach 1994: Vol. III, Bk 4, 1672, 1715). For a fascinating account of the life of Johann Adam Schall von Bell, see Franz 2000.

China's contemporary relations with Europe are governed by these and other historical memories, the country's size and its real, and expected, economic power. The People's Republic of China contains around 1.3 billion people, living on one-fifth of the world's land. Nearly 25 years after Deng Xiaoping (1904–97) promoted decentralization and a 'policy of open doors', contemporary China is also experiencing counteracting processes towards increased restoration, more inequality and corruption (Buruma, *Guardian*, 7 March 2001: 2). Efforts to reform the country's economic and political structures are frequently hampered by considerable regional divergencies in wealth, environmental standards and population. Moreover, a growth in corruption, disorder and crime seem to be the regular by-products of reform. (Weber 1998: 74; Christie and Roy 2001: 231). Contemporary China finds itself in the throes of a twofold transition: from a command economy to a market-based economy, and from a rural to an urban society. Between 1978 and 1995, China achieved economically what took other countries centuries, and the early 1990s saw growth rates of around 10 per cent. In its report on China 2020, of September 1997, the World Bank estimated that, within twenty years, China could be the richest country in the world, a forecast shared by many (e.g. Weber 1998: 86).

In other areas too, post-Deng, China's image of a 'great power on a regional scale' (Yahuda 1999: 650), or of the world's 'unpredictable superpower' (Bauer 1995: 9) changed. The country achieved a foothold in both the Asian camp and in global affairs. It joined the World Bank and the IMF, APEC (1991), the ASEAN Regional Forum (1993) and the CSCAP (1996), and also transformed its ties with India, Pakistan, Central Asia, Russia and Europe. China's participation in a range of international regimes, for example through the signing of the Non-

Proliferation Treaty (NPT) in 1992 and the CTBT in 1996, placed constraints on a Chinese Government, which, in the eyes of some observers, was already challenged by the disparities of the huge country and the dynamics of change (e.g. Yahuda 1999: 654). However, in spite of a strategic economic policy shift in 2000–01, directing more resources towards the country's poorer Western regions, the socio-economic gaps between industrialized eastern seaboard and rural inland areas remained wide, and many loss-incurring state-owned enterprises were in dire need of reform (Buckley 1999: 6-7; see on this topic, Li Cheng 2001: 79-83). Falling short of dealing with the legacy of the Tiananmen Square Democracy Movement (1989), privatization remained high on the agendas of President Jiang Zemin, and Prime Minister Zhu Rongij.[1] Faced with Western challenges on human rights, China continued to channel energy into economic development, regional cooperation and security. When Deng Xiaoping died on 19 February 1997,[2] ex-Commission President Santer paid tribute: 'He initiated a process of market reform, which has now become irreversible. This has enabled Europe and China to build a flourishing relationship in trade and investment and stronger political ties' (*EU-China News*, May 1997). From an Asian point of view, the visit of Chinese Prime Minister Zhu Rongji to the EU on 11 July 2000 marked 25 years of Sino–EU relations in a similarly upbeat way (*Vientiane Times*, 11–13 July 2000).

EU Relations with the People's Republic of China (PRC)

The relationship between the Union and the PRC is one of assessment of, and response to, change. EU–China ties have been characterized by accelerating institutionalization, coupled with occasional stagnation (see Box 6.2). Relations have been delineated as a dialogue between 'strategic friends', 'distant neighbours' (Kapur 1990) or 'nascent superpowers'. The latter reading has proved most appropriate to reflect the multitude of its layers. The key to its understanding is that, in China's eyes, Europe has gone through a transformation from a source of modernist onslaught and imperialist humiliation (Yahuda 1999: 652) to a more attractive partner. The EU is of interest to China, mainly as an

1. Jiang Zemin has been President since 1997; Zhu Rongji has been premier since early 1998.
2. Obituary: John Gittings, *Guardian,* 20 February 1997: 18.

economic model, a way of integration, an emerging external policy, a provider of expertise and a possible catalyst for modernization. The terms 'competitiveness', 'enhanced presence', 'stability' and 'reform' delineate the main European interests in China.

Box 6.2: The Development of the EU–China Dialogue

> Following the 1973 visit by Commission Vice-President Soames and the extension of mutual diplomatic recognition, the EC confirmed China's 'Most-Favoured Nation' preferential trading status and included the PRC in European Political Cooperation (EPC). A second Trade Agreement of 1985 (*OJ* L 250/85, 19 September 1985: 1) received much attention (e.g. Xiao Zhi Yue 1993: 21), and from 1988 the Commission has had a Representation in Beijing. The shots fired on Tiananmen Square on 4 June 1989, reverberated through EU–China relations. But the ensuing EU sanctions were short-lived, and soon EU–China relations moved back from 'sudden freeze' to gradual 'thaw'. The dialogue then entered its current phase of diversification, interrupted again briefly, after a NATO bomb hit the Chinese Embassy in Belgrade during the Kosovo War. The relationship branched out further and incorporated a plethora of institutions and processes, which the EU conceived of as a means of 'engaging China' and supporting reform. Examples of these are the EC–China Economic and Trade Working Party (1993), the EU–China Environment Working Group (1996) or the Human Rights Dialogue (1995). 1998 saw the initiation of the EU–China Business Dialogue, and, on 14 October 1999, an EU–China Chamber of Commerce was launched in Beijing (*EU–China News*, 1/2000).

Between 1978 and 2000 EU–China trade increased more than twenty-fold. Subsequently, trade relations developed into the main catalyst for overall Sino–European contacts. China became the EU's third most important non-European trading partner, and the EU China's second largest export market, with machinery, transport equipment and nuclear technology topping the list. Textiles, clothing and toys continued to be the main Chinese export items to the Union. In the area of anti-dumping rules, the EU no longer characterized the PRC as a 'non-market economy' (*Rapid Database*: IP/98/373). Ferdinand (1995: 28) pointed out the irony that, since Tiananmen, the EU's trade deficit: 'consistently and dramatically worsened'. It stood at €44.4 billion in 2000 (*Far Eastern Economic Review*, 7 June 2001). Alongside this, the EU imposed a host of protectionist measures (e.g. Council Regulation 519/94 of 7 March 1994). But China also acted as one of a number of midwives for the birth of the euro: a copper factory in the PRC won the contract to supply the alloy for euro coins. But the 'euro-train' travelled in both directions, and the EU continued to promote the new currency in China, as a potential reserve currency, an alternative to the US dollar and a means of diversifying debt and avoiding the risks of currency fluctuations. At the beginning of 2002, this strategy was beginning to show first results, with the introduction of the euro coins and banknotes receiving a predominantly positive welcome from Chinese politics and business (*The Economist*, 'Beijing's View', 2 January 2002).

Until the end of 2001, Chinese–EU relations had been decisively shaped by China's 1986 application to join the WTO.[3] Having secured a WTO deal with the USA (1999) and Thailand (2000), the EU was the largest remaining partner for China in this area. On the surface, the Union consistently supported China's accession (see Dent 1999: 118), emphasizing 'cooperation rather than confrontation' (Eglin 1997: 495). By contrast, the 'baggage of human rights and anti-communist lobbies' (Eglin 1997: 497) seemingly played a minor role. The issue was further complicated by the fact that the GATT, the WTO's predecessor organization, tacitly agreed in 1992 that Taiwan would not become a member before China. The WTO 'marathon', as Leon Brittan once termed it (*EU-China News*, April 1995, December 1996) ended on 19 May 2000, when the EU and China finalized the landmark Sino–EU agreement on China's accession to the WTO, following a similar agreement between China and the USA in November 1999. The EU–China accord was, in Chris Patten's words: 'the event in EU-China relations in the last three years which will have most impact' (*Rapid Database*: SPEECH/01/231). It included the settlement of issues surrounding industrial goods, warehouses, agriculture, insurances and other services. A number of obstacles remained to be solved in 2001, in particular in the areas of further tariff reductions, foreign ownership, insurance licences and removal of limitations in currency trading. In the end, and with a 'hint of anticlimax', the 'thump of a rubber stamp' brought closure on 17 September 2001, to China's long quest for membership (*Far Eastern Economic Review*, 27 September 2001); the PRC officially joined the WTO in December 2001, followed by the ROC in January 2002 (*The Economist*, 2 January 2002).

---

3.   Other Asian applicants to the World Trade Organization: Cambodia, Nepal, Laos, Vietnam and Taiwan.

'From Poultry to Pollution': Levels and Initiatives in EU–China Cooperation

The network of mutually reinforcing initiatives (see Box 6.3) that makes up contemporary Sino–EU cooperation was assessed in a mostly positive light by a number of Chinese officials (e.g. Tang Jiaxuan 2000: 22). The dialogue clearly gained from the ASEM process and the annual EU–China summits (from 1996 and 1998 respectively). Additionally, China-related debates in the European Parliament over the last decade revealed a competing agenda and conveyed a more hetero-geneous picture of EU attitudes and policies towards China. Box 6.3 presents a (non-exhaustive) overview of initiatives, ranging 'from poultry to pollution', affecting the EU–China dialogue (see Commission 1999g).

Box 6.3: Sino–EU Programmes and Initiatives (a Non-exhaustive Overview)

Supporting Financial Reform and the Rule of Law and Local Governance in China

Cooperation in the area of Public Procurement

Customs cooperation

Cooperation on registered designation of origin

EU–China Legal and Judicial Cooperation Programme

EU–China Local Authority Linking Programme

EU–China Village Governance Programme (IP/01/733)

Financial Services Reform; Intellectual Property Rights (IPR) Training and Cooperation

Support to economic, social and cultural rights in Yunnan Province

WTO Accession Support Programme

Human Rights and other Initiatives

EU–China Human Rights Dialogue (1997)

EU–China Human Rights Cooperation Programme

EU–China Human Rights Small Project Facility (€840,000)

EU–China Co-operation in combating illegal migration and the trafficking in human beings (2000–01)

Business and Industrial Cooperation

ASEM Trust Fund; Asia-Invest Programme; European Community Invest-ment Partners (ECIP)

EU–China Aviation Cooperation Programme (1999); EU–China Industrial Co-operation in the field of aeronautics

EU–China Chamber of Commerce (Beijing)

Implementation of Telecommunications Working Plan

Intelligent Transport System (Beijing); Networking of Industrial Parks
SeCIM—Second Cooperation Programme in Integration in Manufacturing

Human Resources Development
Basic Education Project in Gansu; Business Internship Programme
China–Europe International Business School Shanghai (CEIBT) (Phase I: 1994, Phase II: 1999)
Commission support for the Chinese Disabled Persons' Federation
Cooperation with Chinese National School of Administration (http://www.ecd.org.cn/eucjmtp)
EU–China Higher Education Co-operation Programme (see Aspinwall 1999: 16-17)
EU–China Junior Managers Programme (*AsiaInvest News* No. 8, November 1999)
EU–China Programme for the Development of Vocational Training for Industry (*EU-China News*, 2/2000)

Science, Technology, Environment and Energy
China Council on International Co-operation on Environment and Development (CCICED)
China-EURATOM Co-operation Agreement on the Peaceful Use of Nuclear Energy (exploratory talks from 2000–01)
China-Europe Biotechnology Network (1998); Environmental Education Television Project for China
Civil Aviation Cooperation Project
EC-China Environmental Management Co-operation Programme (EMCP)
EU-China Norms and Standards Cooperation Programme
EU-China Maritime Transport Agreement (negotiations from September 2001)
Honghe Environmental Protection and Poverty Alleviation Project
Liaoning Integrated Environmental Programme (LIEP, since 10 December 1999, *EU-China News*, 1/2000)
Scientific and Technological Cooperation Agreement (1998)
Synergy Programme (training activities)

Regional Disparities, Poverty Alleviation, Social Cohesion, 'Raising the EU's Profile' in China
China–EC Cooperation in Agriculture (CECA; 1997); Dairy and Food Sector Cooperation (1985)
'Close to Europe' (radio programme)
EU–China Academic Network (ECAN; 1998)
EU–China Local Authority Linking Programme; EU-China Small Project Facility
EU–China STD (sexually transmitted diseases) and AIDS/HIV Training Course Programme (1994)
Ningxia Hui Land Reclamation; Quinghai Livestock Development; Water Buffalo Development Project

Declaratory Policies and their Impact: The Commission's Policy Papers on China

In terms of policy declarations and strategic objectives, the Commission's two major papers on China were a direct result of the 1994 New Asia Strategy; they continued its tone and thrust. *A Long-term Policy for China–Europe Relations* (Commission 1995b) and *Building a Comprehensive Partnership with China* (Commission 1998a) were supplemented by additional proposals on their implementation (Commission 2000m; 2001j) and other significant EU regional strategies, for instance on Hong Kong, Japan, Korea, Indonesia or Macao. *A Long-term Policy for China–Europe Relations* provided the EU–PRC partnership with a single framework. It took into account that the dialogue between the Union and China ceased to be derivative and dependent on Cold War bipolarity. Shambaugh's famous 'marriage' analogy (1996: 5) explained these changes in a convincing manner. A (Chinese–European) wedding had been arranged by two sets of parents (former USSR and USA). It was, however, only after the wedding— and the subsequent divorce of the parents—that the newly-weds began to form a more autonomous and independent relationship. Dent (1999: 149) encapsulated the same phenomenon as 'from cold-war geopolitics to multipolar geoeconomics'.

The 1995 and 1998 China papers introduced a five-pillar framework consisting of: general cooperation, political partnership, economic relations, human rights dialogue, and EU 'presence' in China. The blueprint singles out education, economic and social reform and the private sector as priorities. On human rights, it demands 'dialogue at every opportunity'. The inherent EU vision is one of 'constructive engagement' of the PRC. This contrasts with the new (2001) Bush Administration's view of 'strategic competition' with the People's Republic. The Council approved the 'China Strategy' in December 1995 (12422/ 95, PVD 75, PESC 343), calling its arrival 'timely' and 'a matter of priority'. However, it also reiterated concerns about population, internal reform, human rights and China's WTO accession, and identified immigration—a vital point in the light of the death of 58 illegal immigrants in a truck in Dover in 2000—and European Studies in China as future areas of cooperation. The Economic and Social Committee gave its approval in a 1997 Opinion (*OJ* C 158, 26 May 1997).

A second 'long-term' communication in 1998, *Building a Comprehensive Partnership with China* (Commission 1998a), followed in the
wake of a controversial EU decision not to co-sponsor a UN Resolution
on China. It also came in the midst of the Asian crisis and after the 15th
Congress of the Chinese Communist Party, which had targeted further
market reforms in the PRC. Arguably the most significant novelty of the
EU's updated China policy was the introduction of annual EU–China
summits.[4] According to the 1998 document, China was now both a more
assertive and a more responsible partner, 'deserving a more positive
European response' (Commission 1998a: 25) But the Union's human
rights concerns remained strong. The Commission managed to defend
its basic five-strand approach of the 1995 China communication against
member state criticism, and included a clearer emphasis on linking funds
to policies ('getting value for money') and the promotion of the euro.

In a number of subsequent, 'fine-tuning' communications in 2000
and 2001 (Commission 2000m; 2001j), the Commission reassessed the
progress of the 1998 strategy. In its update on EU–China relations of 15
May 2001, for instance, the Commission left the structure, thrust and
objectives of the earlier documents largely in place. Commissioner
Patten, as ever well-versed in the use of metaphor, added a horticultural
example, prior to his visit to China in May 2001: in his words, the new
Communication: 'did not pull the EU–China Strategy up by the roots. It
was rather a pruning effort, to encourage fresh branches, together with
a dose of eco-friendly fertiliser' (*Rapid Database*: SPEECH/01/231).
The only significant novelty of the paper was in looking towards a
further 'codification' of EU–China relations and in suggesting a number of short- and medium-term 'action-points' across various sectors of
the dialogue (IP/01/700). Among these, the potential issuing of com-
monly agreed 'EU-China Statements', a host of WTO-related cooperation projects and cooperation on the Koreas, Burma, or immigration
looked particularly interesting in the medium-term.

The Issue of Human Rights in EU–China Relations

> Most of the human rights issues China struggles with today stem from the
> great inertia of Chinese traditional attitudes, a product of the country's
> great age, size and pride (Denny Roy, in Christie and Roy 2001: 219).

4.   April 1998 (London), December 1999 (Beijing), October 2000 (Beijing),
September 2001 (Brussels).

The EU–China debate on human rights (see Box 6.4) was still, at best, of a tentative and volatile nature, and the 2001 update on EU–China relations, although giving the issue 'priority focus', diplomatically stated that: 'China 'is not always an easy partner for the EU', and that: 'dialogue is an acceptable option only if progress is achieved on the ground' (Commission 2001j: 7 and 11). Eglin (1997: 497) identified what is, arguably, the key reason for this: 'so far, Europe has not displayed a penchant for linking the quest for new markets to the spread of democracy'. Consequently, relations were 'both improving and deteriorating' (Ferdinand 1995: 26), but continued to be focused sharply on human rights. Relevant sessions in the European Parliament highlighted issues such as: executions (160/88), arms embargoes (324/90), trafficking of body organs (H-890/92), the 'reduction' of 'abnormal births', the Chinese 'one-child-policy' of 1979 (H-111/94), orphanages (H-766/95), Hong Kong (E-476/97) or Taiwan (H-713/95).

Box 6.4: Human Rights, the EU and China

An official EU Human Rights Dialogue (HRD) with China began to be formalized in 1996 and initiated regular talks and conferences. In addition to this, China hosted an ASEM Human Rights Seminar in 1999. The Union wanted to see its human rights stance on China as a 'dialogue backed by action', but did not always present a unified picture. This became clear in relation to the tabling of a Resolution on Human Rights in China at the United Nations Commission on Human Rights (UNCHR). The PRC traditionally prevented adoption of a censoring UN Resolution by securing support for a 'non-action motion', which prohibits a vote. In 1995, the EU's attempt faltered by one vote and, in 1997, the Union was deeply split in Geneva, with Denmark and the Netherlands taking unilateral action and criticizing France and its Spanish, Italian and German allies, for being prepared to 'court' the PRC. France and Germany did not co-sponsor a Resolution in 1997. In 1998, 1999 and 2000, EU member states did not table or co-sponsor a Resolution at all, making them, for many observers, pawns in a Chinese gambit. In 2001, EU Foreign Ministers backed a UN Resolution, but did not join the US in sponsoring it (Council Conclusions on China/Human Rights, 2338th Council meeting, 19 March 2001, point 8). The Union detected improvement in the Chinese signing and ratification of Human Rights Covenants in 1997–98, but also continued to highlight shortcomings regarding the Chinese policy on Tibet, the protection of children, or religious tolerance towards the Falun Gong community or other groups (General Affairs Council Conclusions of 22 January and 19 March 2001). The PRC decided, on 28 February 2001, to ratify the International Covenant on Economic, Social and Cultural Rights, but claimed precedence of Chinese law over the relevant articles on Trades Unions (Article 8:1[a]).

After the Handover-Hangover: The EU and Hong Kong

For some, the British handover of Hong Kong to China on 1 July 1997 meant that the third millennium started prematurely, while for others, the event was 'an anti-climax of historic proportions' (*Time: Special Issue* 1997: 31). Early legal assessments of '1997' had been highly critical of the situation that could be expected. A 1992 report by the International Commission of Jurists was representative of many pre-handover opinions: it focused sharply on issues such as human rights, flaws in the Basic Law, the right to self-determination, the judiciary and the accountability of the executive (International Commission of Jurists 1992: 116-20).

When the 'pearl' finally returned to the 'oyster' (*Times Higher Education Supplement*, 20 June 1997: 22) as the 'Hong Kong Special Administrative Region' (HKSAR), 156 years of colonial rule came to an end. Deng Xiaoping's 'one country, two systems' approach and the Basic Law had stipulated that Chinese-style government would not apply to Hong Kong until 2047. But Tung Che Hwa, Hong Kong's first post-colonial leader, saw reunification as the end to an 'unnatural separation' (*Newsweek*, May–July 1997: 48-49). The quick replacement of Hong Kong's Legislative Council (LegCo) with a hand-picked Provisional Legislature, and the espousal by Tung Che Hwa of 'Asian values' contrasted with many observers' ideas about reforms in Hong Kong and confirmed some anxieties.

Following early sectoral agreements,[5] a more active engagement with Hong Kong had become a necessity for a Union seeking to improve its working relationship with China and Asia as a whole (see Box 6.5). The EU's interests soon extended to a view of Hong Kong as an 'agent for change' in China, a possibility openly questioned by some observers (Tsang 1997: 135), but espoused by many others. On the one hand, former Governor Chris Patten, for example, often reiterated his belief that 'if Hong Kong continues to be successful, the implications for Europe and the catalytic effect on China can be nothing but helpful' (*Die Welt*, 11 November 1996). On the other hand, Patten was also highly critical: 'European ministers and governments were concerned about being tainted by Hong Kong in their dealings with China… They did not want to 'spoil the atmosphere' (Patten 1998: 109).

---

5. For textiles, see e.g. *OJ* L 388/86: 1 and *OJ* L 94/95: 155.

Box 6.5: European Commission Papers on Hong Kong

Commission documents drawn up against the background of these attitudes reflected optimism coupled with watchfulness. In its 1995 China communication, the EU supported a resilient Hong Kong. In *The European Union and Hong Kong—Beyond 1997* (Commission 1997c), the Commission re-stressed the well-known, positive assumptions of Hong Kong as a 'gateway' or a 'catalyst', but also outlined measures for 'maximum vigilance', including an annual report. Resolutions in the European Parliament (*OJ* C 132, 28 April 1997 and *OJ* C 328, 26 October 1998), and an EU Statement of 26 June 1997, backed the demands for 'a high degree of autonomy' in the HKSAR. In its Conclusions of 3 June 1997 (doc. 7892/97; 8627/97), the Council emphasized the desired self-sufficiency of the HKSAR in trade and legal terms. The Amsterdam Council also stated its support for stability and prosperity in Hong Kong. During a Brussels visit, Tung Chee Hwa, the 'Friendly Dragon' (*Guardian*, 16 June 1997: 4), whom Chris Patten had appointed one of his most important advisors in 1992, sought to reassure the Union on these issues. In its 1998 China Strategy, the Commission further defended 'pluralism' and 'political maturity' inside Hong Kong.

The Commission's first annual report on Hong Kong (Commission 1999g), mandated by the 1997 Communication, found no human rights violations and concentrated largely on economic matters. It was followed by the EU-HKSAR Customs Cooperation Agreement, of 13 May 1999 (*OJ* L 151, 18 June 99: 21-26). A second report, published in May 2000 (Commission 2000c), reflected on two years' experience of the handover and re-stated the main concerns: a stronger politicization of life in the HKSAR, and the issue of rights and freedoms. It concluded that, in spite of singular incidents, Hong Kong was clearly 'one of the most free societies in Asia' [*sic*] (Commission 2000c: 10), a sentiment echoed by former Governor Patten in October 2000 (*Rapid Database*: SPEECH/00/383).

In its third annual report on the HKSAR (Commission 2001a), published on 25 July 2001, the Commission reviewed the work of the Legislative Council and the Chief Executive in 2000, the tenth anniversary of the Basic Law. It deemed the Legislative Elections of 10 September 2000 'free and fair' (2001a: section 3). In the area of basic rights and liberties, especially press, academic and religious freedoms, the report looked back at a year that was 'rich in debate and controversy', a fact the Commission saw as 'the best proof that Hong Kong remains a free society' (2001a: point 9).

The European Parliament, by contrast, consistently adopted a much more cautious and critical approach and never ceased to call for continued respect for democracy, the principles of the Basic Law and of the Joint Declaration. (e.g. *EP News*, April 1997).

Following unification, there has been an undercurrent of smooth normality, a 'business as usual' atmosphere in the HKSAR. Anxieties about freedom and Chinese nationalism seem not to have dented optimism about the future of the 'City of Survivors' (*Newsweek*, May–July 1997). To many, the new administration seems mostly to lean on the discreet, not the heavy-handed, side, if one can disregard the controversy over the activities of the Falun Gong practitioners, an issue which would, according to the Commission in 2001, 'no doubt, warrant close attention' (Commission 2001a: point 9).

Did the reality of 'one country' make the mainland more relaxed about the 'two systems'? To many, the HKSAR was beginning to resemble a 'high-tech society' with a 'low-tech' legal order. In areas such as the judiciary, immigration, refugees or the right of abode, a growing influence of Beijing, and of the 'unholy alliance' (So 2000: 379) of Beijing and of the Hong Kong business community was palpable, in the wake of the 2000 elections to the Legislative Council. Observers predicting there would be a 'sidelining' of democratic forces and a tangible increase in Beijing's control, were also proved right. The 2001 resignation of key civil servant Anson Chan, whose reputation extended well into the EU (*Rapid Database*: IP/01/42), and who frequently opposed Tung Chee Hwa's policies, illustrated the fact that a smooth development of democracy in Hong Kong was far from a foregone conclusion. This, and related developments, led some observers to conclude that post handover Hong Kong was best described, with Fenby (2000: 314), as 'one country, one-and-a-half-systems'.

The EU and Macao

> Hong Kong, the last British colony of any size was handed back to China in 1997 in a ceremony stage-managed by Gilbert and Sullivan to mark the final going down of the British sun. Macao, the last Portuguese factory in Asia, by contrast went two years later almost without anyone noticing (Pagden 2001: 159).

Established as a Portuguese trading post from 1555 to 1557, Macao, the 'City of the Name of God', became an important Jesuit missionary outpost. It functioned as a gateway on the south-eastern coast of China (Lach 1994: Vol. I, Bk 1, 295) and a crossroads of trade and European colonial endeavour. Its varying fortunes earned it the name 'Yo-Yo-City' (*AsiaInc*, November 1999: 31). Macao traded with, and constituted a vital counterpart to, the Catholic Spanish empire in the Philippines, yet its territory was only 2 per cent of that of neighbouring Hong Kong. Its return to China, as the Macao Special Administrative Region (MSAR), at midnight on 20 December 1999 (see Box 6.6), ended 442 years of Portuguese administration and represented the end of centuries of European colonialism in Asia. It is an irony of history that the Portuguese, among the first to colonize Asia, were also among the last to let go. As in the case of Hong Kong, the handover was preceded by both a Joint Declaration (1987) and a Basic Law (1993), agreed between Portugal and China, which pledged the 'one country, two systems' rule for 50 years and guaranteed a high degree of autonomy to Macao, with (partial) exceptions in defence and foreign relations.

Box 6.6: EU–Macao Relations

In 2000, the EU was Macao's second largest trading partner, accounting for 28.4 per cent of total exports of goods from Macao, after the USA (48.3 per cent) and before China (10.2 per cent) and Hong Kong (6.5 per cent). In terms of imports, the EU came third (9.6 per cent), after China (41 per cent) and Hong Kong (15.2 per cent) (Commission 2001b: 6). Portugal was still the biggest EU investor (Commission 1999d: 5). The Union's relations with Macao began through sectoral (textile) agreements (*OJ* L 287/87: 46 and *OJ* L 94/95: 237). They were taken further with the Trade and Cooperation Agreement (TCA) of 14 December 1992 (*OJ* L 404/92: 26). Article 16 of this TCA provided for a Joint Annual Committee, meeting even after the handover. Macao, in turn, established the 'Macao Economic and Trade Office' at the EU. The 1998 China strategy of the Commission explicitly referred to the autonomy of Macao (Commission 1998a: 8).

On 12 November 1999, the Commission adopted a more specialized paper on *Relations between the European Union and Macao: Beyond 2000* (1999d), in which it pointed to the function of Macao as a 'role-model' for China, for instance in providing expertise about the WTO of which Macao is a founding member. The terms 'autonomy', 'similar legal system' and 'cultural identity' took centre stage in this Communication, which was also influenced by the possibilities Macao could offer the EU as a 'natural springboard' into China (Commission 1998a: 4). The 7th EC–Macao Joint Committee meeting in June 2000 was the first after the handover, and offered a review of current and future programmes and investments (e.g. Asia-Invest, EU Studies Institute). In its first annual report on the MSAR (Commission 2001b), the Commission continued the tone and thrust of the 1999 Communication. It described Macao as a 'privileged bridge for exchanges of all kinds between the EU and the PRC' (Commission 2001b: section I) and concluded that the MSAR has 'on the whole, got off to a good start'. It is worth noting that the report highlighted the decline in crime in Macao and pointed to future visa-free access of MACAO SAR passport holders to 13 EU member states.

Economics and 'Ersatz-Diplomacy': The EU and the Republic of China (ROC, Taiwan)

The elections in Taiwan on 18 March 2000, called to find a successor to ex-President Lee Teng-hui, were preceded by a war of words between the PRC on the mainland and the ROC. Chinese sabre-rattling stopped short of firing missiles into the Taiwan Strait. On 18 March 2000, the Taiwanese defied the PRC when 39.3 per cent of them voted for pro-independence candidate Chen Shui-ban of the Democratic Progressive Party (cf. *EURASIA Bulletin* 4.3, March 2000: 1-2, 27-28). Fifty-one years of Nationalist rule suddenly came to an end. (Chiang Kai-shek's Kuomintang (KMT) had relocated from Mao's Communist mainland China in 1949). The 2000 vote was seen both as a litmus test for Taiwan's fledgling democracy and the dawn of a new period in cross-Strait relations between the ROC and the PRC (*Taipeh/Free China*

Box 6.7: The Republic of China (ROC, Taiwan) and the EU

In the 1990s, Taiwan developed into the EU's eleventh biggest trading partner and became more significant to the EU than Canada or Australia (Dent 1999: 164). The Union acknowledged the island as a 'Separate Customs Territory', not as a state separate from mainland China. This was a debatable interpretation, which, as Dent pointed out (1999: 165) was based on a kind of de facto 'economic recognition'. However, a declaration by the Finnish Presidency (20 July 1999: 99-125) reaffirmed the EU view on the 'one China' principle. EU relations with the ROC could therefore only take place on the level of annual talks, assisted by the EU Council of Trade and Industry, an EU Information Office in Taipei, and Taipei's representation in Brussels. Relations across the Taiwan Strait and the negotiations for membership of the WTO for both the PRC and the ROC were the main foci for EU–Taiwan relations until both finally joined in December 2001 and January 2002 respectively (see *Financial Times*, 2 January 2002). Much of the three-way dialogue was embedded in an atmosphere, in which interpretations of what constituted 'state-to-state-relations' or 'one-China' often clashed with one another. As far as the EU is concerned, any future aggressive behaviour of the PRC towards Taiwan will have an impact on European business and will increase the challenges for the Union, which ultimately finds itself torn between the two differing historical, diplomatic and economic positions dividing East Asia's second largest and fourth largest markets, caught 'on the horns of a dilemma' (*European Voice*, 6–12 April 2000).

Journal, 24 March 2000). Following the election, however, Chen's government was an uneasy cohabitation, dogged by economic stagnation, conflict between the new President and the KMT-dominated legislature, and the early resignation of Prime Minister Tang Fei on 3 October 2000.

Tibet

Tibet has been called, at best, an internal issue with outward repercussions; at worst, a major external issue and human rights catastrophe, the judgment being relative to the degree to which the legitimacy of China's claim to Tibet, the 1950 invasion, the name Xizang or the Chinese-Tibetan Seventeen-Point Agreement of 1951 are accepted. Mainly on account of the strength of religious identity and national separatism it represented, Tibetan nationalism suffered persistent, massive Chinese repression. EU–Tibet–China relations reflected these issues. Both EU policy statements and EU-delegated visits to Tibet dealt with prison riots, the Chinese destruction of Tibetan cultural heritage, or the role of European states' arms deliveries to the PRC. While most EU pronouncements professed, at least on the surface, to contain 'concern' or 'strong positions', they carefully avoided both firmness and clarity, mostly by referring to the progress of the EU–China human rights dialogue or directly to China–Tibet relations (EUI, *Foreign Policy Review* online: docs. 90/018, 93/229, 93/424, 98/457, 98/462). The fact that Tenzin Gyatso, the fourteenth Dalai Lama, was awarded the 1989 Nobel peace prize and campaigned extensively in Europe (e.g. Finland, Strasbourg)[6] and that many Western observers condemned human rights abuses and supported Tibetan self-rule, did not make the EU fully realize, it seems, that in regard to Tibet, the preservation of an ancient culture and national identity was decidedly inferior to the overall Chinese priority to reaffirm its own power and status (Box 6.8). EU apathy in this area is only explicable, if one wants to leave the lure of business opportunities aside for the moment, by the Union's China policy, especially the support for the 'one-China principle' of the PRC (cf. EUI *Foreign Policy Review* online: doc. 99/125).

---

6.   The Tibetan Government-in-exile opened an office in Brussels on 10 April 2001, which forms an official representation of His Holiness.

Box 6.8: China, Tibet and the 'Policy of Reincarnation'

Diplomatic issues have exacerbated the rifts over 'reincarnation-policy' between Beijing and Lhasa. China and Tibet continue to argue over recognition and appointment of what they see as important 'living Buddhas', such as the Panchen or Karmapa Lamas, second and third respectively in the traditional Buddhist religious hierarchy after the Dalai Lama (although this is a contested area). The PRC's attempts to 'control the process of recognizing, installing and educating major reincarnated lamas' (Hutchings 2000: 436) suffered a blow in 2000, when Orgyen Trinley Dorje, the seventeenth Karmapa Lama, fled Tibet in order to join the fourteenth Dalai Lama in exile in the Indian Dharamsala (*Economist,* 15 January 2000; *Asiaweek*, 16 February 2001: 8; see also Ribes 2000). Meanwhile, the plight of Tibet has entered mainstream popular culture and reached an audience beyond the Free Tibet Movement, the Tibetan Youth Council, and other dedicated pressure groups. Examples for this are two big-budget films about the country, Jean-Jacques Annaud's *Seven Years in Tibet,* based on the book by Heinrich Harrer, and Martin Scorcese's *Kundun,* as well as the success of books such as John F. Avedon's *In Exile from the Land of Snows* (1998).

Conclusion

Among the EU's relations with Asia, its dialogue with the reforming PRC stands out for its diversity. At the beginning of 2002, there were few other individual Asian countries, except Japan, with which the Union was connected through an equally large number of different channels of cooperation on different levels. Given that the majority among those focused on harnessing, in one way or another, the vast market potential that China represents for European business, it was vital for the EU to strive not to sacrifice too many sensitive principles on the altar of business. The EU–China human rights dialogue therefore developed as a necessary alternative forum for debate about the relationship between business and politics. In 2001–02, the EU continued to adhere to the 'one-China-principle', a stance which predetermined many EU–Chinese debates, for example about Tibet or human rights in general. It also put a particular spotlight on EU relations with the ROC in Taipeh, regarded by the EU as a 'Customs Territory', rather than a separate political entity. Any cross-Strait tensions between the PRC and the ROC therefore impacted significantly on the EU's policies, as did the accession of both mainland China and Taiwan to the WTO in December 2001 and January 2002 respectively, a process that the EU supported over many years. After their return to China, the EU's relations with the territories of Hong Kong and Macao developed against a background of concerns for the 'one-country-two-systems' principle and for the preservation of democratic rights and liberties, especially in Hong Kong. Although the former British colony appeared to return to 'business as usual', an increased influence of Beijing in Hong Kong's legal, political and immigration affairs was palpable by the end of 2001.

7 |

Main and Emerging Partners: EU Relations with North-East Asia and South Asia

This chapter contrasts two aspects of the EU's Asia policy: on the one hand, the traditional, highly developed contacts the EU has with its North-East Asian partners, particularly with Japan and South Korea; and, on the other hand, the emerging dialogue with North Korea, South Asia and the members of the South Asian Association for Regional Cooperation (SAARC), notably India, Bangladesh, Nepal, Bhutan, the Maldives and Sri Lanka. Over the last decade, the EU's dialogue with Afghanistan and Pakistan was an important, if exceptional, example of the implementation of a branch of the EU's CFSP in an Asian context. The chapter analyses this development against the background of the war in Afghanistan and the international war against terrorism. The section closes with an investigation of the way these wars, at the end of 2001, not only shaped the EU's future relations with Afghanistan, but were also beginning to contribute to a redirection of the EU's policies towards central Asia and Pakistan, as well as its overall Asia policy.

Trade Imbalance, Knowledge Imbalance: The EU and Japan

For Japan, the second largest global trading power, the 1997–98 crisis heralded a period of recession and a very slow move towards recovery, in spite of parallel political and banking reform. Successive Japanese governments since 1994, under Ryutaro Hashimoto, Keizo Obuchi, Yoshiro Mori (2000) and Junichiro Koizumi (2001),[1] sought to get the economy back on track, to fight unemployment, which rose to a record 5 per cent in August 2001 (*Far Eastern Economic Review,* 6 September

---

1. See J. Watts, 'Lion King', *The Guardian Weekend*, 1 September 2001: 47-57 and *EURASIA Bulletin*, April–May 2001: 10-13.

2001) and to implement successive deregulation initiatives (see EC Delegation to Japan: Speech 23/2000).

EU–Japanese relations have moved on from the failed trade negotiations of the mid-1960s and from the spirit of the infamous 1979 Commission Working Paper according to which the Japanese were a country of 'workaholics living in rabbit hutches' (cf. Gilson 2000: 24; Dent 1999: 91). Nowadays they are founded on institutionalization, a 'habit of interaction' (Gilson 2000: 27) and the common search for geopolitical positions, commensurate with both regions' economic clout. The EU realizes that Japan, perhaps uniquely for Asian states, has moved beyond a trade-off between political and socio-economic rights and now forms the EU's third largest export market. It views Japan as 'the main partner of Europe in Asia' (e.g. Commission 1999b: 8), and currently promotes the Action Plan 'Shaping Our Common Future', constructed during the EU–Japanese summits in 2000 and 2001, and a 'Decade of EU-Japan Cooperation' (*Rapid Database*: SPEECH/00/277). However, Dent (1999: 88) identifies numerous commercial conflicts, and the EU's worsening trade balance with Japan, as key reasons for the 'reluctant and haphazard development of a common EEC policy towards Japan'.

Overall, the 'reduction of ignorance', protectionism, deregulation and a further politicization of the relationship have emerged as the *leitmotivs* of EU–Japanese cooperation. Multilaterally, the EU and Japan liaise through the UN, ASEM, ASEAN ARF, G7/G8, G24 or WTO frameworks, while the bilateral dialogue extends to a very wide range of subjects (cf. Commission 1995a: annex III; Santer 1996: 8-10; Gilson 2000: 100-112). The following are some key areas of EU–Japanese cooperation (see also Box 7.1):

- industry, competition and consumer issues, science and technology, R&D;
- telecommunications, information technology, services, transport, social affairs;
- cooperation between the European Atomic Energy Community (EURATOM) and Japan on the peaceful use of nuclear energy (Commission 1988; *OJ* L 57/89: 62);
- non-proliferation and disarmament, crime, drugs and sexual exploitation;
- The environment, health, legal dialogue, culture and education.

Box 7.1: EU–Japanese Cooperation Initiatives

Among the many EU–Japan initiatives (see Dent 1999: 99 for an overview), are an EU–Japan Business Dialogue Round Table (EUJBDRT), the EU–Japan Consumer Dialogue (EJCD, 1999), a Trade-Assessment Mechanism (TAM, 1993), a Science and Technology Fellowship Programme (1986) and Forum (1993), EU–Japan Cooperation Weeks (1997) and a Euro–Japanese Information Technology Month (October 2000). The EU's 'EXPROM' export promotion campaign, in particular, seeks to stimulate European exports to Japan through the organization of trade fairs and seminars. It consists of the Executive Training Programme (1979), linguistic and cultural familiarization programmes, ad hoc initiatives, the EU–Japan Centre for Industrial Cooperation (Tokyo, 1987, Brussels, 1996), and Gateway to Japan, billed as the 'largest EU export promotion campaign' (*Rapid Database*: IP/94/138). Its main thrust is the provision of a 'competitive edge' for companies, through presentations and market studies in a range of sectors from medical equipment to food or information technology. The programme connects with Japanese import schemes and targets EU exports thought to have the best chances of success in the competitive Japanese market.

The establishment of an EC Delegation in Tokyo in 1974 was followed by early initiatives such as the Executive Training Programme (*Background Report,* BR ISEC/B19/89), but also by the imposition of EC anti-dumping duties. The 1991 Hague Joint Declaration (Hill and Smith 2000: 440, Doc. 4c/35; Gilson 2000: 173-75) became both the seminal codification of the partnership and, as Gilson (2000: 98) states, its '*de facto* point of departure'. In its 1995 communication 'Europe and Japan: The Next Steps' (Commission 1995a), the Commission realized 'cultural and linguistic barriers' still had to be overcome, and political relations improved, to counteract US influence (1995a: 6, 14). The European Parliament (*OJ* C 304, 6 October 1997) and the General Affairs Council have broadly affirmed this approach. In addition, a 1999 Commission Working Document on Japan (Commission 1999b), noted the positive repercussions of the euro and the Treaty of Amsterdam on EU–Japan relations, but found that its desired 'diversification' and 'politicization' were still incomplete. It recommended discussions in the 'key areas' of regional security, FDI, the euro or the 'Deregulation Dialogue'. The ninth Japan–EU summit, of 19 July 2000, looked towards future issues such as an EU–Japan cooperation agreement in the area of competition, or a EURATOM–Japan agreement on nuclear energy (see *OJ* L 57/89: 62). On 4 April 2001, the EU and Japan signed a new agreement aimed at facilitating trade in pharmaceuticals, chemicals, telecommunications and electrical equipment, which included mutual recognition in relation to testing standards and conformity assessment (Commission 2001k). The tenth EU–Japan summit in Brussels on 8 December 2001 resulted in a comprehensive, ten-year action plan. The scheme, 'Shaping Our Common Future', was inspired by the desire for enhanced EU–Japanese security cooperation and assumed a much wider, global approach to EU–Japanese relations than many earlier documents (*European Voice*, 13–19 December 2001). Although the action plan contains references to human rights (at point 1.3), and in spite of the EU's calls on Japan, early in 2001, to abolish capital punishment (*EU News* 04/2001, 16 February 2001), human rights do not form part of the core of the EU–Japanese dialogue, particularly when compared with the significance of issues such as FDI. Overall, however, deregulation and market access for European goods form the central themes in EU–Japanese economic diplomacy, and an official EU–Japanese 'deregulation dialogue' began in 1994. According to the Commission's Delegation in Japan, deregulation is 'no sinister battering ram used by a foreign invader to assault Japan's markets', but a priority in the midst of intensive, ongoing work on defining a new EU–Japan partnership (*EU News,* 03/2001, 9 February 2001). This issue, in spite of an otherwise 'healthy' association, was said to 'sour' EU–Japanese relations (*European Voice*, 12–19 May 1999: 9). In the Union's view, deregulation still 'moves in fits and starts' (Commission 1999b: 11). The Japanese, on the other hand, pointed to the EU's own history of anti-dumping measures against Japan. Annual lists of regulatory reform proposals identified agriculture, transport, distribution systems, competition policy, the investment situation and a host of sectors such as financial services, cars, telecommunications or insurance for further deregulation (*European Voice*, 1–7 March 2001: 22; Commission Delegation to Japan: Speech 23/2000, 7 November 2000).

The 1994 New Asia Strategy pointed to another set of problems: lack of 'cultural awareness' between the EU and Japan (Commission 1994a: 19). Similarly, the 1995 Communication on Japan spoke of a 'knowledge imbalance' to the detriment of the EU (Commission 1995a: 15; 1999b: 16, 19). On top of this, there are differences in values, evident in the way business is conducted in Japan, for example through the tightly knit, opaque Japanese *keiretsu* enterprise networks. The situation regarding FDI is another case of divergence, with the figure given for Japanese FDI in Europe ranging from five to seven times that of European FDI in Japan. These discrepancies laid open differences, both in networking structures, and regarding strategic alliances (Dent 1999: 114).

Thaw along the Last Cold-War Frontier? The EU and the Republic of Korea (ROK, South Korea)

The Korean War (1950–53) had important repercussions on Europe's common security identity, and the commonalities of the historical and human-suffering experience between Korea and the EU (particularly Germany) are obvious. Slogans such as 'We Are One People' in 2000 (*Asiaweek*, 23 June 2000: 22) were strongly reminiscent of European/ German developments a decade earlier. The apparent thaw along the 'world's last Cold-War frontier', accelerated by an inter-Korean summit and Joint Declaration (13–15 June 2000), was welcomed by the Commission. It entailed an unprecedented North Korean 'diplomatic blitz',[2] and, from July 2000, Korean membership in the Asian Regional Forum (*Rapid Database*: IP/00/625). Moreover, EU involvement in KEDO, the ASEM 3 in Seoul, and the award of the 2000 Nobel peace prize to South Korean President Kim Dae-Jung shifted the goalposts of EU–Korean relations. Chris Patten claimed in January 2001 that: 'North Korean government and society are out of the cold' (Remarks in the European Parliament, 17 January 2001). However, the absence of a Peace Treaty, the presence of US military personnel and of a 'demilitarized zone' were stark reminders of the political reality between the two Koreas, despite embryonic attempts at reconciliation.

Following the 'suspension' of hostilities in the Korean War, diplomatic EU–ROK contact was initiated in 1963. An EU chamber of Commerce opened in Seoul in 1986, and a Delegation followed in 1989. Apart from WTO, ASEM or IMF contacts, bilateral relations with South Korea, which was in 2001 the eighth largest exporter to the EU and Europe's third largest export market in Asia, continued to unfold against the backdrop of trade disputes and the threat of WTO action, most notably in the field of shipbuilding.[3] EU anti-dumping measures,

---

2.   Involving both European states and the USA; Kim 2001: 25-26.

3.   See *Rapid Database*: IP/00/1301; *European Voice*, 23–30 May 2001 and 26 July–1 August 2001; EU–Korea relations regarding shipbuilding are founded on an 'Agreed Minutes' Accord, initialled by the Commission and the Korean Govern-

even a temporary suspension (1989–92) of GSP preferences, had been implemented towards South Korea. Dent (1999: 205) summarized that: 'as with most of its other economic relations with East Asian countries, the EU's main concerns continued to relate to Korea's 'internal' barriers to international trade'. But issues of protectionism were paralleled by three counteracting developments: first, a steep rise in general EU–Korea trade and investment flows; secondly, the Joint Declaration and Framework Agreement of 1996, plus the Telecommunications and Customs Cooperation agreements (*OJ* C 188/96, 28 June 1996: 11; *OJ* L 321/97: 30; *OJ* L 121/97: 13); and, thirdly, the Commission communication, *European Union Policy towards the Republic of Korea* (Commission 1998b).

The Asian crisis, the new Kim Dae-Jung Government and the dissolution of military authoritarianism proved catalytic, both for economic liberalization and for South Korea's relations with the EU. The Commission's 1998 communication and Council conclusions of 19 July 1999, therefore prioritized democratization, reform and support for the Four Party Talks (between the two Koreas, the USA and China, the former antagonists in the Korean War). In economic affairs, the Commission demanded the inclusion of the ROK in regional programmes such as AsiaInvest or ECIP. A new 'EU-Korea Trade and Cooperation Framework Agreement' entered into force in April 2001 (*Rapid Database*: IP/01/477). This agreement, and the activities of the EU–Korea Business Cooperation Network, exposed possibilities and drawbacks of the dialogue, in which the obstacles included differences over human rights—long the focus of European Parliament debates—and diverging attitudes towards market access and multilateral trade cooperation.

Distance or Engagement?: The EU, KEDO and the People's Democratic Republic of Korea (DPRK, North Korea)

The DPRK was, in 2001, in the eighth year of a food crisis, which cost the lives of at least one million people. The country was a recipient of EU humanitarian aid from the mid-1990s, but no bilateral agreements emerged between the EU and the DPRK. In 2001, seven EU member

ment on 10 April 2000, and on a subsequent Council Decision; cf. *EURASIA Bulletin* 4.4-5, April–May 2000: 25; 4.10, October 2000: 29.

states (Austria, Denmark, Finland, Italy, Portugal, Sweden, UK) maintained diplomatic relations with the DPRK, and Germany, Spain and the Netherlands were about to initiate them (*Financial Times*, 22 October 2000).

Overall EU trade volumes with North Korea were small, but the European Union was a partner—in conjunction with the founder members South Korea, Japan and the USA—in the Executive Board of the Korean Peninsula Energy Development Organization (KEDO). KEDO was established in March 1995, the year of the EU's first New Asia Strategy (Commission 1994a), as an instrument for the implementation of the US–North Korea Agreed Framework of October 1994. The immediate aim of KEDO was the closure of North Korea's Russian graphite-moderated nuclear reactors, which are capable of producing weapons-grade plutonium (see Gilson 2000: 129-32). But the wider objectives of the organization included 'denuclearization', the strengthening of nuclear safety, the promotion of the peaceful use of nuclear energy and of the use of energy sources outside the nuclear option. The programme's aims comprised the construction of more 'proliferation-resistant' nuclear reactors in North Korea and the supervision of the dismantling of the nuclear weapons programme of the DPRK. After initial confusion over who should represent the Union in KEDO, it was agreed in January 1997 that Euratom would fulfil this function, with one vote in KEDO, and that the Council and the Commission would authorize one delegate each. The Euratom–KEDO Accession Agreement was signed on 19 September 1997 and entered into force a year later, shortly after a missile test undertaken by North Korea on 31 August 1998 pressed home the *raison d'être* of the entire KEDO exercise. Until 2000, the Union's involvement in the KEDO programme entailed around €75 million in EU funding (*Rapid Database*: IP/96/896; IP/00/99). From 1996 onwards, the Council supported EU membership of KEDO through two main CFSP instruments:

- By means of Joint Action 96/195/CFSP, of 13 March 1996, the Madrid Council approved of the EU's participation in KEDO. Article 1 of the Joint Action, which was worth an initial €5 million, committed the Union to non-proliferation and enhanced nuclear safety, by means of contributing towards the financing and supply of 'interim energy alternatives in the Korean Peninsula'.

- Common Position 97/484/CFSP, adopted on 24 July 1997,[4] considerably facilitated the decision-making process within the KEDO Executive Board, by covering decisions falling outside the area of competence of EURATOM.

The European Parliament, although approving of the EU's participation in KEDO on 23 March 1999, regretted nevertheless that it had not been consulted on the accession. (*OJ* C 177, 22 June 1999).

In a more general context, the Council stated in 1999 that there were no basic objections to improving the EU's relations with North Korea, subject to progress on issues like nuclear activities or human rights. A wider political dialogue between the EU and North Korea had been inaugurated in 1998, marking a further step for the country, led by President Kim Jong-Il and Prime Minister Hong Song Nam, on the road from 'rogue-state to vogue-state' (*Far Eastern Economic Review,* 10 August 2000: 16; *EURASIA Bulletin* 5:1-2, January–February 2001). By the end of 2001, unification seemed more than the 'distant prospect' foreshadowed by the Commission's Communication on Korea (1998b: 10). Further Council Conclusions of 9 October and 20 November 2000 (2308th Council Meeting (13430/00, *presse* 435), reiterated the Union's support for reconciliation and for President Kim Dae-Jung's North Korea engagement ('sunshine') policy towards the North. This contributed to a more coherent EU policy towards the DPRK, which continued to be fully dependent on further North–South *rapprochement* (*Rapid Database*: MEMO/01/159). However, also in 2001, member states like France or Ireland continued to block initial EU–DPRK diplomatic efforts, mainly on human rights grounds (*European Voice,* 1–7 February 2001). Following the 2001 visit to Pyongyang by an EU *troika* (the Presidency of the Council of Ministers, the European Commission and the Council Secretariat), which was led by Swedish Prime Minister Göran Persson, the EU expressed its hope for the establishment of full diplomatic relations with the DPRK in the near future (Commission: *Midday Express* 14 May 2001; *European Voice,* 17–22 May 2001).

---

4. Joint Action 96/195/CFSP: *OJ* L 63, 13 March 1996; Common Position 97/484/CFSP, *OJ* L 213, 5 August 1997; *OJ* L 70, 10 March 1998; Parliament approval: *OJ* C 177, 22 June 1999; GR 1997, points 722 and 982; GR 1998, points 539, 895, 911.

After 'People Power II': The EU and the Philippines

The Philippines, independent since 1946, were shaped by the Marcos dictatorship, martial law, economic crises and civil unrest. In 1985, the 'People Power' revolt successfully motivated Corazon Aquino, widow of the assassinated Benito Aquino, to run against Ferdinand Marcos. Although this fostered positive change towards democracy, violence and coup attempts continued. Successive presidents, Fidel Ramos (1992) and Joseph Ejercito Estrada (1998), faced allegations of a return to Marcos-style 'crony' capitalism, which brought 'people power' back to the streets of Manila from 1999, and, eventually, led to Estrada's impeachment and removal from office (cf. *EURASIA Bulletin* 4.10, October 2000; 5.1-2, January–February 2001). In 2001, the new President, Gloria Macapagal Arroyo, the daughter of former Philippine President Diosdalo Macapagal, had to face not only internal reform, but also the hostilities of the Moro Islamic Liberation Front (MILF), which, in 2000 and 2001, included several hostage crises involving European citizens.

Box 7.2: The Development of EU–Philippine Relations

> Beginning with NGO co-financing arrangements in 1976, EC development aid to the Philippines increased incrementally, particularly after 'People Power I' in 1985–86. The 1980 ASEAN Cooperation Treaty formed the central axis of EU–Philippine relations, and an EU Delegation operated in Manila from 1990. The first ever European Business Information Centre (EBIC) in Asia was established in Manila in 1993. There was a textile accord in 1990 (*OJ* L 339/90: 1), but 'integrated rural development' was the main focus of overall assistance. In this area, EC funding was the highest within South-East Asia (Commission 1997g: 84). Most programmes had a 'local community-' and 'human resources-' dimension. They included schemes for Credit Facilities for Women (CFWP), Standards, Quality and Conformity Assessment Schemes and Business Information and Development Services. EU–Philippine cooperation was the subject of a Resolution in the European Parliament on 14 January 1999 (*OJ* C 104, 14 April 1999).

Common Values and Entrepreneurship: The EU–India Dialogue

Consider this: the European Union is India's largest trading partner. It accounts for nearly half of total foreign direct investment (FDI) flows into the country, and is the largest source of grant aid. And yet EU-India relations are a pale shadow of what they should be (*EURASIA Bulletin*, 5.1-2, January–February 2001: 5).

Modern India, under Prime Minister Atal Bihari Vajpayee, has been called a 'rising force' (Commission 1996b: 3) or a 'giant on the move' (*Asiaweek*, 11 August 2000). With a population of 1.2 billion, India is the world's second most populous country. It became an 'Asian super-power' and made vital contributions in the Non-Aligned Movement, the UN, as an ASEAN 'Dialogue Partner', in the ARF, the WTO and the Group of 77. In terms of GNP and purchasing power parity, India represented the fifth largest global economy, with an average growth of 5 per cent over the last decade of the twentieth century (*The Economist*, 9 December 2000: 94). Since the widely analysed economic reforms under Narasimha Rao from 1991–96 (Chakravartty 1997: 83), many observers invoked the 'Indian Tiger'. More appropriately, Vandenborre (1999: 283) preferred to relate India to an elephant: 'this animal has more difficulty in getting itself in motion because of its size and weight but once it reaches full speed it becomes an irresistible force'. It appeared, however, as an ambivalent giant: on the one hand, more than half of the population lived on less than US$1 a day; on the other, there was an expanding IT-literate middle-class and substantial, productivity-led, growth.

The EU's 'Prospects for EU–India Relations' (*OJ* C 207/163, 21 July 1999, 1999/C 207/225) emphasized that 'South Asia has an important and increasing role in the world'. In the case of India, sheer size, population density and a European colonial heritage impinge on its present-day relations with Europe. But although the EU is India's biggest trading partner, with bilateral trade flows at a level of €23 billion (*European Voice*, 6–12 July 2000: 6), India attracted less external EU trade than small Singapore. By contrast, India was the largest recipient of development aid in the developing world, with human resources and education assuming high priority. Because of these imbalances, Chris Patten called the EU–India dialogue a 'unique success story that is still undersold' (*Rapid Database*: SPEECH/01/36). Similarly, for the Commission, Indian dynamism 'has to overcome a number of challenges to fulfil its full potential' (Commission 1996b: 4). And from an Asian point of view, more decision-makers in India are now beginning to perceive the EU as more than a mere German-French-British assembly.

India's 'escape' from the 1997–98 Asian financial crisis, a large Indian community in Europe and India's democracy itself, all provided a strong rationale for the EU–Indian partnership (see Box 7.3). These factors consolidated what the EU called its 'automatic sympathy' for the country that represents the largest democracy in the world. This was a significant change of approach from a period of indifference which frequently amounted to no more than a 'dialogue of the deaf'. India was, more often than not, the 'poor cousin' among EU partnerships in Asia. There were some sector-specific agreements (*OJ* L 273/81; 301/90: 46; *OJ* L 94/95: 191), and South Asia bought arms from Europe, but the EU did not initiate any significant trade initiatives. The 1994 New Asia Strategy incorporated South Asia only half-heartedly, and only as an afterthought. The fact that India—and the other members of SAARC—were left out at the ASEM 1 summit, both raised eyebrows and provoked questions about whether the process truly deserved its name as an 'EU–*Asia*' meeting (*OJ* C 297/02, *Question* E-0086/96; *OJ* C 273/34 *Question* E-1685/95).

In spite of the boost to bilateral relations, EU-Indian irritations over 'Fortress Europe' or anti-dumping duties continued to surface throughout 2000 (*European Voice*, 27 January 2000). The Comprehensive Test Ban or Non-Proliferation Treaties too remained thorny issues. Against the background of an EU Common Position on Non-Proliferation and Confidence-Building in the South Asian Region,[5] both the Council and the European Parliament condemned the territorial conflict between India and Pakistan, the nuclear tests of June 1998[6] and the hostile episodes in the Kargil area of the disputed state of Kashmir from 1999 to 2002 (see Ramdas, Ahmar and Samad 2001: 26-42). Parliament regularly called for (a partial) autonomy for Kashmir and noted the existence of executions, child labour, forced prostitution, police brutality and the worrying tensions between religions, castes and ethnic groups. The future, partners on both sides agreed, would lie in a further, 'phased' extension of EU-India dialogue, a point Commissioner Patten was at pains to stress during his visit to the region from 25–29 January

---

5.   98/606/CFSP, *OJ* L 32, 6 February 1998; *OJ* L 290, 29 October 1998: 1; see also Decision 98/623 CFSP relating to the implementation of Joint Action 97/288/CFSP, on the EU contribution to the promotion of transparency in nuclear-related export controls.

6.   2097th and 2104th Council Meetings (General Affairs) 25 May 1998 and 8–9 June 1998; European Parliament, *OJ* C 210, 6 July 1998: 205.

2001. Kirpalani and Seristo (1998: 97-98) concluded that: 'thus the time is clearly appropriate for the EU and India to do far more trade and for Multi-National Corporations in the EU to seriously consider investing more in the Indian market'.

Box 7.3: India and the EU

Concerned about keeping UK Commonwealth preferences (Singh 1962: 275-76), India was one of the first countries to establish a mission to the EC in 1962. By 1971, India had become a major GSP beneficiary, largely offsetting any losses. A 1972 EC–India Joint Declaration and the 1993 EU–India Joint Statement on Political Dialogue (11390/93, *presse* 246-G*)* reinforced shared democratic values and foreshadowed the Commercial Cooperation Agreement of 1973 (*OJ* L 82, 27 March 1974). A second EC–India Economic and Commercial Cooperation Agreement (*OJ* L 328/5, 16 November 1981) covered trade, environment, energy, science and industrial cooperation. However, the exclusion of the relevant provisions of Lomé II was criticized (Sundaram 1997: 110).

The 1994 third-generation 'EU-India Cooperation Agreement on Partnership and Development' (*OJ* L 223/23, 27 August 1994) was the most far-reaching accord so far, containing many non-aid issues. A Commission communication, *The EU–India Enhanced Partnership* (1996b) reaccentuated shared values and singled out arms control, terrorism, illegal immigration, environmental degradation and WTO objectives for further cooperation (Council, 12440/96 *presse* 366: II, V; European Parliament, *OJ* C 175, 21 June 1999). In 1998–99, regional hostilities and nuclear testing propelled all of South Asia higher up the EU's agenda (European Parliament A4-0066/99 lit. G), and in 2000 India finally joined the ranks of the five countries—USA, Canada, Japan, Russia and China—with which the Union holds regular summit meetings. The first ever EU–India Summit of 28 June 2000, under the aegis of the Portuguese presidency, added significant political weight to the dialogue and demonstrated 'shared interests and adherence to shared principles' (Singh 2000: 15).

Following the summit, EU–India relations were more wide-ranging than ever. An *Agreement for Scientific and Technological Co-operation* (Commission 2001 [l]), an EU–India Round Table and talks about human rights, IT, biotechnology, culture, the environment, nuclear proliferation (cf. Commission, *General Report* 2000: point 982) or education were all embedded in wider frameworks such as the EU–India Economic Cross-Cultural Programme (ECCP), the District Primary Education Initiative, *Asia Urbs*, AsiaInvest, the Management Exchange and Cooperation Programme, the EU–India Business Forum or the European Community Investment Partners (ECIP) scheme.

The EU and the South Asian Association for Regional Cooperation (SAARC)

The EC–India cooperation agreements of 1973 and 1981 were emulated in similar accords with SAARC member states, particularly Bangladesh, Pakistan and Sri Lanka (Sundaram 1997: 107). However, the SAARC, formed in 1985,[7] was more than a mere extension to EU–India cooperation. EU relations with the grouping were also based on diplomatic contacts and a 1996 Memorandum of Understanding on Administrative Cooperation. On 23 October 1998, the EU *troika* and the Commission met SAARC representatives in the margins of a meeting in New York.[8]

Bangladesh

The 1976 Commercial Cooperation Agreement between the EU and the People's Republic of Bangladesh,[9] ensured the proper functioning of future sector-specific agreements, such as those of 1979 and 1986 on textiles.[10] In 2001, the EU was the biggest trade partner for Bangladesh. After independence in 1971, Bangladesh's relations with the Union concentrated on poverty alleviation, rural development and disaster prevention (see Box 7.4). The Commission and seven member states were represented in Dhaka,[11] and the country, under Prime Minister Sheikh Hasina Wajed, was the second largest recipient of EU development assistance in Asia, after India. It was included in the DIPECHO First Action Plan for Disaster Preparedness for South-East and South Asia in 1998 and 2000. Food security, that is, access to food, remained of over-arching importance and accounted for two-thirds of EU-Bangladesh projects.

7.   The seven members of SAARC are: Bangladesh, Bhutan, India, the Maldives, Nepal, Pakistan and Sri Lanka.
8.   Commission, *General Report* 1998, point 899; see also European Parliament, Doc. PE DOC A2-212/88.
9.   Council Regulation (EEC) No. 2785/76, 16 November 1976, *OJ* L 319/1, 19 November 1976.
10.   Council Regulation (EEC) No. 2558/79, 30 October 1979, *OJ* L 298/38, 26 November 1979, cf. also: *OJ* L 325/90: 1 and *OJ* L 94/95: 24.
11.   Denmark, Germany, France, Italy, the Netherlands, Sweden and the UK.

Box 7.4: The EU and Bangladesh

Based on the EC Food Aid/Food Security Regulation 1292/96, EU–Bangladesh projects concentrated, from 1997, increasingly on cash resources, replacing traditional food aid. This method was anticipated to achieve an increase in incomes and production in the agriculture and forestry sectors. The 1999 European Strategy to Support Food Security Policy for Bangladesh was designed to run for three years and spawned initiatives against malnutrition, valued at €80 million (Commission, *EC-Bangladesh Development Cooperation*, 1999). In 1999–2000, a 'third-generation' Framework Cooperation Agreement (Commission 1999c; *OJ* C 143, 21 May 1999) coincided with a general EU development policy overhaul (*Rapid Database*: IP/00/1525). The agreement focused on poverty, 'trade for development' and regional integration. It included a human rights conditionality clause, inserted on account of traditionally high levels of political violence among Bangladesh's political parties. In addition, the general elections in Bangladesh on 1 October 2001 (*EURASIA Bulletin*, 5.10-11, October–November 2001: 1-2, 39-42, 55) were accompanied by an EU-funded Electoral Observation Mission which delivered a positive assessment of their outcome (EOM, *Rapid Database:* IP/01/833; SPEECH/01/125).

Afghanistan, the EU and the 'First War of the Twenty-first Century'

To read the illustrated *London News* of 1879 is to see that Afghanistan then, as now, is a place that operates in a different universe of belief. It is a place where our assumptions cannot be taken for granted, and it is a lace where military adventures are usually disastrous. Smoking the evil ones out of their caves is not going to be any easier than it was 120 years ago. In Afghanistan, perhaps more than anywhere, it is true that those who cannot remember the past are condemned to repeat it (Justin Cartwright, 'Familiar Ground', *Guardian*, Saturday Review, 3 November 2001: 3).

In 2001–02, Afghanistan became the location of a prolonged military campaign, on account of the terrorist atrocities in New York and Washington on 11 September 2001.[12] The American- and British-led military action in a country which had seen more than its share of wars over the last decades, was accompanied by a volatile international

---

12. See *Far Eastern Economic Review*, 4 October 2001: 16; and for a comprehensive overview of the war until the end of 2001, see *EURASIA Bulletin*, 5.10-11, October–November 2001: 10-33.

coalition and introduced further elements of change and unpredict-ability to the state of international relations. The new regional turmoil rendered the political situation in Afghanistan extremely fluid. It affected all aspects of the EU's relationship with Afghanistan, from the fight against terrorism, to the provision of aid, and from the establish-ment of a future, comprehensive political and military strategy, to the facilitation of a viable post-Taliban settlement (*Rapid Database*: IP/01/1389 and SPEECH [C. Patten] 01/429).

The history of structured EU–Afghanistan relations, however, pre-cedes the 2001 conflict. Coordinated from the offices of the EU Delega-tion to Pakistan, relations did not benefit from any formal cooperation agreement. Since 1976, they were rather based on food aid, interrupted only temporarily until the end of the Soviet occupation of Afghanistan in 1989. Subsequently, other areas of cooperation were added to the agenda of EU–Afghan relations: drug abuse rehabilitation, refugee matters and issues of resettlement or displacement. Afghanistan, like few other Asian countries (with the exception, perhaps, of Burma), is a revealing example of how a section of the EU's Asia policy can be shaped by the implementation of the instruments of the CFSP.

Box 7.5: Case Study: The EU's Common Foreign and Security Policy in Afghanistan

In 1996, Common Position (CP) 96/746/CFSP (*OJ* L 342, 31 December 1996) moved to the core of the Union's CFSP initiatives towards Afghan-istan. It took into account the new political realities created by Taliban rule since 1994. The CP imposed an embargo on the shipment of arms, munitions and military hardware to Afghanistan. In several successive CPs, the Council fine-tuned the Union's basis objectives for Afghanistan. CP 98/108/CFSP, for instance, adopted on 26 January 1998, continued the earlier embargo and introduced the five pillars of the Union's strategy towards the country: to provide humanitarian aid, bring about peace, promote respect for human rights, fight terrorism and combat illegal drug trafficking.

Between 1998 and 2001, the Council adopted a number of further CPs on Afghanistan (e.g. CP 98/108/CFSP, *OJ* L 32, 6 February 1998; CP 1999/73/CFSP, *OJ* L 23, 30 January 1999; CP 1999/727/CFSP, *OJ* L 294, 16 November 1999; CP 2000/55/CFSP, *OJ* L 21, 26 January 2000). CP 1999/73/CFSP, replacing CP 98/108/CFSP, re-emphasized these aims, particularly the struggle against ethnic- and gender-based persecution, and stressed the vital role of the UN in the search for peace, while CP 1999/727/CFSP was one of the first in a number of successive instruments introducing restrictive measures against the Taliban, pursuant to United Nations Security Council

Resolution (UNSCR) 1267/99 of 15 October 1999 (Commission, *General Report* 2000: point 986; Council: *Annual Report CFSP* 1999: points 12 and 12n). Sanctions included a flight ban and the freeze of Taliban-held funds abroad. The Council also called on the regime to hand over Osama bin Laden (CP 98/108/CFSP, *OJ* L 32, 6 February 1998; CP 1999/73/CFSP, *OJ* L 23, 30 January 1999 [see *General Report* 1999: point 835]; CP 1999/727/CFSP, *OJ* L 294, 16 November 1999; see also Commission 1999h and Regulations [EC] No 337/2000, *OJ* L 43, 16 February 2000 and EC No. 1272/2000, *OJ* L 144, 17 June 2000).

In CP 2000/55/CFSP, which repealed CP 1999/73/CFSP, the Council, once again comprehensively restated the EU's objectives, condemned terrorism and highlighted the importance of the UN Special Mission to Afghanistan (UNSMA) and the rights of women and children. It also called for enhanced 'intra-Afghan dialogue', at a time of an unprecedented anti-Hindu edict by the Taliban, and of a campaign of destruction against both the country's agricultural infrastructure and Buddhist heritage at Bamiyan (cf. *EURASIA Bulletin* 5.3, March 2001: 1). In CP 2000/55/CFSP, the Council made the fight against drugs and terrorism, mine clearance and peacemaking further priority areas (Commission 1997g: 59; see also Council Regulation [EC] No. 443/97, 3 March 1997; *European Voice*, 20 December 2001–9 January 2002; CP 2000/55/CFSP, *OJ* L 21, 26 January 2000: 1-3).

Through supplementary CPs in 2001 and 2002, especially 2001/56/CFSP and 2001/154/CFSP (CP 2001/56/CFSP, 22 January 2001 and 2001/154/CFSP, 26 February 2001) the Council succeeded and repealed CP 2000/55/CFSP, extending the range of arms- and funds-related sanctions towards the Taliban, but, importantly, exempting 'non-lethal military equipment needed solely for humanitarian or protective use', in compliance with a further UNSCR (1333 [2000]) of 19 December 2000. By CP 2001/771/CFSP, the Council sought to bring the EU's CFSP instruments towards the country in line, both legally and linguistically, with the new UNSCR 1333 (2000).

In a number of Resolutions from 1999 to 2001, the European Parliament had given its broad support to these Council policies and to the EU's efforts to step up relations with opposition forces in Afghanistan, placing, as always, a particularly strong emphasis on human rights, democracy and the situation and future of women in Afghanistan (e.g. *Resolution A5-0340/2000*, 30 November 2000: point 38, or Resolution A5-0332/2001, 25 October 2001: point 34; for earlier initiatives: *OJ* C 339, 10 November 1997 [*General Report* 1997: point 974] or *OJ* C 80, 16 March 1998 [*General Report* 1998: point 903); *Rapid Database*: IP/01/1652).

Pakistan

Three wars between Pakistan and India (see Ramdas *et al.* 2001: 27) mean that in 2000, 'the possibilities of a thaw seem distant' (*Asiaweek*,

5 May 2000: 27). On 12 October 1999, a *coup d'état,* led by General Pervez Musharraf in Pakistan (cf: *EURASIA Bulletin* 4.4-5, April–May 2000: 7-10), was met with surprisingly little internal condemnation. It resulted in the replacement of the government of former Prime Minister Mian Nawaz Sharif (Ahmar 2000: 62). There can be few areas of EU foreign policy which have undergone as rapid a change as the relationship between the Union and Pakistan. In the period of time between the *coup d'état* in Pakistan, in October 1999, and June 2001, when General Musharraf also appropriated the Presidential office,[13] (*Financial Times,* 21 June 2001: 10), the EU intensified its association with India, while relations with Pakistan were said to be 'going through a period of uncertainty' (Commission, *General Report* 1999: point 651). Although not entirely discontinuing the aid for the most needy or for refugees from Afghanistan, based on Council Regulation 443/92 of 25 February 1992, the Union did not, until the end of 2001, advance a 1986 co-operation agreement with Islamabad beyond a 'Draft Proposal' of 22 April 1998. However, by September 2000, the EU had decided to re-open a cautious ad hoc dialogue with Pakistan.[14] The war in Afghanistan and the ensuing refugee crisis from 2001 onwards, resulted in a significant intensification of EU–Pakistan relations. The dormant cooperation agreement was finally signed during Commission President Prodi's visit to Islamabad on 24 November 2001 (14350/01 Press 435 P 183/01). This was accompanied by accelerated EU pledges for economic assistance to Pakistan, including a €1.4 billion package of trade concessions, designed to considerably improve the access for Pakistani exports to the EU (*Guardian*, 26 September 2001; *European Voice,* 18–24 October 2001: 25). Through the trade deal and the inclusion of Pakistan in the EU's special GSP-related drugs regime, the Commission clearly expressed its view of trade as a 'weapon of peace', rewarding Pakistan for its 'courageous decision' to side with the West in the fight against terrorism.[15]

13. Generals Ayub Khan and Zia ul-Haq had previously seized the Pakistani Presidency in 1958 and 1977.

14. *OJ* L 108/86, July 1985: 1; COM (98) 357 final; *OJ* C 17, 22 January 1999; see also Council Regulation (EEC) No. 2561/79, 30 October 1979, *OJ* L 298/143, 26 November 1979 and *OJ* L 352/90: 74; *OJ* L 94/95: 285, 306 (textile agreements).

15. GAC Conclusions of 17 October 2001, point 6; Ghent European Council Conclusions, of 19 October 2001, point 3; *Rapid Database* IP/01/1426, 16 October 2001, for details of the new EU–Pakistan preferential trade package. Following

The Wider Implications of the War in Afghanistan for the EU's Future Asia Policy

Owing to these developments, and as one result of the war in Afghanistan from 2001, the Council redefined its position towards countries in the region, following the premise that 'peace in Afghanistan is a guarantee of security for the entire region' (2386th General Affairs Council Conclusions of 19 November 2001, first paragraph). In its previous conclusions of 17 October 2001—'Action by the European Union Following the Attacks in the United States of America'—the GAC issued a firm declaration of 'total solidarity' with the USA. The unprecedented wording was a significant bone of contention and came about, in part, as a result of pressure from the UK and Germany, preferring 'total solidarity' over the alternative wording which referred to an EU action 'perfectly in solidarity'. Ministers from some bigger members states thus adopted a more determined stance, brushing aside reservations over the bombing of Afghanistan on the part of smaller member states and the (Belgian) presidency (see: *Independent*, 18 October 2001). Questions of diplomacy aside, the GAC conclusions of 17 October, in conjunction with the Ghent European Council Declaration two days later, represent a concerted EU effort to fight terrorism in all its forms, including the biological option. The EU planned to achieve this mainly through a strengthening of its relevant initiatives and bodies, such as a new, common European definition of terrorism, the European arrest warrant, Eurojust or Europol. Enhanced, reciprocal EU–US assistance and judicial cooperation programmes were other alternatives. The GAC Conclusions and the Ghent European Council conclusions of October 2001, in conjunction with similar, later, documents (e.g. the 2386th GAC Conclusions of 19 November 2001), assumed a significance far beyond these narrower strategies. They constituted a new milestone, not only in the development of the EU's relations with Afghanistan or Pakistan, but regarding the Union's Asia policy as a whole. Preferring a 'dialogue of equals' over a widely debated 'clash of civilizations', the Union confirmed, in Ghent, the role of the UN in Asia, as well as the centrality of the Middle East Peace Process and of EU dialogue with its Arab partners to a solution of the crisis.

Commission proposals for reform, the EU's new GSP Scheme, covering countries 'combating drugs' was on track for adoption by the Council on 1 January 2002; see also, *Rapid Database* MEMO/01/362 on Pakistan.

But the Council also, tentatively, mapped out a much wider EU approach pointing towards a more comprehensive and inclusive future policy. It highlighted a number of strategic elements of a future EU Asia Policy and a regionally focused CFSP.[16] The blueprint the Council outlined in October 2001 almost appeared to take the form of concentric circles, with more immediate concerns, following from the Afghanistan war, in the centre, and the more long-term aims and ambitions for general Asia policies more on the outside, backing up and complementing recent shifts in policy and laying the groundwork for future CFSP actions. The model the Council suggested, rested, in the first place, on humanitarian aid to Afghanistan (in excess of €310 million by mid-October 2001: *Rapid Database:* SPEECH/01/472; IP/01/1708; *European Voice*, 15–21 November 2001: 8). This was designated an 'absolute priority', in view of the need for the eventual reconstruction of Afghanistan, including a future 'stabilisation with a regional dimension'.[17]

Next to the provision of aid, however, the Council also stated its 'staunch support' for military operations in Afghanistan. According to the Council Conclusions of October 2001, the 'elimination' of the Al Qua'eda terrorist network and the 'freeing' of the country of the terrorists remained very much an EU objective, as did the establishment of a stable, legitimate and 'broadly' representative government in the country. To this end, but also clearly going beyond that, the Council announced that it would upgrade its ties with states neighbouring Afghanistan. This would include a further strengthening of EU–Pakistan ties (see above), and a more active development of relations between the EU, India, Iran and the Central Asian Republics, for which a more general EU strategy was envisaged. In connection with the Commission's Asia strategy of 4 September 2001 (Commission 2001c) and relevant European Parliament Resolutions on individual regions or countries in Asia, the European Council's conclusions of October 2001 had implications beyond the problems of the moment; they had the potential to shape the EU's medium- and long-term policies—and its

16. Declaration by the Heads of State and Government of the European Union and the Presidency of the Commission: Follow-Up to the September 11 Attacks and the Fight Against Terrorism, Brussels, 19 October 2001, SN 4296/2/01 REV 2 (OR.fr): for example at points 4-9.

17. The GAC Conclusions of 19 November 2001 (2386th General Affairs Council Conclusions) are the latest example for this prioritization.

CFSP activities—towards a variety of West, South and Central Asian states.

Bhutan

Relations between the EU and the Kingdom of Bhutan (see Box 7.6), an independent hereditary monarchy, began with a plant protection scheme in 1982. A similar scheme in 1992 concentrated on medicinal plant collection. An EU-supported trade development project was also completed. Individual sector-specific agreements covered civil aviation and tourism. Questions on Bhutan asked in the European Parliament frequently surrounded human rights and refugee issues,[18] and, on 21 January 1997, the Commission participated in a round-table on Bhutan (*General Report* 1997: point 974). In general, EU projects largely accorded with the priorities of Prime Minister Lyonpo Yeshey Zimba's Government in Thimphu and prioritized the problems of the *lotshampas* (Bhutanese of Nepalese origin),[19] as well as refugee matters, health, export diversification and agriculture.

Box 7.6: EU-supported Projects in Bhutan

The Development of Agricultural Support Activities (DASA) Project in rural Bhutan targeted training and promotional activities related mainly to bioscience. The scheme aimed to improve infrastructure, information and services and further strove to open markets. It was conducted in collaboration with the Bhutanese National Agricultural Extension Service and involved more than 20,000 people. The desired results of higher crop yields and incomes were largely achieved (Commission 1997g: 23).

Nepal

The then EEC established diplomatic relations with the kingdom of Nepal in 1975. From 1977, cooperation assistance began with a live-stock development project (Commission 1987: 4). A 1996 EU–Nepal Framework Cooperation Agreement consolidated relations and aimed at trade, sustainable economic development, the fight against drugs and

18. For example, EUI, *Foreign Policy Review* online, question No H-620/95, Doc. 95/260.
19. See Mathou 2001: 135-36.

AIDS and the improvement of living conditions.[20] After 1990, Nepal developed into a constitutional monarchy,[21] a status quo the EU expressly welcomed (EUI, *Foreign Policy Review* online: doc. 90/179, 12 April 1990). At the beginning of 2002, the outcome of recent EU–Nepalese Joint Commission meetings demonstrated that support for human rights issues, tourism development, help for Bhutanese refugees, poverty alleviation and rural infrastructure continued to be high on the agenda of relations between the EU and Kathmandu (Box 7.7).

Box 7.7: EU-supported Projects in Nepal

The Bagmati Watershed Project encompassed infrastructure improvement, conservation activities and the enhancement of agricultural productivity in a number of Nepalese villages. The aim was to diversify production in areas suffering from environmental degradation. Measures included the construction of rope bridges to facilitate the transport of goods (Commission 1997g: 39). On 13 September 1999, the Council decided to implement provisionally a EU–Nepalese Textile Agreement (*OJ* L 32/1, 7 February 2000, 2000/72/EC). In a 1999 statement the EU welcomed the abolition of the death penalty in Nepal (Commission, *General Report* 1999: point 651). However, it later also affirmed the right of the Nepalese state to use force against insurgents (EUI, *Foreign Policy Review* online: doc. 00/116). The salience of this was confirmed in April 2001, when Maoist rebels, in opposition since 1996, defied the government of former Prime Minister Girija Prasad Koirala and launched widespread attacks against Nepalese security forces. The attacks continued under the new government of Prime Minister Sher Bahadur Deuba.

The Maldives

EU cooperation with the more than 200 inhabited islands of the Maldives was of a limited nature after the inception of diplomatic contact in 1983. However, financial, technical and health cooperation (1980) preceded even this date. The 1995 EU–Maldive project for the empowerment of women constituted one of the most distinctive aspects

20. van der Geest (1999); *Rapid Database*: IP/95/760; Council Decision, 96/354/EC, 20 May 1996; *OJ* C 338, 16 December 1995; *OJ* L 137, 8 June 1996: 14.

21. In a bizarre and tragic incident on 1 June 2001, ten members of the Nepalese Royal Family—King Birendra and Queen Aishwarya among them—were murdered with an automatic weapon, in a drink-induced killing spree by the Nepalese Crown Prince Dipendra (cf. *EURASIA Bulletin*, 5.6-7, June–July 2001: 11-16; *Sunday Times*, 28 April 2002: 8).

of the relationship: it incorporated education, income generation, child-care, employment initiatives and elements of gender awareness among local Maldive populations. The tourist and fisheries industries were further targets of economic cooperation with Male, since tourism over-took fishing as a mainstay of the Maldive economy from about the mid-1980s.

Sri Lanka

The development of the Democratic Socialist Republic of Sri Lanka (Ceylon) under President Chandrika Bandaranaike Kumaratunga (*EURASIA Bulletin* 4.1, January 2000: 16-25; Saravanamuttu 2000: 219) had a 'darker side' (*EURASIA Bulletin* 5.3, March 2001: 6). It was weighed down by protracted Tamil-Sinhalese hostilities, which claimed more than 60,000 lives from 1983.[22] The roots of the conflict pre-dated independence in 1948 by far. Lach (1994: Vol. I, Bk 1: 272) refers to the arrival of the Portuguese in 1505 and notes: 'then as now, Ceylon was divided into two religious and cultural spheres, the Sinhalese-Buddhist area of the south and central territories, and the Tamil-speaking Hindu areas of the north'. Sri Lanka, literally the 'Resplendent Isle', was one of the first Asian countries to initiate relations with the EC in 1971. Textile agreements followed between 1978 and 1990 (*OJ* L 301/90: 1) and commercial relations were based on a 1975 cooperation agreement (Commission 1984: 2-4). A 'third-generation' Partnership and Development Agreement (*OJ* C 86, 23 March 1994: 5-13; *OJ* L 85, 19 April 1995: 32) was concluded in 1994. The bulk of EU–Sri Lankan programmes aimed at poverty alleviation, food security and rural development, with an emphasis on irrigation projects (Commission 1997g: 77, 86). In addition, the elections in 2000 were observed by an EU Electoral Observation Mission (EOM). Referring to the activities of the Liberation Tigers of Tamil Eelam, the Commission stated that 'it is unfortunate that co-operation funds cannot always be disbursed efficiently'. More directly, a recent UK law branded the 'Tigers' a 'terrorist organization' (*Far Eastern Economic Review*, 15 March 2001).

---

22. On the effect of the sectarian violence on rural Sri Lankan communities and on the country's national identity, see Spencer 2000: 23, 232.

Conclusion

EU relations with East and South Asian states present a diverse picture. There is no doubt that the EU's dialogue with Japan, South Korea or the Philippines is differentiated and comprehensive, in spite of ongoing discussions about market liberalization in Japan, Islamic fundamentalism in the Philippines or shipbuilding in South Korea. The East and South Asian regions also hold a diverse number of countries which have in the past played only a small part in the EU's Asia policy. Examples for those are some of the members of the Association for South Asian Regional Cooperation (SAARC), such as Bhutan, Nepal, the Maldives or Sri Lanka. However, continued Tamil-Sinhalese hostilities in Sri Lanka, refugee, environmental and gender equality issues in Bhutan or the Maldives, as well as considerable political unrest related to a Maoist insurgency in Nepal, and the assassination of the Nepalese Royal Family in 2001 meant that these Asian partners of the EU moved quickly up the EU agenda. The same is true for North Korea, linked to the EU through a nuclear safety programme, KEDO. Following an inter-Korean summit, ASEM 3 in South Korea and an ensuing thaw in North–South relations, the Democratic People's Republic of Korea seemed to have 'come in from the cold' in 2001, which resulted in a cautious upgrading of the EU's relations with the country, and an increase in diplomatic activity and humanitarian aid. The story of the EU's relations with other members of SAARC, notably India, Pakistan and Bangladesh, is one of long neglect, followed by a sudden realization of improved relations. India, in particular, now a regular summit-partner of the EU, was the focus of renewed attention and EU strategy papers. One effect of this was that the debate about South Asian membership in ASEM was brought to the fore again. Following the nuclear testing by both India and Pakistan in 1998–99 and the beginning of the anti-terrorism war in Afghanistan, the EU's relations with Pakistan were considerably upgraded in 2001–02. Events during and after the Ghent European Council in December 2001 showed that the war in Afghanistan was beginning to profoundly re-shape the EU's dialogue with other partners in the region, for instance the Central Asian Republics, and that it would alter the direction and thrust of much of the EU's future Asia policy.

8 |

The EU and South-East Asia

> The historical and cultural links between Europe and Asia could be
> analogized as an 'umbilical cord' kind, but one in which the cord is
> never severed. On the contrary, the cord has thickened and enlarged as
> the baby grows to become an adult, and now an aging adult, bringing
> both sustenance and complications for both because the flow is not
> necessarily one-way (Shamsul 2001: 30).

Following on from the assessment in Chapter 4 of the EU's relationship
with ASEAN as a whole, this chapter investigates the EU's diverse
policies towards individual countries in South-East Asia and assesses
their success. On account of global events, developments in newly
independent East Timor and the processes of change and democratization in Indonesia, there is a first emphasis on Indonesia, the world's
largest Islamic country, relations with which were part of a new,
comprehensive Commission strategy paper in 2000. Malaysia and
Singapore form other parts of the analysis; the concern here is with the
unique brand of 'constrained democracy' or 'Asian authoritarianism'
pervading the political systems of these countries, and the way this
affects their dialogue with the EU.

Among all the Asia policies of the EU, the one towards Burma is
probably the best known, on account of the human rights record of the
political leadership in Burma and because of the determination of the
EU not to 'reward' the Burmese military leadership for its longevity
(Patten, *Rapid Database*: SPEECH/00/276). The EU–Burmese relationship is determined, to a large degree, by the chances for more
democratization in Burma, human rights considerations and the implementation of a large number of CFSP measures towards the country, all
of which are assessed in this chapter.

Thailand, one of the very few countries in the scope of this book
which has never been subjected to European colonialism, occupies a
unique position in Asia–Europe relations. This will be explained with
reference to diplomacy, the Thai tradition of European contacts, and the

way both of these have resulted in a thriving, contemporary intellectual exchange and academic discourse about Europe.

The countries of Indochina—Laos, Cambodia and Vietnam—are included in this chapter in the context of a number of EU cooperation initiatives with these countries, covering more basic issues such as infrastructure, preservation of cultural heritage, health and the environment. Among those countries, Cambodia is the subject of particular scrutiny, as the country in many ways reflects problems and prospects of EU relations with the whole of South-East Asia. The analysis in this part is determined by the reality of the violent historical legacies of Vietnam, Laos and Cambodia, and by the way this perpetuates itself today in the problems concerning landmines, small weapons, war tribunals and local infrastructure.

Last, but definitely not least, there is a short section on Australia and New Zealand explaining their relationship with the EU before and after the Commission's 2001 Asia paper and touching on the question of whether these countries can be explained with reference to 'Asian', 'European' or other identities.

Merdeka Means Freedom: Indonesia and East Timor

Indonesia, ASEAN's 'strongman' and, according to the EU, a 'key player in the Asia-Pacific region' (Commission 2000a: 4), is South-East Asia's biggest state with the world's largest Muslim population. But the 5000 km-wide archipelago is fraying at the seams, despite *pancasila* ('unity in diversity'), its integralistic *Staatsidee*, which envisages the state as the embodiment of the entire people (Christie and Roy 2001: 126).

In 1949, the Dutch acknowledged Indonesia's sovereignty asserted by Muhammad Hatta and Sukarno. Sukarno's strong brand of nationalism was revealed during the violent period of *konfrontasi*, with Malaysia from 1963. Following a coup and anti-Chinese massacres in 1965, Sukarno's protégé, Suharto, became head of state in 1968, counteracting increased demands for freedom, *merdeka* (Reid 1998: 141-60) with an Indonesian brand of the 'development-before-democracy' dictum. Suharto's *Golongon Karya* (Golkar) party ruled, unopposed, from 1971 onwards, overseeing the invasion of East Timor (see Box 8.1) in 1975, a massive forced resettlement and migration programme, as well as the massacre in Dili/East Timor, in 1991.

Suharto was eventually forced from office in May 1998, amid economic disaster, forest fires and street rioting.

Box 8.1: East Timor

In 1999, new President Bacharuddin Jusuf Habibie hinted at independence for East Timor, long the centre of international human rights concerns. A Portuguese colony since 1701, East Timor had been occupied by Indonesia and annexed as its 27th province on 17 July 1976. After nearly 25 years of bloodletting and struggle by the *Frente Revolucionaria do Timor Leste Independente* (*Fretilin*), the province went to the polls on 30 August 1999, under the auspices of the UN Assistance Mission to East Timor (UNAMET). Of the 98.6 per cent of voters who turned out, 78.5 per cent preferred independence over limited autonomy (Haji-Ahmad and Ghoshal 1999: 776). The Referendum and its aftermath of civil war, refugee crises and ethnic violence focused attention on the role and function of ASEAN, human rights and regional security. On 19 October 1999, the Legislative Council, *Majelis Permusyawaratan Rakyat*, declared the 1978 decree incorporating East Timor into Indonesia null and void and released the territory into the administration of the United Nations Transitional Administration in East Timor (see Carnegie Council 2001: 12-13).

The world's youngest state was left to come to terms with its past, to build bridges within ASEAN, and to prepare for elections for a Constituent Assembly. These took place on 30 August 2001 and, according to the European Union Election Observation Mission, were a 'remarkable success'. The June 1999 elections in Indonesia, the first democratic vote since 1955, did little to remove internal divisions. On 20 October 1999, the frail civilian and Muslim cleric Abdurrahman Wahid (nicknamed 'Gus Dur') was nominated president. He was known to sympathize with Burmese opposition leader and Nobel prize laureate Aung San Suu Kyi and began to curb the powers of the army, the key to Indonesian politics. The EU aided the transition in Indonesia with €38.8 million in humanitarian assistance between 1999 and 2001 (*Rapid Database*: IP/01/778).

An attempt to put Suharto on trial on corruption charges ended in a declaration by a panel of judges that he was medically and psychologically unfit to stand trial. According to Indonesia analysts like Ramstetter (2000: 7), this meant 'the effective end' to any moves to deal with Indonesia's immediate past in the courts, at least as far as criminal charges against the former president were concerned. The battered economy—Indonesia was the hardest-hit state during the 1997–98 financial crisis—as well as individual incidents such as the bombing of the Jakarta Stock Exchange Building on 13 September 2000, were also seen as slowing down progress. More generally, the challenge of managing the ethnic mix that holds together Indonesia was frequently confounded by the spectre of further disintegration, and ethnic and sectarian violence in provinces such as Aceh, Irian Jaya and in the Moluccas. This made President Wahid's political fate very short-lived. His term was overshadowed by impeachment threats and frictions with Vice-President Megawati Sukarnoputri, the daughter of Indonesia's founding father, who eventually replaced him as President of Indonesia in July 2001.

The EU's Involvement in East Timor and Indonesia

Indonesia's trade and investment relations with the EU are the most highly developed among the ASEAN states. While ASEAN countries engage on average 9–12 per cent of their trade with the EU, for Indonesia, this figure was 15 per cent or more throughout the 1990s (EU Delegation to Indonesia 2000: 1). Christie and Roy (2001: 152) maintain that 'after Myanmar, the main target of western pressure for changing Human Rights in Southeast Asia is Indonesia'. Not unlike the case of Burma, it is the human rights situation which largely shapes progress and stagnation in the EU–Indonesia dialogue. At the time of the December 1996 Dublin summit, for instance, the ASEAN–EU Senior Officials Meeting (SOM) called on Indonesia to improve its human rights record in East Timor. The EU's 1996 and 1999 Common Positions on Indonesia and East Timor[1] reinforced this point. In successive declarations, the Council called for the release of political prisoners, praised the signs of democratization, deplored rising levels of violence, praised the involvement of the UN and the International Force, or welcomed the release of East Timor.[2] EU concern—and humanitarian aid—also revolved around violence and insecurity in West Timor, the Moluccas and Aceh. The Prodi Commission asserted both its support for East Timorese independence and its financial

---

1.   CP 96/407/CFSP (*OJ* L 168); CP 1999/479/CFSP, *OJ* L 188, 21 July 1999 and CP 1999/624/CFSP, *OJ* L 245, 17 September 1999: 53.

2.   See Council Press Releases 10757/98 (*presse* 275) P.88/98, 12 August 1998; 6970/99 (*presse* 90) P 33/99, 8 April 1999; 7213/99 (*presse* 99) P 36/99, 12 April 1999; 11129/99 *presse* 278 P 94/99, 21 September 1999; 11942/99 (*presse* 311) P 107/99, 21 October 1999.

assistance and humanitarian aid for the former colony.[3] No EU–Indonesian cooperation agreement had been signed by 2001, but a number of development cooperation schemes existed in the areas of irrigation control, food self-sufficiency or forest fire and 'haze' prevention.

The elections on 7 June 1999, which the EU assisted with 135 observers and €7 million and which it was clearly impressed with,[4] a visit by the (then) newly elected President Wahid to Brussels in February 2000 and the decision to release East Timor contributed to an upgrade in EU–Indonesian relations. The Union showed itself keen to 'kick-start' the EU–ASEAN dialogue, long frozen because of Burma, and to involve Indonesia in this. The EU seemed to rely on a smooth transition to democracy in the country and there was considerable evidence for an opening up of the relationship: an arms embargo and a Regulation on its implementation[5]—equal in scope to the one still covering Burma—were not renewed for Indonesia after September 1999 (*EURASIA Bulletin* 4.1, January 2000: 3-4), but were replaced, on 17 January 2000, by a Code of Conduct. In addition, the Consultative Group for Indonesia, a World Bank-led group, comprising, among other members, Japan, and the EU, pledged, in early 2000, up to $4.7 billion in loans to Indonesia (*Asiaweek*, 18 February 2000: 20-21).

In a Commission communication, *Developing Closer Relations Between Indonesia and the EU* (Commission 2000a; see *Rapid Database*: IP/00/98), the EU comprehensively redefined its multi-faceted relationship with a democratizing Indonesia, to include dialogue in five main areas: security, constitutional reform, eradication of corruption, detachment of the army from their political functions and the restructuring of the economy. The EU's updated approach appeared more holistic than before. In terms of human rights, Indonesia was seen by the EU as a kind of 'role-model' for Burma; human rights work was projected to take place in conjunction with NGOs and Indonesia's National Human Rights Commission. The paper stated that:

3. Press: 321-Nr.11425/1/00, 20 September 2000; *Rapid Database*: IP/00/294, IP/00/389.

4. CFSP Presidency Statement, 9 June 1999, Nr. 8878/99 (*presse* 187), CFSP: 58/99.

5. CP 1999/624/CFSP; *OJ* L 245, 17.9.99; Regulation 2158/1999, *OJ* L 265/1, 13 October 1999.

a basic assumption of the Union should be that Indonesia cannot wait to address environmental problems until the financial situation gets better. The risk of environmental degradation becoming the cause of the next crisis is too great.[6]

The Politics of Judicial Revenge: Malaysia

EU relations with Malaysia, Singapore and Brunei are largely derived from, and constitute a part of, the wider EU–ASEAN dialogue. The 1980 EU–ASEAN Agreement and the 1996 communication on *A New Dynamic in EU–ASEAN Relations* are the main reference documents in this context. Since 1996, the EU is also linked to these states though the ASEM process.

In spite of a three-party opposition, Malaysian politics, at the start of the new millennium, was governed by the ruling United Malays National Organization (UMNO) which existed since 1957. UMNO dominates a multi-party coalition (Barisan Nasional), organized along racial and religious lines. The Federation of Malaysia, incorporating Malaya, Singapore, North Borneo (Sabah) and Brunei was created in 1963 on the initiative of Tunku Abdul Rhaman, who was succeeded, in 1981, by Mahathir Mohamad. The latter remained in office ever since. But three developments began to change the political landscape: first, political Islam, particularly in the Malay heartlands of Terangganu and Kelantan; secondly, the cumulative 15-year sentence, delivered in April 1999 and August 2000, on former deputy prime minister Anwar Ibrahim for 'abuse of power' and 'unnatural sexual acts'[7] and, thirdly, the aftermath of the November 1999 snap general election, which was 'neither fair, nor free' (Weiss 2000: 433). Although UMNO kept its two-thirds majority, it bled votes to the Justice Party (KeADILan) of Wan Azizah Ismail, Anwar Ibrahim's wife, and especially to PAS, the conservative Islamic opposition. Particularly among the younger Malays, former UMNO youth leader Anwar Ibrahim and slogans like KKKN (*kolusi, korupsi, kronisme, nepotisme*) or *reformasi*—which hardly require any translation—became icons. The universally condemned trial of the vocal Ibrahim, who was ousted because he dis-

---

6.   Commission 2000a: point 4.3; see also *OJ* L 219/82: 56; *OJ* L 329/90: 1; *OJ* L 94/95: 214; *OJ* C 296, 18 October 2000.

7.   See *EURASIA Bulletin* 4.8–9, August–September 2000: 15-18. Some remaining charges against Anwar Ibrahim were finally dropped on 12 May 2001.

agreed with Prime Minister Mahathir over who was 'to blame' for the Asian crisis in 1997, left stains on the credibility of Malay politics. The repercussions of the Ibrahim case, called a 'travesty of justice' (Christie and Roy 2001: 39), also caused friction in EU–Malaysian relations. In Declarations, like the one of 14 April 1999 (Council 7217/99 (*presse* 103) P39/99), the EU registered its reservations over the trial, especially the alteration of the charges against Ibrahim in mid-trial, and the mistreatment of Ibrahim in police custody. Members of the EU mission to Malaysia also expressed doubts about the proceedings.

In the absence of an EU–Malaysian Cooperation Agreement, bilateral relations tended to focus on economics trade, investment and the environment. Malaysia received no EU development aid, but some development cooperation assistance for the environment and forestry started in 1987. A European Business Information Centre (EBIC), promoting inter-regional business-to-business cooperation, was inaugurated in Kuala Lumpur in mid-1996. Commission funding for a new University of Malaya European Studies Programme (UMESP) started in 1998 within the framework of EU–ASEAN economic cooperation. European partners included universities from Spain, Italy and Austria. The scheme was established a year later at the University's Asia-Europe Institute and enabled the University to acquire an EU studies related stock of materials, to build up a documentation centre, launch a journal and develop courses, as well as organizing conferences on the subject (Commission 2000i; UMESP Prospectus). A Malaysian–EU joint seminar on Europe and the Islamic World on 24–25 March 1998 sought to dispel misunderstandings and stereotypes in the relationship between Europe and the Islamic world. It was hosted by Oxford University's Centre for Islamic Studies and the Institute of Islamic Understanding (Malaysia), founded in 1992. The conference aimed to put relations into (historical) perspective and to define the current and future agenda of the dialogue (see also *OJ* L 339/90: 42; *OJ* L 94/95: 262).

'Personalized Politics', or the Prisoner in the Amusement Park: Singapore Inc.

In the late twentieth century, multicultural Singapore was one of South-East Asia's big performers. Lee Kuan Yew, one of the most outspoken exponents of 'Asian values', became prime minister of the new state in

1959 and entered the Malaysian Federation with the people of Malaya, Sarawak and North Borneo (now Sabah) in 1963. Differences between Lee's People's Action Party (PAP) and UMNO, the growing supporter of Malaysian nationalism, over the extent of a 'Malaysian Malaysia' (Low 1998: 42), led to the island state's departure from the Federation in 1965, to become a Republic, in spite of its size. The PAP governed Singapore for 40 years. In 1990, Lee Kuan Yew handed over the prime ministerial reins to Goh Chok Tong, but Lee remained elder statesman and 'Senior Minister', (as well as being the father of deputy prime minister Lee Hsien Loong). Singapore escaped relatively unharmed from the 1997–98 currency turmoil, but faced some signs of an over-aging population and urban poverty. The Government was a blend of economic liberalization and 'soft' authoritarianism, resistance to reform and 'personalized politics' enforced through the extremely controversial Internal Security Act (ISA), the libel courts and through the systematic and widespread practice of the 'bankrupting' of opponents (Christie and Roy 2001: 65, 71; *Guardian*, 10 February 1999; *Far Eastern Economic Review*, 19 July 2001). A 'Speaker's Corner', initiated in 2000, made little impact on freedom of speech in Singapore, or rather the lack of it (Huxley 2001: 204). The description of '*Mal Preußen, mal Konfuzius*' ('Prussia at times, at times Confucius', *Die Welt*, 13 March 1997) accurately depicts the atmosphere in this neat, organized, multi-cultural, high-tech, and efficient city-state, which, from 1966 to 1998, kept former lecturer and MP Chia Thye Poh, the longest-serving political prisoner of modern times, partly confined to his off-shore exile in the theme park of Sentosa Island.[8]

Singapore may be just a 'dot on the map', as Indonesia's ex-President Habibie put it (Buckley 1998: 14), but at the beginning of the third millennium, it was both a gateway into Asia and the largest trader with Europe among the ten ASEAN member states. The overall trade in goods in 1999 amounted to €25 billion, or 29 per cent, of the EU–ASEAN total, and Singapore was the top destination for European investors in Asia, before Japan and Hong Kong (Delegation of the European Commission, 'The EU and Singapore: Trade and Investment Relations', 2000: 1, 2). In addition, Singapore, site of the Asia–Europe Foundation, was active in the area of inter-regional environmental technology exchange (see also *OJ* L 329/90: 1; *OJ* L 94/95: 415).

---

8.   See on this episode: Christie and Roy 2001: 61-62; Sesser 1994: 32-35.

Brunei-Darussalam

The resource-rich, and strategically important, Sultanate of Brunei-Darussalam on the northern tip of the island of Borneo became independent of Britain in 1984. The country's 350,000 people are ruled by one of the world's longest-serving heads of state, Sultan Haji Hassanal Bolkiiah. Brunei is connected to the EU through the 1980 EU–ASEAN Agreement—which was extended to Brunei on 21 March 1985—and joint projects derived from it. The oil-rich country, which, in 2000, saw its own share of financial scandal involving the royal family (*Asiaweek*, 10 March 2000), never received development aid, but benefited from European funding for the ASEAN–EC Management Centre), located in its capital, Bandar Seri Begawan.

Thailand: Challenged by the Speed of Change

Thailand–Europe relations (Thongswasdi 1993) and 'European Studies' in Thailand have a long tradition (see Box 8.2), reaching back well into the nineteenth century and the reigns of Kings Mongkut (Rama IV, 1851–68) and Chulalongkorn (Rama V, 1868–1910). Economic ties with Thailand were initiated on a bilateral level long before European integration began. Portugal, for example, traded and contracted with the kingdom of Siam when it was still governed from the former capital of Ayut'ia (Ayutthaya). However, as Breazeale (1999: 10) notes, most of the former Portuguese, Dutch or English trade was indirect and part of the intra-Asian coastal trading network. Thailand is the only country in the scope of this book, except Japan and Nepal, which has avoided colonial rule. This had its causes in the skilful actions of Thai monarchs, and a combination of diplomacy, sympathetic accommodation of Asian nationalist activities on Thai soil, and an effort not to antagonize its colonial neighbours, a method which has been termed 'benign neutrality' (Wyatt 1984: 238). Sandwiched between the former British and French spheres of influence in Asia, Thailand accepted territorial losses and went through a transition from absolute to constitutional monarchy in 1932. During the Vietnam War, Thailand provided the USA with air bases for bombing campaigns targeting neighbouring Indochina.

Thai politics from 1973 to 1991, punctuated by the Thammasat University killings in 1973, was characterized by alternating military and civilian governments. Only the Chakri-Dynasty king, Bhumibol Adulyadej (Rama IX), remained a figure of integrity and authority throughout. He is the longest-reigning monarch in the world. A military putsch in 1991 took General Suchinda Kraprayoon to power. During violent demonstrations in 1992, army and police created a bloodbath on Bangkok's Sanaam Luang Square. Only through the king's intervention did the country return to democracy. Following annual growth rates of around 9 per cent from 1992 to 1996, the late 1990s brought problems with corruption. The economic débacle of 1997–98 took a heavy toll on Thailand, leading to an increase in political instability, reverse migration from Bangkok to the countryside and social deterioration. During 2000, a number of violent clashes fed criticism of the government's handling of dissent in Myanmar and the methamphetamines trade out of the 'Golden Triangle' at Thailand's north-western border with Burma. The elections for a new Senate on 4 March 2000 were the first under Thailand's new, 1997 Constitution, which also spawned a National Human Rights Commission. Some observers (Christie and Roy 2001: 159 n. 1) have seen Thailand as representing the 'nearest approximation to Western-style bourgeois democracy'. However, 'money-politics', globalization, reform and accountability in Thai politics were mayor issues in the general election on 6 January 2001. The vote brought telecoms tycoon Thaksin Shinawatra (Thai Rak Thai Party) to prime ministerial power, to succeed Chuan Leekpai (Democrats) but seemed not to have injected more long-term political or economic stability into Thai politics (cf. *EURASIA Bulletin* 5.1-2, January–February 2001: 8-12).

The Commission maintained a Delegation in Bangkok since 1979. Against the background of ASEM and ASEAN and the shift, during the early 1990s, from development aid to economic cooperation, bilateral relations tended to focus on trade, economics, intellectual property rights, AIDS and the environment. When a confederation of bilateral Chambers of Commerce (the European Communities Business Association) was formed in 1993, the European Business Information Centre, forming a part of it, was supported by Commission funding. The EC–Thailand Framework Cooperation Agreement dates back to 1981, the year after its EC–ASEAN equivalent. Relations following the 1997 IMF 'Economic Adjustment Programme' existed in a scenario in which EU FDI actually rose (in 1998) and lending from EU banks remained relatively stable. The EU banks' share of total credit even increased (from 28.5 to 33 per cent) between June 1997 and June 1998. (Commission 2000h: 4-5). Academic exchange and cooperation on many levels, and through the Thai European Community Studies Association (ECSA), became prominent aspects of EU–Thai relations (see Box 8.2).

Box 8.2: Higher Education Cooperation and European Studies at Chulalongkorn University, Bangkok

Chulalongkorn University is the oldest Thai University. Its European Studies Programme (CUESP) in Bangkok has run, with EU support approximating €4 million, since 1992. It attracted large numbers of students, as well as scholars, researchers and visiting scholars from Thailand and Europe. On 6–7 November 1997, for instance, CUESP organized a conference on King Chulalongkorn's famous tour of Europe in 1897. The Centre developed a BA Programme and, from June 1997 onwards, offered a 'multi-disciplinary' MA route in European Studies, which, it is claimed, is the first of its kind in South-East Asia. In 1999, the programme was upgraded to a Centre for European Studies, which benefits from its own European Documentation Centre (EDC), a *Journal of European Studies* and other publication outlets. Teaching incorporates study trips to Europe for the participants, perpetuating, in a modern context, the tradition of the voyages of King Chulalongkorn at the turn of the twentieth century (Commission 1995e: 14; EU, Bangkok Delegation: News Release, 21 September 1999 and *EU Today*, No. 5, January–March 1998: 15).

A number of EU humanitarian aid programmes to Thailand, operated through ECHO and NGOs, frequently focused on the issue of displaced persons. This group consisted of hundreds of thousands of Burmese refugees on the Thai/Burmese border in the north-west, who originated from ethnic minorities in Burma (Karen, Mon, Shan) and were persecuted by the Burmese government. EU aid was also allocated to members of ethnic minorities who have recently relocated to Burma, in the hope of finding peace and freedom from fear (*Rapid Database*: IP/97/55). The EU and Thailand are further linked through a number of important initiatives (see Box 8.3), embedded in the Asia-Invest and other overarching schemes (ECIP, EBIC, SME development). The agenda of the March 2001 EU–Thai SOM was exemplary of the scope of contemporary EU–Thai relations. Having moved on, beyond humanitarian assistance, it comprised issues such as trade, investment, economic and market access issues, scientific, technological and environmental cooperation and human resources. However, much of the cooperation, funded through the member states and the EU budget, targeted the rural economy, poverty, SMEs and industrial development:

Box 8.3: EU-supported Projects in Thailand

The 2000–05 Social Support Project for Thailand, initiated after the financial crisis of 1997–98, was described as the biggest project launched by the EU in Thailand in the last decade. It provided more than €15 million in grants. Aiming at the enhancement of rural productivity and the initiation of new rural economic activities, particularly in the Thai countryside, the programme's administrators hoped to achieve an increase in rural incomes while counteracting reverse migration from the cities, which had occurred after the crisis (Commission 2000h: 7 and *EU Today* No. 14, September 2000: 12).

The Huai Mong Project, supported by the EU, Denmark and Belgium, was a two-phase pump irrigation and drainage scheme in Nong Khai in the north-east of Thailand (Isaan), the least developed region of the country, where Thai, Khmer and Lao cultures merge. The programme's objectives of strengthening farming institutions and agricultural output were achieved through engineering work and 'on-farm development'. With the major drainage infrastructure being built from 1982 to 1987, phase two of the scheme (1990–98) focused on crop diversification and self-reliance of the regional farmers. (Commission Delegation Bangkok, 'Huai Mong Project' and News Release, 2 February 1998: 'EU-MoAC Projects').

The EU-assisted (€12 million) DEVSILK Project (1995–2000) aimed to improve the yield of sericulture in over 200 villages in Thailand's Khon Kaen, Marasarakham, Buriram and Nakhon Ratchasima provinces. This was achieved through empowerment of local farmers, training and study visits. The project contributed to a higher real value of the product for which Thailand is justly famous (Commission Delegation Bangkok, *EU Today*, No. 4, October–December 1997: 5). The DEVSILK project and the €6.1 million Pilot Project for the Development of Rubber Tree Cultivation in the North-East (RUTCINE) were finally handed over to Thai authorities in 2000 (Commission Delegation Bangkok, *EU Today*, No. 15, January 2001: 10-11 and *Development of Silk Production in the North East*, September 2000).

From 1998, the EU provided €970.000 for the Small and Medium Enterprises Development Project in Southern Thailand, in conjunction with Thai authorities. The integrated scheme aimed at supporting SMEs in the southern peripheral provinces of Songkhla, Trang, Phattalung, Satun, Yala, Pattani and Narathiwat, and at encouraging cross-border trade with Northern Malaysia, through training and awareness-building within the Southern Thai business community (Commission Delegation Bangkok, *EU Today*, No. 8, October–December 1998: 12).

Rich Country Gone Awry: Burma (The Union of Myanmar)

Independent of British rule since 1948, multi-ethnic and resource-rich Burma was taken over in 1962 by a 'Revolutionary Council', led by General Ne Win. He subsequently prescribed a 'Burmese Way to Socialism'. Military régimes have ruled the largest South-East Asian country ever since (Fink 2001). In 1988, the Orwellian-sounding State Law and Order Restoration Council (SLORC) under General Saw Maung was constituted. In 1997, it transmogrified into the no less awkwardly named State Peace and Development Council (SPDC).[9] In 1988, the army perpetrated a massacre among civilians in Rangoon (Yangon), an event which, unlike the events on Tiananmen Square in the PRC a year later, went largely unnoticed by the world.[10] The Union of Myanmar, as the country has been called since 1989, challenges perceptions about Asian nations, international relations and the role of values. The opposition National League for Democracy (NLD), under Nobel prize laureate Aung San Suu Kyi,[11] was continuously harassed and persecuted. In the 1990 elections, the NLD scored 82 per cent of the vote, but was never allowed to govern nor was the Pyithu Hluttaw (National Assembly) permitted to work. The sole party is the Taingyintha Silonenyinyutye (National Unity Party). The National Coalition Government of the Union of Burma, formed in December 1990, operates from Washington DC and has 'repeatedly, yet unsuccessfully' contested SLORC's seat in the United Nations (Aung San Suu Kyi 1997: 75, 241).

These developments and the country's status as a 'human rights pariah' continued to provoke international and EU sanctions. Aung San Suu Kyi was put under arrest for six years (20 July 1989–15 July 1995)

---

9. See on this the Council of Minister's Decision 98/107/CFSP, *OJ* L 32, 6.2.98 and the list of key members of the Burmese junta in Commission 2000n: 11-17 (annexe II).

10. With the exception of the feature film *Beyond Rangoon*. For a widely-noticed literary treatment of the events surrounding the 1989 Tiananmen Square killings see Wang 2001.

11. Who was also awarded the *Rafto* Human Rights Prize in 1990. Aung San Suu Kyi is the daughter of Aung San, the hero of Burmese independence, who was murdered, in unclear circumstances, in 1947. See Aung San Suu Kyi 1995 and J. Pitman, *The Times*, 2 March 1996: TM 10.

in her house at No. 54 University Avenue, Rangoon, but, undeterred, continued resisting (Kelly and Reid 1998: 187-203). In the context of the *tatmadaw* (military) keeping her politically involved, she has—not without irony—called the ruling SLORC her 'unpaid PR' (Aung San Suu Kyi 1997: 48). Regarding 'PR' on the other side, the Government proclaimed 1996 a 'Year of Tourism', but widespread use of forced labour, tolerance towards drug-trafficking and the unexplained prison death in 1997 of James Leander Nichols, an Honorary Consul to Denmark, Norway, Finland and Switzerland,[12] aggravated the country's isolation. Notwithstanding this, Burma was admitted into ASEAN on 23 July 1997 (see below). Continued human rights concerns prompted some companies to withdraw from the country, and a lawsuit against a US energy company with presence in Burma set a groundbreaking precedent in the area of corporate liability for human rights abuses by military dictatorships.

The Politics of Non-politics: The EU and Burma
EC cooperation with Burma started with a palm oil development scheme in 1979, but a coherent EU–Burma Cooperation Programme did not come about. A look at current funding reveals that the pattern of EU relations with Burma has concentrated on purely humanitarian aid, HIV/AIDS prevention and repatriation help for returnees and refugees on the Thai/Burmese and Bangladeshi/Burmese borders. A cross-section of written questions to both Commission and Council shows that the human rights situation in Burma overwhelmingly dominated the EU's dealings with that country. The following are some examples for 'EU-Burmese' topics on the European Parliament agenda.

- Prison camps (Written Question E-2846/95, *OJ* C 9/63, 15 January 1996 and E-3278/95, *OJ* C 91/53, 27 March 1996).
- Forced labour (Commission 1996i; *OJ* C 15/3, 20 January 1996, 96/C 15/03; see also IP/96/44 and *Financial Times*, 2 June 2000).
- Ethnic minorities (E-1596/98, *OJ* C 50/53, 22 February 1999).
- General human rights and political prisoners (E-3957/97, *OJ* C 187/101, 16 June 1998).

12. Written Questions to the Council E-2274/96, *OJ* C 217/7, 17 July 1997, 97/C 217/10 and E-3534/96, 17 July 1997, 97/C 217/11; *The Observer*, 1 March 1998: 20; *Bangkok Post*, 29 July 1998: 4.

- The need for stronger EU sanctions (E-2743/97, *OJ* C 134/20, 30 April 1998).
- EU member state investment sanctions regarding Burma (E-2119/98, *OJ* C 96/41, 8 April 1999).

EU measures against Burma complemented sanctions imposed by the ILO (e.g. on 14 June 2000), the USA and the international community. The EU's arsenal included the imposition of an arms embargo (1991), and the severing of defence links in 1992. The fact that, over and above Western objections, Rangoon was embraced—'constructively engaged' —by ASEAN in 1997, led to the controversial statement by former Commissioner Mañuel Marin, that part of the new agenda between Europe and ASEAN might be to accept that 'some Asian values differ from European values' (*Financial Times*, 31 July 1996: 6). Following the first Asia–Europe Summit in 1996, however, Dick Spring at the helm of the Irish presidency was quoted as having said 'Burma is welcome to join the ASEAN Regional Forum'. Following renewed pressure on Aung San Suu Kyi and the NLD, the Union tightened the sanction screws further and decided on the following further measures.[13]

- The suspension of EU non-humanitarian aid, with certain exceptions.
- The withdrawal of GSP trade preferences for Burmese agricultural and industrial exports (Commission 1996i, Regulation (EC) No. 552/97 of 24 March 1997, *OJ* L 85/8, 27 March 1997).
- CP 96/635/CFSP, *OJ* L 287, 8 November 1996, endorsed by the Council on 28 October 1996, on the basis of Article J.2 TEU. It formally adopted existing measures and decided not to grant entry visas to Burmese officials and ban high-level visits.
- Council Regulation banning sale of equipment which might be used for repression or terrorism in Burma and freezing foreign funds of Burmese officials (Commission 2000n; (EC) No. 1081/2000 of 22 May 2000, *OJ* L 122/29, 24 May 2000).

Common Position 96/635/CFSP (*OJ* L 287, 8 November 1996; Hill and Smith 2000: 438, Doc. 4c/33), the EU's main instrument on Burma,

---

13. Foreign and Commonwealth Office, 2000: 5; *European Voice*, 17–23 September 1998.

was extended every six months.[14] It was also amended to include a ban on transit visas. A group of Eastern European and other accession candidates, Turkey and European Economic Area (EEA) states, associated themselves with the Common Position on 7 November 1996. The lifespan of the arms and funds embargo was linked to that of the Common Position. These sanctions, not unlike US sanctions against Iraq, did not go unquestioned, on the grounds of their ability to encourage an 'Asian solidarity', because of their efficiency, and on account of their likely effect on the population of Burma (e.g. *Financial Times*, 19 December 1996; *Asiaweek*, 11 August 2000). In connection with the débacle over Burmese participation in the EU–ASEAN Joint Co-operation Committee, resulting from the country's position as a new ASEAN member, individual member states, such as Sweden, Portugal or Denmark, made public statements about Burma's human rights record. At times, however, they found little solidarity from their European neighbours, giving the impression of a Union that lacked a common policy over Burma, but worked on the basis of case-to-case *Realpolitik*.

At the beginning of 2002, the situation was largely unpredictable, in spite of faint signs of hope (see Box 8.4). Pressure on SPDC leader Than Shwe, from both ASEAN and Malaysian Prime Minister Mahathir Mohamad increased, and, in July 2000, newspapers reported that Burmese Universities would open again (*Bangkok Post*, 12 July 2000). In 2001, the first talks since 1994 between Aung San Suu Kyi and Generals Kyaw Win and Khin Nyunt, engineered by Malaysian UN special envoy Razali Ismail, were cautiously welcomed by the international community.[15] Preceding the 2001 visit by the EU Delegation, some 80 political prisoners, including NLD Vice-Chairman Tin Oo were released from detention. However, the West was also urged to tone down expectations. Later in 2001, Aung San Suu Kyi was again put under house arrest and the NLD's activities remained severely restricted.

---

14. For 1999: Decision 1999/289/CFSP, *OJ* L 114, 1 May 1999 and CP 1999/670/CFSP, *OJ* L 267, 15 October 1999. For 2000: CP 2000/346/CFSP, *OJ* L 122, 24 May 2000 and 2000/601/CFSP, 9 October 2000.

15. *Far Eastern Economic Review*, 25 January 2001; *Asiaweek*, 19 January 2001: 12; *EURASIA Bulletin* 5.1–2 January–February 2001: 19-20.

Box 8.4: A Thaw in EU–Burmese Relations?

Following the earlier EU mission of July 2000, a five-strong EU *Troïka* Delegation, led by Swedish Foreign Ministry Official Börje Lunggren, again visited Burma from 29 to 31 January 2001, in a gesture that was judged to potentially 'make or break the military regime' (*The Nation*, 30 January 2001). The groundwork for this renewed fact-finding mission had been laid by Burmese Foreign Secretary Win Aung, during the EU–ASEAN ministerial level meeting in Vientiane in December 2000. (*European Voice*, 25–31 January 2001: 5; *Bangkok Post*, 18 January 2001). The Delegation consisted of the representatives of the two 2001 presidencies (Sweden and Belgium), the Council and the Commission. Participants talked to SPDC First Secretary Khin Nyunt, Foreign Secretary Win Aung, Aung San Suu Kyi, representatives of Burma's ethnic political parties, intermediaries of cease-fire groups, Rangoon-based UN and NGO personnel, and diplomats from Australia, the USA, Britain, India and Japan. During the visit, Western diplomats urged: 'hopefully the EU will not be too hot, with too many short-term expectations (*The Nation*, 30 January 2001), and: 'it is to be hoped that before the EU mission renders any credit to the junta, the team is 100 per cent sure that the junta is serious about national reconciliation' (*The Nation*, 30 January 2001). The EU's assessment of the visit and its attitude towards Burma was seen to constitute 'a barometer' for the international community for how to base its own policies. The EU called reconciliation talks 'fragile', contacts 'promising, but not yet irreversible'. It kept much of the content of the talks confidential, but judged the trip as the most 'interesting' and 'significant' development in more than a decade (*The Nation*, 12 February 2001: *Bangkok Post*, 29 January 2001; *The Nation*, 31 January 2001). This assessment also informed subsequent EU policy towards Burma.

Fragile Democracy on Trial: The EU and Cambodia

Following the Lon Nol dictatorship (1970–75), Cambodia lost around one-fifth—and quite possibly much more—of its population between 1975 and 1979, when it was renamed Democratic Kampuchea.[16] Far from benefiting from any kind of democracy, millions of Cambodians died in the neo-feudal, social engineering by the Khmer Rouge (or 'Red Cambodians', a phrase coined by Prince Sihanouk in the 1960s) and during the Vietnamese invasion in December 1978, which gave birth to the People's Republic of Kampuchea under the Vietnamese Hun Sen puppet regime. The argument may never fall silent over which

---

16. The 1984 film *The Killing Fields* remains the most gripping depiction of a Cambodia, which was returned to 'Year Zero' by Pol Pot and his followers.

superpower bears greater responsibility for the 'killing fields': China, which sent advisors and US$1 billion in aid, or the USA, which supported the Lon Nol dictatorship, drew Cambodia into the Vietnam War and did little more than express verbal disapproval when the Khmer Rouge were in power. The 'mosaic' of human skulls, forming a rough outline map of Cambodia, and the other exhibits in the extraordinary Tuol Sleng Genocide museum, a former torture site in Phnom Penh, are poignant reminders of those times, in a country which has no lack of tragic places.

Against the backdrop of the US-brokered 1991 Paris Peace Treaty, UN-sponsored elections in May 1993 and years of 'tandem government' involving two prime ministers, the state was going to be invited to join ASEAN during the association's 30th anniversary in 1997. But on 5–6 July 1997, the leader of the Cambodian People's Party, former Khmer Rouge Commander and second Prime Minister, Hun Sen, ousted Prince Norodom Ranariddh, King Sihanouk's son, and his royalist party, the 'United National Front for an Independent, Neutral, Peaceful, and Cooperative Cambodia' (FUNCINPEC). Again, rocket-launchers could be heard among the temple ruins of Angkor Wat.

The Cambodian elections of 26 July 1998 were the subject of two European Parliament Resolutions (*OJ* C 104, 6 April 1998 and *OJ* C 210, 6 July 1998). The EU also sent 200 observers, led by Glenys Kinnock, MEP. The new coalition agreement resulted in a—frequently violent—consolidation of power by Hun Sen, the sole prime minister, while Norodom Ranariddh became president of the National Assembly. ASEAN finally embraced Cambodia on 30 April 1999, fulfilling its vision of an 'ASEAN-10'.[17] But the spectre of Cambodia's past still loomed large, and socio-economic conditions improved but slowly. Cambodia's nemesis, Saloth Sar (*nom de guerre*: Pol Pot), who was last seen in public in 1979, was condemned to a life-long house arrest by a disgruntled faction of his own Khmer Rouge and died in unclear circumstances in April 1998.[18] Following initial governmental resistance, the National Assembly approved a law, on 2 January 2001, enabling the leaders of the now defunct Khmer Rouge to be tried (*Asiaweek*, 18 February 2000, *Guardian*, 16 January 2001; *Far Eastern*

17. Commission Proposal regarding the Extension Protocol: Commission 2000o.

18. For an outstanding analysis of Saloth Sar and his regime of terror see: Chandler 1999.

Economic Review, 24 May 2001). The European Parliament welcomed this development in a Resolution of 18 January 2001. However, the EU argued that an interference-free domestic trial was problematic because of a lack of human and other resources. Similarly, Christie and Roy (2001: 215) maintained that 'once its institutions are entrenched, Cambodia is likely to head towards an illiberal form of democracy'.

EU–Cambodia relations developed against the background of rising odds. The annual floods of the Tonle Sap lake and the Mekong river, the legacy of wartime economy and conflict and urgent problems of poverty and child prostitution, spilling over from neighbouring Thailand, made it more difficult for the country to seek justice and come to terms with its recent past, and more challenging for the EU to develop the partnership further. From 1994 onwards, EU activities and projects were administered by a Technical Coordination Office in Phnom Penh. In 2002, the EU established a fully-fledged Delegation in Phnom Penh (*Rapid Database*, IP/01/1909). Major EU projects comprised the revitalizing of institutions and infrastructure rehabilitation, food aid, or health projects concentrating on AIDS or malaria. Later, but no less urgent priorities, were education initiatives, the observation of local elections (*Rapid Database*, IP/01/1669) and the preservation of the country's unique archaeological sites around Siem Reap, Angkor Wat and elsewhere (see Box 8.5).

Box 8.5: The Cambodian Cultural Heritage at Siem Reap and Angkor

> The EU's three-year, €1.5 million *REPLIC Programme* aims at assistance with the provision of vocational training for young Cambodians involved in trades. Perhaps the most visible aspect of the programme is the *Artisans d'Angkor* initiative, an EU-funded system of rural workshops, in which artefacts and everyday items taking their stylistic cue from the temple complex at nearby Angkor are sold at fair prices, reflecting the skill and training involved in their production. The initiative was recognized by the Cambodian Prime Minister, Hun Sen, when he put his signature under its Charter on 4 May in Siem Reap, near the site of the eighth- to fifteenth-century temples (Commission Delegation Bangkok, *EU Today*, No. 14, September 2000: 10).

Humanitarian aid provided by the EU had its origins in the more general support programmes for developing countries (e.g. Commission 1993d: 12). From 1992–94 the (€67.1 million) European Rehabilitation Programme for Cambodia and related projects (see Box 8.6), such as the Rehabilitation and Support Programme for Cambodia's Agricultural Sector, known under its French acronym (Programme de Réhabilitation et d'Appui au Secteur Agricole du Cambodge—PRASAC) were initiated.

Box 8.6: EU-supported Agricultural Rehabilitation Initiatives in Cambodia

With €79 million overall, PRASAC was the biggest such initiative in Cambodia. The 1994 Cambodian Programme for Rehabilitation and Development (NRPD) and the EU Rehabilitation Programme for Cambodia (PERC) formed the origins of the scheme. PRASAC covered six provinces around Phnom Penh: Kampong Chaam, Kampong Chhnang, Kampong Speu, Takeo, Prey Veng and Svay Rieng.

A second phase commenced in 1999, to end in 2003. The new €39 million pledge prioritized six areas: safe water supplies, irrigation rehabilitation, agricultural production, rural credit schemes, local entrepreneurship and instruction of local government staff and mine victims (Commission 1999e: 3-11). These activities took into account the fact that some 85 per cent of Cambodians live in the countryside, farming, on average, one hectare of land as subsistence farmers (Commission 2000f: 16-17; Commission Delegation Bangkok, *EU Today*, No. 4, October–December 1997 and No. 11, July–September 1999: 13-14; Commission 1999e; Commission 2000: *PRASAC II: From Emergency Relief to Sustainable Development*).

The Cambodia Institutional Support Programme, worth €4.9 million, aimed to encourage capacity building, the improvement of institutional infrastructures and delivery of public services in six key Cambodian Ministries, all concerned with the abolition of poverty, legal and administrative reform. The programme functioned through technical advisors, participating in the work of the ministries and assisting with training and the initiation of policies (Commission Delegation Bangkok, *EU Today*, No. 14, September 2000: 12).

Funding for rehabilitation of refugees and returnees (from Thailand) has formed a crucial part of the EU's involvement. A wide-ranging cooperation agreement (*OJ* C 107/97, 5 April 1997: 6; Commission 1997b), 'offering an opportunity to strengthen the Human Rights clause, on which all relations with Cambodia hang' (p. 2), was signed on 7 November 1996, interrupted by the 1997–98 events and approved by the Council on 4 October 1999 and the European Parliament on 14 April 1999.[19] It entered into force on 1 November 1999. EU support, worth some €10.5 million, focused on voter registration kits, training, a PR campaign and monitoring of the elections on 26 July 1998 (EU

19. *Rapid Database:* IP/96/998; *OJ* L 269/99, 19 October 1999: 17; 1999/677/EC; *OJ* C 219/99, 30 July 1999.

Delegation Bangkok, *EU Today*, No. 7, July–September 1998: 12). It had been controversial because of concerns over fairness and widespread intimidation by a newly assertive Hun Sen government. (*European Voice*, 9–15 April 1998; 9–15 July 1998). In July 1999, the extension of the EC–ASEAN Cooperation Agreement to Cambodia was initiated. It was signed in July 2000. Combating the proliferation of small weapons in the country appeared as one of the Union's most urgent concerns (see Box 8.7). This helped to promote tourism, culture and economic development and was reflected in a number of Union activities, such as the Commission Statement on Arms Exports of 2 October 2001 (*Rapid Database*: SPEECH/01/430) or the Council Decision on Small Arms of 15 November 1999.

The Lao People's Democratic Republic (Laos, Lao) and Lao–EU Relations

Luang Prabang, capital of the former 'Kingdom of the Million Elephants' and a UNESCO World Heritage site since 1995, used to be the cultural centre of Laos.[20] The modern state of the Lao PDR was centred on its capital, Vientiane, in the south. In spite of being a crossroads of cultures, the country became a 'geographical doormat' and one of South-East Asia's poorest states, with an average per capita GDP at the turn of the millennium of US$350 (Freeman 2001: 101). Eighty-five per cent of the population were subsistence farmers. After independence from France in 1953, the first government, under Prince Souvannaphouma, was established in 1957. However, the country was drawn into the Indo-China wars and became a battlefield for the USA and North Vietnam from 1964 to 1973. Since 1975, when the Communists took power, the country existed as a landlocked one-party state, overshadowed by its more powerful neighbours Vietnam, Cambodia, China, Burma and Thailand.

When, from 1986, the Lao People's Revolutionary Party (the Pathet Lao) drove forward limited economic reform in the shape of the New Economic Mechanism, hopes rose that Laos would become a trade hub connecting China, Thailand and its close ally Vietnam. In 1991, Prince Souphanouvong was succeeded as Laotian Head of State by Kaysone Phomvihan and Nouhak Phomsavan. At the start of the twenty-first

---

20. For an insightful introduction to contemporary Laos, see Kremmer 1997.

Box 8.7: The EU's CFSP and the Problem of Landmines and Small Arms in Cambodia

Council Resolution 'Cambodia I' (1999/730/CFSP; *OJ* L 294/99, 16 November 1999) implements Joint Action 1999/34/CFSP (*OJ* L 9, 15 January 1999) and is worth €500,000. In 2000, Resolution 'Cambodia II' (2000/724/CFSP; *OJ* L 292/3, 21 November 2000), extended the funding to €1.3 million. This represents an effort to help Cambodia to try to come to terms with its recent past and to return to some kind of normality. The availability of high numbers of small arms in the country and a related 'gun-culture' are salient reminders of the work that still needs to be done to achieve some degree of stability and—like the extraordinarily high proportion of young men with amputated limbs—symbolize Cambodia's torment. The Decision targets the 'destabilizing accumulation' of weaponry and, in pursuing it, the EU cooperates with local NGOs and appoints a 'project manager' to oversee its implementation (Commission Representation Bangkok, *EU Today*, No. 13, May 2000: 4, 7; *EURASIA Bulletin* 4.11–12, November–December 2000: 33; Commission 2001, *Small Arms and Light Weapons: The Response of the European Union*: 5, 14-15, 21).

Based on the Ottawa Convention on the Use, Stockpiling, Production and Transfer of Anti-Personnel Mines and their Destruction, which entered into force on 1 March 1999, and in conjunction with UN and other bodies, 'mine actions', especially the clearing of millions of anti-personnel landmines and unexploded ordnances and related R&D activities, have been among the worldwide external activity priorities for the Union since 1995. On 14 March 2000, the Commission adopted further proposals to intensify EU action against landmines (*Rapid Database*: IP/00/250), based on relevant CFSP Joint Actions and European Parliament Resolutions of 1996–97. (For instance: Joint Action 97/817/CFSP, *OJ* L 338, 9 December 1997; and 96/588/CFSP, *OJ* L 260, 12 October 1996. The European Parliament passed Resolutions on increased aid and the EU role in this area on 17 July and 18 September 1997 [*OJ* C 286, 22 September 1997 and *OJ* C 304, 6 October 1997]).

The Union is supported in these efforts by the EU Joint Research Centre and Laboratories in Ispra, Italy. On 17 July the Joint Research Centre signed a memorandum, with Belgium, Canada, the Netherlands, Sweden, the UK and the USA, on the 'International Test and Evaluation Programme for Humanitarian De-mining', an international research effort, to render de-mining more reliable and cost-effective (*Rapid Database*: IP/00/792). With China holding the world's largest stockpile of mines and South and South-East Asian countries such as Afghanistan, Laos, Vietnam or Cambodia still riddled with them, the task is enormous. Cambodia is among the territories most affected by mines and unexploded ordnances, with more than 2000 sq. km of land known, or suspected to be, mined (Commission 2000k: 18).

century the country, under Prime Minister General Sisavath Keobounphan lingered on, in a state of 'suspended anticipation', awaiting improved infrastructure, exploitation of its hydroelectric power generating potential and a general economic upturn (*Far Eastern Economic Review*, 27 July 2000: 48). Freeman (2001: 102) has pointed to the rise and subsequent contraction of cumulative FDI inflows into Laos in the 1990s and has identified some of the reasons for it: the Asian economic downturn of 1997–98; the decline of Thailand, the major investor; domestic legal incompatibilities; red tape; and failing expectations. Defections of high-ranking politicians such as Khamsay Souphanouvong (Bourdet 2001: 166; *Financial Times*, 8 November 2000: 8), pointed to an apparent power struggle within the Communist Party, and a bombing campaign in summer 2000 inflicted severe damage on the ambitions of the 'Visit Laos 2000' year. For these reasons, events like the opening of the 'Friendship Bridge' with Thailand in 1994, a promotion of Lao-Chinese relations (*Vientiane Times*, 18–20 July 2000) or the building of new roads and hydroelectricity projects have been eagerly awaited.

Laos joined ASEAN in July 1997,[21] but EU–Lao relations, like those between the EU and Cambodia, often developed through the actions of member states such as France, Germany, the UK and Sweden. EU–Lao contacts have also been influenced by the Mekong's annual flooding and the related, recurring crop damage, which has necessitated disaster relief, relocation assistance and other humanitarian aid, provided through ECHO. Diplomatic EU–Lao relations began in 1986. The co-operation agreement signed on 29 April 1997 (*OJ* C 109, 8 April 1997; *OJ* L 334/97, 5 December 1997: 14), concentrated on rural matters, development, health and human resources. Following the EC–Lao PDR Joint Commission meeting in Vientiane on 25–26 June 1998, a working group on development and economics moved issues such as rural development, forest conservation, health, infrastructure and irrigation higher up the EU–Lao partnership agenda. Initiatives were accompanied by 'tripartite meetings' of the EU, the Lao Government and EU-funded projects in the country, for reasons of liaising and maximizing of benefits. The opening of an EU Office for Technical Coordination and Institutional Stability in Vientiane was initialized in 2000.

---

21. Commission Proposal regarding the Extension Protocol: Commission 2000o.

However, individual assistance programmes in Laos often were quite 'pointillist' in scope, that is, they did not, traditionally, cover a larger area. This was, above all, a reflection of the fact that in Laos, life has often changed little over centuries and the average life expectancy among the 47 ethnic groups from four linguistic families is around 56 years. But this situation was changing and projects were beginning to have a wider impact (see Box 8.8). Box 8.8 gives examples of significant EU–Lao cooperation programmes in the areas of infrastructure, mine-clearance, textile exports and the fight against communicable diseases.

Box 8.8: EU Projects in Laos

The second phase (1996–2003) of the Micro-Projects Luang Prabang (MPLP) aimed at poverty alleviation in the agricultural sector through a number of priorities like the sustainable integration of agriculture and forestry, the strengthening of institutions and provision of social services for all main Lao population groups, particularly ethnic minorities. The 'Micro-Projects' targeted infrastructure, health and sanitation, farmers' incomes, cultivation and processing, marketing, communications, credit and training. MPLP I had affected hundreds of villages from 1990 to 1995. MPLP II, to which the EU contributed €43.6 million, began operations in Luang Prabang and Northern Laos. It was conceived of as a demand-driven initiative and aimed to respond to needs among the local population. As was the case with other schemes, 'community participation' and 'empowerment' were pillars of the project's philosophy. In a country where only 4 out of 17 provinces had infrastructure, its success was crucial for locals and future investors alike (Commission 2000g; Micro Projects Luang Prabang, Phase II, 2000; Commission Delegation Bangkok, *EU Today*, No. 4, October–December 1997: 8 and No. 15, January 2001: 6-8; Commission 1997g: 32).

Laos holds the—unenviable—record of being the most bombed country in history, with over 9 million pieces of unexploded ordnance (c. 500,000 tons) still in the ground. Humanitarian de-mining was therefore a priority activity for the EU (Commission 2000k: 22). For conservation projects and *'La Maison du Patrimoine'* (Heritage House) in Luang Prabang, see Commission Representation Bangkok, *EU Today*, No. 9, January–March 1999: 6.

In the last few years, exports of high-quality textiles to the EU were worth more than €85 million for Laos. The EC–Lao Textile Agreement, initialled in Brussels on 16 June 1998 (*OJ* L 321/98: 41 and *OJ* L 208/99: 1), therefore represented a significant step forward in relations. Next to textiles, livestock-rearing is vital for a rural society such as Laos. EU support for this area assumed a high priority. The Strengthening of Livestock Services and Extension Activities Project in Lao PDR started in 1998, and was planned to run until 2004, with an EU contribution of €5.7 million. It was executed by

Lao authorities and directed at farmers, particularly smallholders, to consolidate their financial security. Among its aims were the improvement of laboratory services and animal health and the upgrading of veterinary legislation and information systems relating to regional animal production. For its duration, the programme was supported by a documentation centre in Vientiane (EU-Lao PDR Project ALA/96/19).

In a (globally) worsening malaria situation, thousands of people die from the disease every year in Laos and Cambodia alone, especially in border areas. In Laos, some 80 per cent of the population suffer from some form of the disease. The Regional Malaria Control Programme (EC-RMCP), which encompasses Laos, Cambodia, Vietnam and regional coordination groups of health ministers, has therefore been—literally speaking—a vital part of EU–Lao relations. RMCP lasts from 1997–2001, with an overall budget of €29 million of which 18 per cent (or €5.1 million) went to Laos. Since 5 July 2000, EC-RMCP has a Working Group on Border Malaria sited in Vientiane (Laos). The EC-RMCP overlaps with related schemes, like the Asian Collaborative Network for Malaria or the website/newsletter initiative Mekong Malaria Forum. Collation of data, training, disease management, networking, prevention, medical advice and improving health systems are cornerstones of the project (Project websites: http://www.mekong-malaria.org or http://www.ec-malaria.org, Commission Representation Bangkok, *EU Today*, No. 6, April–June 1998: 6-7 and No. 10, April–June 1999: 13. Additional information: *Rapid Database*: IP/96/74; IP/97/872; IP/98/1110; IP/00/185, *OJ* L 321/98: 41 and *OJ* L 208/99: 1).

The Socialist Republic of Vietnam and EU–Vietnamese Relations

Following the French Indo-China War and the battle of Dien Bien Phu in 1954, the Geneva Accord divided Vietnam along the 17th Parallel. South Vietnam was led by Ngo Dinh Diem, who was assassinated in 1963. North Vietnam was dominated by the Communist Ho Chi Minh, who died in 1969. During the 1960s, the southern Communists, the Viet Cong, grew considerably in strength. In the middle of that decade, the USA started bombing targets in North Vietnam. The years from 1973 to 1975 saw the Paris Ceasefire Accords and the end of the US military presence. In 1975, North Vietnamese forces entered Saigon, and the South Vietnamese Government surrendered. The Socialist Republic of Vietnam was founded in 1976. Following incursions by the Chinese-supported Khmer Rouge on the Vietnamese border, Vietnam invaded Cambodia in 1978–79. The Cambodian Government under Pol Pot was overthrown when Phnom Penh fell and the Vietnamese established a government consisting mainly of defectors from the Khmer Rouge. In the 1980s, a programme of socio-economic reform, called *Dôi Moi* ('openness and renovation') was initiated and, by the end of the decade, Vietnamese troops had left Cambodia.

In the 1990s, Vietnam enhanced and diversified its diplomacy towards Europe, the EU (see Box 8.9) and China, and, on 28 July 1995, the country became ASEAN's first communist member (*AFTA Reader*, IV: 33-34). Ironically it was the Vietnam War which provided the initial *raison d'être* for the creation of ASEAN. However, the Vietnamese Communist Party (VCP) remained paramount in Vietnamese politics and the impact of bilateral trade agreements with the USA or Japan remained unclear. Investors pulled out, deterred by corruption and bureaucracy. The country's potential therefore remained largely unfulfilled (*Asiaweek*, 14 April 2000: 34), in spite of attempts by Prime Minister Phan Van Khai's Government to lure foreign investment back into the country. In April 2001, Vietnam finally replaced Le Kha Phieu with Nong Duc Manh as secretary-general of the VCP. The new leader was said to be a more moderate consensus-broker. This might have amounted to a 'silent palace revolt' (*Die Welt*, 21 April 2001), but in the first quarter of 2002, any implications of this change of guard were hard to gauge.

Box 8.9: The EU and Vietnam

EU relations with Vietnam started with a rural development scheme in 1977. They were discontinued, on account of Vietnam's invasion of Cambodia. The *Dôi Moi* economic reform initiatives, inaugurated in 1986, opened doors again, and EU–Vietnam diplomacy 'normalized' (Commission 1997a: 3) in 1990. A textile agreement followed in 1992. It was revised in 1995, 1997 and 2000. The EU–Vietnam Cooperation Agreement dated from 17 July 1995 (Commission 1995g; IP/95/552; Council Decision of 14 May 1996, 96/351/ EC; *OJ* C 12, 17 January 1996; *OJ* L 136 7 June 1996). An EC Delegation opened in Ha Noi in 1996. The EU-Vietnam Technical Assistance Programme, which ran from 1995 to 1998, prioritized Vietnamese accounting and insurance systems, standards and quality control (Commission 1995e: 17). The extension of the EC-ASEAN Cooperation Agreement to Vietnam (Commission 1997a; *OJ* C 95, 24 March 1997, *OJ* C 325, 27 October 1997) came into force on 1 May 1999. The Mekong floods of 1999 were the subject of a European Parliament Resolution on 16 December 1999 (*General Report*, 1999: point 838). In early 2002, More than 70 per cent of EU–Vietnam projects still found their rationale in poverty-reduction (Commission 1997g: 90). The 1992 textile agreement was revised again in 2000 (Commission 2000p). These amendments concerned, for example, the area of quantitative restrictions.

Out of Asia? The EU, Australia and New Zealand

In the context of EU–Asia relations, what position can Australasia hold? The Commission's new Asia blueprint of September 2001 contained for the first time, in a document of this kind, the beginnings of an answer, in the form of references to Australasia and the EU's relationship with, in particular, Australia and New Zealand (Commission 2001c: 24, point 4.3) (see Box 8.10). On the one hand, it is impossible for Australia and New Zealand to deny their long-standing connection with Europe, and a heritage of cultural, historical and people-to-people ties. But on the other hand, one result of Britain joining the EC (1974), and of the overall decrease of the Anglo-Saxon protective presence in Asia after the fall of Saigon, has been a further engagement of Australia and New Zealand towards Asia, in combination with considerable migratory movements from Asia into Australia and New Zealand. Regarding Australia, 70 per cent of its exports go to Asia and the Pacific (Funabashi 1993: 109).

What does this mean for the domestic policies and identities of these countries, and for their European relations? Elijah, Murray and O'Brien (2000: 28) have pointed to the dichotomy of the 'history or geography' debate in Australia during the 1980s and 1990s, which revolved around 'values' and 'the need to "choose"' affiliation with either Europe or Asia.[22] And they observe elsewhere (2000: 16): 'Australia's shift towards greater engagement with the Asia-Pacific region and its attempts to be accepted as a Asian actor can be seen in the context of a perceived shift away from Europe'. In spite of parts of Australia looking to the future as an 'integral part of Asia' (K. Hamlin, *Asia Times*, 19 June 1997) Australia has not, so far, joined the ASEM process and, on the question of ASEM enlargement, the Chinese Foreign Secretary, Qian Qiuchen has made it quite clear that China would be prepared to vote against Australia (and New Zealand) on the grounds that these are 'not Asian countries' (*Agence Europe*, 17 February 1997). For the EU on the other hand, the case has always been quite unambiguous:

> Its political system, socio-economic structure and cultural traditions place Australia, notwithstanding its geographic isolation, firmly in the same system as Western Europe, from which its population and values so

22. See, in this context, Milner and Quilty 1996.

largely derive (Europe Information External Relations, *The European Community and Australia*, 55/82, February 1982: 1).

Where then, do Australia and New Zealand belong? The question is inextricably connected to another: how can these countries be conceptualized in terms of identity? Are they 'European', 'Asian', 'Pacific' or, indeed, 'Other'? This is an intractable question, but issues of multiculturalism, 'belonging' and identity continue to inform and shape the discourse about culture, literature and politics in Australia on many levels.[23] For Australian–EU relations (see Box 8.10), Elijah *et al.* (2000: 29-30) and many others have argued that, notwithstanding APEC, or the amount of 'Asianization' of Australia, the continent has the potential to become a more, rather than less, interesting dialogue partner for the EU, as an Asian-European middle-power, an intermediary or investment locale. Changes in political emphasis from the Keating to the Howard Governments under the slogan of 'Asia first, but not Asia only', (cf. *Far Eastern Economic Review*, 8 June 2000: 38), the high-profile engagement of Australian soldiers in East Timor,[24] the Asian financial crisis of 1997–98 and the continuing phenomenon of 'broadening' of the Euro-Australian relationship all appear, generally, to bear out this hypothesis, but economic relations are still asymmetrical.

Box 8.10: The Evolution of EU–Australia and EU–New Zealand Relations

At the end of the second millennium, the EU was Australia's largest economic partner and 14 per cent of Australia's exports were to the Union. However, the Australasian Continent accounted for a share of just 1 per cent of the EU's imports and exports (Murray 2000). Consequently, as Heather Field pointed out in a rather diplomatic way (1997–98: xii): 'The imbalance between exports and imports has tended to encourage a colder view of Australia-EU relations than has been justifiable because of an over-simplistic expectation of reciprocity as being desirable in trade relations'. The EU was Australia's largest merchandise trading partner, exporting mainly passenger motor vehicles, pharmaceutical products and telecommunications equipment, in return for Australian products such as wool, coal and wine.

23. See, as one example, Nuttall 1997; for an unsurpassed fictional treatment of questions of Australian identity and 'otherness', see Malouf 1993.

24. Formerly secret Government documents revealed in 2000 that Australia knew of the 1975 Indonesian invasion of East Timor, in advance of the event (e.g. *Guardian* 13 September 2000: 16).

Beyond trade relations, the widening scope of the contemporary EU–Australia relationship reflected both the quickening pace of EU integration and the perceptual shrinking of the 'distance' between Europe and the Asia-Pacific. The dialogue was extended to security issues, competition and consumer affairs, development cooperation in the South Pacific, education, environmental dialogue and other matters. The Commission's new Asia paper of September 2001, therefore, could state that: 'our relations with Australia and New Zealand have developed positively in recent years and are no longer dominated to the same extent as previously by agricultural trade issues' (Commission 2001c: 24). However, given the EU's current preoccupations and Australia's 'Asian interests', it is no surprise that some authors still deplored a 'mutual comprehension deficit' in the relationship (Murray 2000: n. 4).

A majority of the early Australian attitudes towards European integration were characterized by historical ties and the view through the 'British lens': tentative support, accompanied by fears over a loss of Australian interests, as well as export markets and Commonwealth preferences (Elijah *et al.* 2000: 3). Following the establishment of diplomatic relations from 1962 and Britain's EC accession in 1973, the EU–Australian partnership became more independent, although the Common Agricultural Policy (CAP) and related European protectionism caused much friction and impasse (Elijah *et al.* 2000: 7-15). The CAP led to a wide variety of Australian responses (overview: Benvenuti 1998–99: 75-76), including international campaigning, diplomacy and persuasion.

Subsequent high-level consultations and inter-parliamentary contacts since the mid-1970s produced a threefold pattern of themes: trade, investment and technology transfer, and development cooperation in the South Pacific. Export diversification, e.g. to minerals or steel, and later GATT concessions partly compensated for the loss of traditional markets such as the British agricultural market (which was subsumed by the CAP) or the sugar market (much of which shifted to ACP countries following the Lomé I Convention).

A Commission Delegation to Canberra started operations in 1981, the year the EURATOM-Australia Uranium Agreement was signed. A number of bilateral agreements on issues such as wine exports (1994, *OJ* L 86, 31 March 1994: 1-93), scientific and technical cooperation (1994, updated 1999) or industry cooperation followed. 1998 saw the signing of a Mutual Recognition Agreement on Standards Certification and Conformity Assessment (*OJ* L 229, 17 August 1998: 1-60; see *European Voice*, 18–24 June 1998), covering eight product sectors, including telecommunications and automotive products. A proposed Framework EU-Australia Trade and Cooperation Agreement failed to materialize over the EU's insistence to include human rights conditionality. Unfortunately this led to all the connected budgetary consequences for cooperation activities in areas such as education or science. However, a less ambitious Joint Declaration was signed in Luxembourg on 26 June 1997, opening up avenues towards new fields of cooperation.

From the time of the British presidency of 1998 onwards, Australia also held talks about Asia with the EU *troika*. Multilateral contacts developed through a range of Ministerial and Senior Officials Meetings, as well as the 1994 Energy Charter Treaty, and also within the ARF and ASEAN Post-Ministerial Meeting formats, but not through the ASEM-process. In 1999, the people of Australia decided in a referendum, not to relinquish their constitutional-legal links with the UK, which remained Australia's major partner in the EU (*Guardian*, 8 November 1999; *The Economist*, 13 November 1999; http://www.dfat.gov.au/geo/european_union/jointdec.html).

In 2001, the EU was the second largest market—after Australia—for New Zealand (Aotearoa*)* and took some 17 per cent of New Zealand exports, such as 'sheep meat' (lamb, mutton), fruit, wine or butter. The negotiation of special terms for New Zealand butter in the EU's Single Market entered the Union's regulatory framework on several occasions (Council Regulation EEC No. 3841/92, *OJ* L 390, 31 December 1992: 1-2; Commission 1989; 1992). EU relations with New Zealand were traditionally rooted in strong bilateral commonalities and ties, in particular with the UK. The New Zealand Government believed that: 'productive bilateral relationships with the three key Member States of the EU—Germany, Britain and France—can support our political and economic objectives in Europe' (see: http:.www.mft.govt.nz/foreign/regions/Europe/ overview.html). There were a number of EU–New Zealand bilateral agreements, for instance on science and technology (1991), veterinary standards (1997) or mutual recognition of conformity assessments (1998). However, the main point of reference, after 1999, was the new Joint Declaration on Relations, identifying, as in the case of its EU–Australia equivalent, a number of new areas for cooperation, based on shared interests and the economic significance of the Asia-Pacific (see http://www.mft.govt. nz/foreign/ bilat.html#eur).

Conclusions

At the end of 2001, relations between the EU and South-East Asian countries constituted a mosaic. The dialogue involved South-East Asian partners of great diversity and therefore presented a mirror-image of the varying intensity of EU-Asia contacts on a wider scale.

The EU continued to expand its successful dialogue with some countries in the region. EU–Thai relations, for instance, based on a long, mutual tradition of contacts, experienced a further expansion following the 1997–98 Asian financial crisis, and a stronger emphasis on cultural and educational contacts; while the EU–Brunei partnership benefited from the work of the ASEAN-EU Management Centre in Brunei.

The EU further intensified its dialogue with selected states in South-East Asia. In the case of Indonesia, this was due to ongoing processes of democratization in this country and to the events leading to the independence of East Timor; in the cases of Malaysia, Singapore or Brunei, the reasons were to be found in economics and strong invest-ment relations by European businesses with those countries. The tension between the lure of business opportunities for European companies and the silencing of the opposition, especially through the judiciary in Malaysia and Singapore, continued to present the EU with a dilemma, accentuated by the fact that the political leaders of these countries, alongside China, tend to be consistently vocal proponents of an 'Asian values' concept, which, more often than not, masked repres-sion and authoritarian practices. This was particularly true in the case of EU–Burma relations, which were again dominated by the implementation of a large number of CFSP measures and sanctions. At the end of 2001, the SPDC, the Burmese military leadership seemed unperturbed in their intransigence, but appeared increasingly keen to end their isolation, in the face of renewed contacts between the EU, the Burmese opposition leader Aung San Suu Kyi and government representatives.

The EU's relations with the countries of Indochina, Laos, Cambodia and Vietnam, were beginning to overcome the legacies of war and genocide and moved towards broader partnerships, which encompassed the preservation of cultural heritage, health, the environment, the prevention of the spread of small weapons and the fight against the ubiquitous scourge of landmines.

Pacific Asia—outside the EU's relations with the ACP group of states—was beginning to make a bigger impact on the EU's agenda. In 2001, the New Asia Strategy of the European Commission included more references to Australia and New Zealand (Aotearoa) than previous, comparable, documents. The new EU–Australian and EU–New Zealand Joint Declarations, in conjunction with a number of bilateral agreements moved the EU's dialogue with these countries out of the narrow debates of the past, which were frequently dominated by the effects of the CAP. The intensity with which Australia and New Zealand wished to deepen their ties with the EU continued to fluctuate, in line with domestic discussions in these countries about issues of asylum, identity, European heritage and Asian re-orientation.

9 |

Overall Conclusions and Outlook: Prospects, Priorities and Perspectives on EU–Asia Relations

Where did the EU's relations with Asia stand at the beginning of the third millennium? The preceding chapters have sought to illustrate that they had developed beyond all recognition when compared to the situation about a decade earlier. This chapter attempts to summarize the extent of that development. It also presents one observer's view on what the future looked like from the perspective of 2001.

EU–Asia relations, and the EU's Asia policies, had by 2001 transcended what, not too long before, could still be termed an initial, 'fledgling' or 'emerging' stage (Wiessala 1999: 96). Following a hesitant start and in the wake of an unprecedented change of major geopolitical parameters, the EU–Asia partnership went through institutionalization and crisis, but, on the way, gained significant momentum in a number of areas. Decision-makers on both sides were approaching one another across a cultural and linguistic divide which was still considerable, but was constantly being narrowed by confidence-building measures such as the ASEM summits, by enhanced economic relations and by political dialogue. This dialogue, born out of new global political and strategic considerations and greatly increased economic—and therefore political—weight on the side of the Asian countries, was much more firmly on course. It was beginning to be conducted through a more regular EU–Asian bilateral framework of working groups, summit meetings, foreign ministers' briefings and cooperation programmes, as well as in multilateral fora such as the WTO, the UN and APEC.

To the same degree as the realization of the growth, inescapability and scope of global interdependence had dawned on decision-makers in both the Western and the Eastern hemispheres, EU–Asia contacts had grown into a much more systematic and coherent relationship. This made the EU–Asia partnership less reactive and more proactive. There remained, however, some constraints. The element of 'commonality' in the EU's CFSP, although growing, remained a largely untested—and undervalued—issue. This unavoidably affected Asia–Europe relations. Analysts of the EU's global reach and ambition, such as Algieri (1999: 93, 96) found that, due to a coherence dilemma in the area of the EU's general external relations, the EU's Asia policies were but a mirror of the different quality between economic and political integration of European states. This realization led to speculation about whether the development of the EU's Asia policy would be dependent on the activities of single European states.

It seemed clear at the start of the new millennium that individual states' relations with the Asian region would, indeed, continue to be significant, would continue to be determined by individual histories regarding Asia, and would continue to cause friction and divergencies in European perceptions of Asia. But, as was also shown in this book, in the same way as general Europe–Asia contacts had matured from the exploitation of former stereotypes of 'threat' and 'competition' to the re-exploration of potential mutual interests, the relationship between the EU as a whole and Asia was taken more seriously, as opposed to just being taken for granted. It had graduated from political expediency to being seen as a necessity for the future. That the EU should not only have relations with Asia as a desirable aspect of its emerging foreign policy, but should also actively seek to maintain, expand and diversify them, was indicative of how far partners in East and West had emerged from the long shadows of imperialism, colonialism, the Cold War and, more recently, the financial turmoil of the late 1990s. But the fact that this more independent 'maintaining', 'expanding' and 'diversifying' was happening at all, and that it was happening to a very significant degree among an ever-growing number of actors, is perhaps, the main conclusion to be drawn from this book.

By the turn of the century, the EU had reassessed and streamlined its partnership with Asia. The Union's New Asia Strategy of 1994 and its successor strategies had been substantially reinterpreted, updated and reformed in the light of economic and political developments in Asian countries, and the way these changed their relationship with Europe. The Commission's first agenda concerning Asia as a whole, the New Asia Strategy of 1994, was followed by detailed blueprints covering

EU–ASEAN relations, the ASEM process, and by individual, country-specific policies, such as those for China, Hong Kong, India, Indonesia or Macao. Last but not least, the second general Asia Strategy of September 2001 took into account the rapid change of the parameters of EU–Asia relations since the early 1990s. From the perspective of 2001, it could be expected that this agenda would be both enlarged and refined in the time leading up to ASEM 4 in 2002. The whole process of adaptation seemed set to continue in 2002, and to result in at least one major new 'Asia Strategy' to be proposed by the Commission in due course.

The war in Afghanistan in 2001, and the Ghent European Council, resulted in a realignment of the EU's wider Asia policies. From this it could be anticipated that the Union's dialogue with Afghanistan, China, Central Asia, India and Pakistan, in particular, would be worked out in much more detail and would go through a further phase of intensification, realignment and consolidation.

In this context, and given the way the ASEM meetings were determining priorities for the dialogue, there were grounds in 2001 for cautious optimism. It could be concluded that the often-heard concern that too much of the relationship was still devoted to 'the business of doing business' (e.g. Bridges 1999: 200) would recede into the background a little. The areas of culture, education and training, R&D, environmental and human rights cooperation seemed most likely to stand out. These areas seemed destined to become more comprehensive and more entrenched in the ASEM process, next to the more 'traditional' fields of business promotion, development aid or humanitarian assistance. This would make EU–Asia relations more 'holistic' and fruitful in the medium- to long-term, as long as the ASEM process could be fine-tuned as to its function and identity, and, perhaps, pruned in its ambitions and its mushrooming institutionalization.

Among the main objectives of these and future political 'roadmaps', it seemed, would also be a more wide-ranging economic cooperation, enhanced EU 'presence and profile' in Asia and renewed political and human rights talks. The Union had already made a start in exploiting the accelerating pace of its reformed Asia relations and seemed more than likely to continue to seek to shape and deepen the partnership over the next decade.

However, some of the obstacles on this course looked formidable. Above all, there seemed a considerable likelihood that Asian and European interlocutors would continue to underestimate the significance of the necessary 'values' discourse, and therefore under-rate the importance of a continued search for commonality on terms such as 'rights', 'values' or 'democracy'. Further neglect in this area had a very real potential to undermine future EU–Asia relations in all fields. The enormous diversity and heterogeneity among Asian states themselves and the changeable political, social and economic situation in some of them were clearly going to present further challenges. In addition to this, the danger of European unemployment was looming large, and strong US and Japanese competition never seemed far away in the Asian region. Last but not least, following the Asian crisis of 1997 and 1998, the repercussions of which were still being acutely felt in 2001, enhanced volumes of intra-regional trade, new foreign policy and security realignments among the Asian nations, and the sheer proportions of ongoing economic change had both increased the need for the EU to keep up the momentum of its Asia dialogue and indicated the challenges of the future.

In the new world ('dis-)order', lying beyond the colonial past of the Europeans in Asia, the Europeans were often faced with very divergent concepts of 'democracy', 'civil liberties' or 'tradition', and with different mentalities, negotiating styles, priorities and tactics, in spite of a semblance of commonality on the surface. Developments in Indonesia, China, Burma or Hong Kong seemed likely to continue to highlight this in the years to come. The debate about the morally and politically justifiable, the 'right' or even the preferred route for human rights dialogue —isolation and sanctions or 'constructive engagement' of individual states—remained very much a characteristic of overall EU–Asia relations and seemed likely to be so for some time to come, in spite of likely improvements in the EU–Burma dialogue and of a more constructive institutionalization of EU–Asian, EU–Chinese or EU–Indonesian human rights talks.

In 2001, the European Union seemed likely to continue on the way it had chosen so far, vigorously and in a focused way, but needed, perhaps to make more use of the supposedly 'Asian' characteristics of patience, calm, serenity and a well-developed sense of balance, harmony, equilibrium and proportion.

Appendix 1
EU Relations with Asia: A Chronology

1958   First European Development Fund (EDF) established
1963   First Yaoundé Convention with 18 African states and Madagascar
1967   Association of South-East Asian Nations (ASEAN) established in Bangkok
1969   Second Yaoundé Convention
1971   Generalized System of Preferences (GSP) extended to non-ACP developing countries
1972   Paris Summit: worldwide development policy outlined
1974   Commission Report proposing extension of aid to non-ACP countries
1975   First Lomé Convention signed with 48 countries
1976   Financial and Technical Cooperation with Asia (and Latin America) budgeted
        First Asian Development Projects funded (304 projects totalling 2.120 million ECU to date)
        First ASEAN Summit in Bali. Members sign Treaty of Amity and Co-operation in South-East Asia
1978   First meeting between European Union and ASEAN foreign ministers
1980   EU–ASEAN Economic and Commercial Cooperation Agreement; Trade Agreement with China
1981   Council Regulation about financial and technical aid
1984   Brunei Darussalam joins ASEAN
        COMPEX compensation scheme introduced for least developed Asian/Latin American countries
1985   South Asian Association for Regional Cooperation (SAARC) established
        Second Trade and Cooperation Agreement with China
1987   Third ASEAN Summit in Manila, Manila Declaration signed
1988   European Community Investment Partners (ECIP) Scheme launched
        STABEX export earnings assistance programme extended to ALA countries
1989   Commission Report on 13 years of EEC/ALA cooperation; first APEC meeting near Seattle, USA
1991   Resolutions on Human Rights, Democracy and Development (Council, EP)

1992 Regulation: Developing Countries of Asia and Latin America
   Fourth ASEAN Summit in Singapore, AFTA and CEPT decisions
1993 European Investment Bank (EIB) starts operations in Asia; China: programme on IPR initiated
   Philippines: First European Business Information Centre (EBIC) opened
1994 ASEAN Regional Forum (ARF) set up: security and political dialogue
1994 New Asia Strategy formulated by the Commission (COM (94) 314)
1995 Commission Communication: *A Long-Term Policy for China-Europe Relations*
   36 new development aid programmes launched for Asia; 5th ASEAN Summit in Bangkok
   Vietnam joins ASEAN, EU Technical assistance programme with Vietnam
1996 EURO-ASIA FORUM in Venice (January) brings 'civil societies' closer together
   First Asia-Europe NGO Conference on the Future of Asian-European Relations
   First Asia–Europe Meeting (ASEM 1) in Bangkok, Thailand
   First Ministerial Meeting of the World Trade Organization (WTO) in Singapore
1997 Commission Document: *The European Union and Hong Kong: Beyond 1997*
   EU–ASEAN and ASEM Foreign Ministers Meeting in Singapore (February)
   30th anniversary of the foundation of ASEAN (July).
   EU–ASEAN Foreign Ministers' Meeting in Kuala Lumpur (28 July)
1998 2 April: First-ever summit meeting between China and the EU in London
   3–4 April: second Asia–Europe Meeting (ASEM 2) In London, England
   Commission communication: *Building a Comprehensive Partnership with China*
1999 21 December: Second EU–China Summit in Beijing
   Commission communication: *Relations between the EU and Macao: beyond 2000*
2000 20–21 March: Third Asia–Europe Meeting (ASEM 3) in Seoul, Republic of Korea
   Chinese PM Zhu Rongji on first-ever visit to the Commission in Brussels
   Commission communication: *Developing Closer Relations with Indonesia*
   Commission strategy on communicable diseases and poverty
2001 The EU reforms its system of development aid and establishes the new EuropeAid office
   Significant EU visits to India, China, North Korea and Burma (Myanmar)
   January: New EU Common Position on Afghanistan
   19 March: Council Conclusions on human rights; new human rights communication by the Commission
   April: EU–Japan Mutual Recognition Agreement
   EU–Korea Trade and Cooperation Agreement comes into force

EU Electoral Observation Mission (EOM) to Bangladesh

3 May: third UN Conference on the least developed countries (LDC) hosted by the EU

15 May: Commission reports on implementation of the 1998 China Strategy

New Commission Action Programme on malaria, HIV/AIDS and tuberculosis

4 September: Communication from the Commission (COM [2001] 469: *Europe and Asia: A Strategic Framework for Enhanced Partnerships*, overhauls and extends the 1994 New Asia Strategy

2002   Fourth Asia–Europe Meeting (ASEM 4) in Copenhagen, Denmark

Appendix 2
Selection of Useful Addresses

ASEAN-EC COGEN Programme
Asian Institute of Technology
COGEN Programme Secretariat
Outreach Building 301
PO Box 4, Klongluang
Pathumthani, 12120, Thailand
Fax: 0066-2-5245396
E-mail: cogen@ait.ac.th
Internet: http://www.cogen.ait.ac.th

**ASEAN-EC Energy Management
Training and Research Center
(AEEMTRC)**
PO Box
Jakarta
Indonesia
Fax: (0062-21) 7398279
Internet: http://www.aseansec.org/
economic/aeemtrc.htm

ASEAN-EC Management Centre
Sinpang 347
Jalan Pasar Baru
Gadong 3186
Brunei Darussalam
Fax: (00673-2) 445856
E-mail: aemc@pso.brunet.bn
Internet: http://www.brunet.bn/php/
aemc/aemc.htm.bn

ASEAN University Network
Room 210, Jamjuree 1 Building
Chulalongkorn University
Phyathai Road,
Bangkok 10330
Thailand
Fax: (0066) 2 2168808
E-mail: aun@chula.ac.th
Internet: http://www.aun.chula.ac.th

**Asia-Europe Vision Group
Secretariat**
PO Box 112
Korea World Trade Centre
Seoul,
Korea 135-729
Tel: (822) 720-4043/4
Fax: (822) 722 1480
E-mail: aevg@chollian.dacom.co.kr

Asia-Invest Secretariat
Rue Archimède 17/
Archimedesstraat 17
B–1000 Brussels,
Belgium
Tel: (0032-2) 2821750/1756
Fax: (0032-2) 2821760
E-mail: asia.invest@asia-invest.com
Internet: http://www.asia-invest.com;
http://europa.eu.int/en/comm/
dg1b/asia-invest.html

Asia University Network (AUN)
Office of the AUN Secretariat
Ministry of University Affairs
Building
328, Si Ayutthaya Road
Ratchathewi
Bangkok, 10400
Thailand
Fax: (0066-2) 2458289
E-mail: auns@mua.go.th

Asia-Urbs Secretariat
205, Rue Belliard
B–1040 Brussels,
Belgium
Tel: (0032-2) 230-7688
Fax: (0032-2) 230-6973
E-mail: secretariat@asia-urbs.com
Internet: http://www.asia-urbs.com

Centre for Euro-Asian Studies
The University of Reading
PO Box 218
Reading RG6 6AA
UK
Tel: +44 (0) 118 931 6205
Fax: +44 (0) 118 931 6274
Internet: http://www.rdg.ac.uk/
AcaDepts/le/CEAS/main/contact.htm

**Europe-Asia Cooperation
Programme in Information and
Communication Technology (IT&C)**
Programme Management Office
Europe
Avenue Albert Elisabeth 62
B–1200 Brussels
Belgium
Tel: (0032-2) 7391160
Fax: (0032-2) 7391166
E-mail: info@asia-itc.org
Internet: http://www.asia-itc.org

**European Union: Delegations of the
European Commission**

Australia and New Zealand
18 Arkana Street
Yarralumla ACT 2600
Australia
Fax: (0061-2-)6273-4445
E-mail: Australia@ecdel.org.au or
        newzealand@ecdel.org.au

Bangladesh
House/Plot 7, Road 84, Gulshan
Dhaka 1212, Bangladesh
E-mail: mail to@bgd.eu.del.com;
eudelbgd@bd.drik.net
Internet:
http://www.eudelbangladesh.org

*Burma (Myanmar), Cambodia, Lao
PDR, Malaysia and Thailand*
Kian Gwan House II, 19th Floor
140/1 Wireless Road
Bangkok 10330, Thailand
Fax: 0066-2-255-9114
E-mail: mailto@tha.eudel.com;
ecdelbkk@ksc15.th.com;
mailto@deltha.cec.eu.int
Internet: www.deltha.cec.eu.int

China
15 Dong Zhi Men Wai Daije, Sanlitun
100600 Beijing, China
Fax: (0086-10)-65 32 43 42
E-mail: ecdel@public.bta.net.cn
Internet: http://www.ecd.org.cn

*Office of the European Commission in
Hong Kong*
19/F St John's Building, 33 Garden
Road
Central Hong Kong, China
Fax: (00852) 2537-6083
E-mail: eurocornhk@hk.super.net
Internet: http://www.ust.hk/~webeu/

India, Nepal and Bhutan
65, Golf Links
New Dehli 110003, India
Fax: (91-11)-4629206
E-mail: eudelind@giasdl01.vsnl.net.in
Internet: http://www.eudelindia.org

Indonesia, Singapore and Brunei-Darussalam
PO Box 6454 JKPDS
Wisma Dharmala Sakti, 16th floor
JI Jendral Sudirman 32
Jakarta 10064, Indonesia
Fax: (0062-21) 570-6075
E-mail:
tioria.silalahi@delidn.cec.eu.int;
ecrep@uninet.net.id

Japan
Europa House, 9-5 Sanbancho,
Chiyoda-ku
Tokyo 102, Japan
Tel: (0081-3-) 3239-0441
Fax: (0081-3-) 3261-5194

Pakistan
PO Box 1608, House No. 9, Street No.
88, Sector G-6/3
Islamabad, Pakistan
Fax: 0092-51-822-604
E-mail:
husnain@eurocompak.sdnpk.undp.org

Philippines
7th floor, Salustiana D. Ty Tower
104 Paseo de Roxas
Legaspi Village, Makati City 1200
Metro Manila, The Philippines
Fax: (0063-2-812-6686/87)
E-mail: eudelphl@info.com.ph

Sri Lanka and The Maldives
81 Barnes Place
Colombo 7, Sri Lanka
Fax: 0094-1-698820
E-mail: adas.eudelka@itmin.com;
hdel.eudelka@itmin.com

Vietnam
The Metropole Centre
56 Ly Thai To Street
Hanoi, Vietnam
Fax: 00844-9341361
E-mail: oriol@netnam.org.vn

Eurochambres: European Association of Chambers of Commerce and Industry
5, Rue Archimède bte 3
1000 Brussels, Belgium
Tel: (0032-2) 2820850
Fax: (0032-2) 2800191
E-mail:
eurochambres@eurochambres.be

European Commission: Unit for Relations with China, DG I / F / 2
Rue de la loi 200
B–1049 Brussels, Belgium
Tel: + 32-2-296-0214
Fax: + 32-2-295-1028
E-mail: unit-f-2@dg1.cec.be

European Documentation Centre (EDC) at Chulalongkorn University
Centre for Academic Resources, Main Library
5th Floor, Chulalongkorn University
Phya Thai Road
Bangkok 10330
Thailand
Tel: (00662) – 21829523
E-mail: cuesp@netserv.chula.ac.th
Internet: http://www.car.chula.ac.th

European Institute for Asian Studies (EIAS)
35, Rue des Deux Eglises
B–1000 Brussels
Belgium
Tel: (0032-2-) 230-8122
Fax: (0032-2) 230-5402
E-mail: eias@eias.org
Internet: http://www.eias.org

Institute for Commonwealth Studies
University of London
28 Russell Square
London WC1B 5DS, UK
Tel: +44 (0) 171 862 8844
Fax: +44 (0) 171 862 8820

Institut für Asienkunde
Rothenbaumchausee 32
D-20148 Hamburg
E-mail: ifahh@uni-hamburg.de.
Internet: http://www.duei.de/ifa

International Institute for Asian Studies (IIAS)
PO Box 9515
2300 RA Leiden
The Netherlands
http://www.iias.nl

Junior EU-ASEAN Managers Exchange Programme (JEM)
JEM Programme Office Europe
Rue du Trône 51
B-1050 Brussels, Belgium
Tel: (0032-2) 5510770
Fax: (0032-2) 5120197/5121651
E-mail: info@jemasean.org
Internet: http://www.jemasean.org

Master of Arts Programme in European Studies (International)
Chulalongkorn University, 3rd floor,
Vidyabhathana Building
Phya Thai Road, Bangkok, 10330
Thailand
Fax:(0066)22183907
E-mail: maeus@cula.ac.th
http://www.chula.ac.th/international/m
aeus/prog.html

Micro Projects Luang Prabang Phase II
PO Box 535
Luang Prabang,
Lao PDR
Fax: (00856)71-212776

Nordic Institute of Asian Studies
Leifsgade 33
DK-2300 Copenhagen S
Denmark
Tel: (+45) 32 54 88 44
Fax: (+45) 32 96 25 30
E-mail: jcs@nias.ku.dk;
sec@nias.ku.dk
Internet: http://www.nias.ku.dk

Office for the Third Asia-Europe Meeting
ASEM Tower, 6th floor
Trade Center, Kangnam-gu
Seoul
Republic of Korea
Tel: (+822)6001-6600
Fax: (+822)6001-6666
E-mail: m_asem3@asem3.go.kr

PRASAC Head Office
No. 6 L Street 21
Tonle Bassac, Chamkarmon, PO Box 2412
Phnom Penh 3,
Cambodia
Fax: 00855-23216293
E-mail: prasac2@bigpond.com.kh

Regional Institute of Environmental Technology – Asia Eco Best
3, Science Park Drive
PSB Annex (Science Park)
#04-08 Singapore 118223
E-mail: riet@pacific.net.sg
Internet http://www.riet.org

Regional Malaria Control Programme in Cambodia, Lao PDR and Vietnam
34 Hang Bai Street
Hanoi
Vietnam
Tel: (00844) 9341642
Fax: (00844) 9341641
E-mail: ec-rmcp@netnam.org.vn

Strengthening of Livestock Services and Extension Activities Project in Lao PDR
The Project Management Unit
Department of Livestock and Fisheries
P.O. Box 8330
Vientane
Lao PDR
Tel/Fax: (00856)21217869
E-mail: eu.livestock@laonet.net

Technical Coordination Office of the European Commission in Cambodia
1, rue 21 Chamkamon (BP 2301)
Phnom Penh, Cambodia
Tel: (0085523) 216 996, 360 877
Fax: (0085523) 216 997
E-mail: sophea@tco.forum.org.kh

The European Business Information Centre (EBIC) Malaysia
Level 7, Wisma Hong Leong, 18 Jalan Perak
50450 Kuala Lumpur, Malaysia
Tel: (60 3) 26 26 298
Fax: (60 3) 26 26 198
E-mail: ebic-kl@mol.net.my

University of Malaya European Studies Programme (UMESP)
Asia-Europe Institute (AEI)
University of Malaya
50603 Kuala Lumpur, Malaysia
Tel: (0060) 37594645
Fax: (0060)37540799
E-mail: umesp@umcsd.um.edu.my

Appendix 3
Selection of Internet Resources

General Sources and Documents

Asia House, Essen (Germany)
http://www.asienhaus.org/englisch/eu-asia.htm

Association of Southeast Asian Nations (ASEAN)
http://www.aseansec.org

ASEM (EU-ASEM relations)
http://europa.eu.int/comm/dg01/euasem.htm

ASEM I (Bangkok, 1996)
http://asem.inter.net.th

ASEM II (London, 1998)
http://asem2.fco.gov.uk

ASEM III (Seoul, 2000)
http://asem3.org

ASEM: Science and Technology Cooperation
http://www.cordis.lu/asem/home.htm

ASEM Investment Regulations
http://www.asem.vie.net

ASEM Child Welfare Initiative, Resources Centre
http://www.asem.org

Bibliography on Buddhism and human rights
http://jbe.la.psu.edu/2/rightbib.html

Documents relating to South-East Asia
http://www.mtholyoke.edu/acad/intrel/seasia.htm

European Commission Delegation China
http://www.delchn.cec.eu.int

European Commission Office Hong Kong
http://www.ust.hk/~webeu/

European Commission Delegation Japan
http://www.jpn.cec.eu.int//

European Commission Delegation India, Nepal, Bhutan
http://www.eudelindia.org

European Commission Delegation Indonesia, Singapore, Brunei-Darussalam
http://www.delidn.cec.eu.int

European Commission Delegation Philippines
http://www.euphil.org

European Commission Delegation Thailand, Cambodia, Burma/Myanmar, Lao PDR and Malaysia
http://www.deltha.cec.eu.int

EU-Australia relations
http://europa.eu.int/comm/dg01.euaus.
htm (Commission)
http://www.ecdel.org.au (Delegation)
http://www.dfat.gov.au/geo/europe/ind
ex.html (Australian Department of
Foreign Affairs and Trade)

EU-Japan relations
http://europa.eu.int/comm/dg01/eujap.
htm (Commission)
http://www.jmission-eu.be (Japanese
Mission to the EU)

EU-New Zealand relations
http://europa.eu.int/comm/dg01/eunz.h
tm (Commission)
http://www.ecdel.org.au (Delegation)

External Relations Website
(Commission)
http://europa.eu.int/comm/dgs/external
_relations/index_en.htm

EU and Asia sub-site
http://europa.eu.int/comm/external_rel
ations/asia/index.htm

European University Institute
Florence (Foreign Policy Bulletin
Online)
http://www.iue.it

RAPID Database
http://europa.eu.int/en/comm/spp/rapid
.html (log-in as 'guest', password
'guest')

South Asian Association for Regional
Cooperation (SAARC)
http://www.saarc.com

The Korean Peninsula Energy
Development Organization (KEDO)
http://www.kedo.org

EU–Asia Related Programmes and
Institutes

ASEAN-EC Energy Management and
Training Centre (AEEMTRC)
http://www.aseansec.org/economic/aee
mtrc.htm

ASEAN-EC COGEN Programme at
the Asian Institute of Technology in
Bangkok
http://www.cogen.ait.ac.th

ASEAN-EC Management Centre
http://www.brunet.bn/php/aemc/aemc.
htm.bn

Asia-Ecobest
http://www.riet.org/aeb/aeb.htm (see
RIET)

Asia-Europe Environmental
Technology Centre (Bangkok)
http://www.aeetc.org

Asia Europe Foundation (ASEF)
http://www.asef.org/

Asia-Europe Vision Group (AEVG)
Report 1999
http://www.mofat.go.kr/aevg

Asia-Europe Young Leaders'
Symposium II
http://www.aeyls-ii.bka.bv.at/

Asia Initiative for Reproductive Health
(RHI)
http://www.asia-initiative.org

Asia-Invest
http://www.asia-invest.com

Asia Society
http://www.asiasociety.org

Asia-Urbs
http://www.asia-urbs.com

Centre for Euro-Asian Studies (CEAS), Reading
http://www.rdg.ac.uk/AcaDepts/le/CEAS/main.htm

Europe-Asia Cooperation Programme in Information and Communication Technology (IT & C):
http://www.asia-itc.org

European Institute for Asian Studies (Brussels)
http://www.eias.org

EU-India Economic Cross-Cultural Programme
http://www.euforindia.org

EU-Japan Centre for Industrial Cooperation
http://www.eu-japan.gr.jp/base/index1.html
Executive Training Programme (Japan)
http://www.etp.org

Gateway to Japan
http://www.eu-gateway-to-japan.be

Institute of Commonwealth Studies (ICS), London
http://www.sas.ac.uk/commonwealthstudies/

Institute for Southeast Asian Affairs (ISEAS - Singapore)
http://merlion.iseas.ac.sg

Investment Promotion Action Plan (IPAP- ASEM)
http://europa.eu.int/comm/external_relations/asem_ipap_vie/intro/

Junior EU-ASEAN Managers Exchange Programme
http://www.jemasean.org

Mekong Malaria Forum (MMF)
http://www.ec-malaria.org

Regional Institute of Environmental Technology (RIET, Singapore)
http://www.riet.org (see Asia-Ecobest)

Regional Malaria Control Programme (Indochina)
http://www.mekong-malaria.org

Southeast Asian Studies Center (Illinois)
http://www.niu.edu/acad/cseas/seasia.html

Asia Coverage (General)

Asia Daily
http://www.asiadaily.com/

Asia Now (CNN USA)
htpp://cnn/ASIANOW/Asiaweek

Asia Observer   ·
http://wwwasiaobserver.com

Asia Source
http://www.asiasource.org

Asia Times
http://www.atimes.com

Asiaweek
http://*Asiaweek*.com

BBC World Service (Asia-Pacific)
http://www.bbc.co.uk/worldservice/asiapacific/index.shtml
CNBC Asia
http://www.cnbcasia.com

Far Eastern Economic Review
http://www.feer.com

Time Asia
htpp://cnn.com/ASIANOW/time

Washington Post: Asia-Pacific
http://www.washingtonpost.com/wp-srv/inatl/asia.htm

General Links to Asian Newspapers

http://dir.yahoo.com/News_and_Media
/By_Region/Countries/ (very
comprehensive)
http://www.newspapers.com
(newspapers by country, worldwide)
http://www.newsdirectory.com/news/p
ress/as (Asian Newspapers)
http://www.members.spree.com/sip/wa
ytoshop/apacnews.htm

Individual Newspapers, by Country

Asahi Shimbun (Japan)
http://www.asahi.com/english/english.
html

Bangkok Post (Thailand)
http://bangkokpost.net/

*Burma Project: Burma Net News
(Myanmar/ Burma)*
http://www.soros.org/burma/burmanet
_news.html

Channel News Asia (Singapore)
http://www.channelnewsasia.com

China Daily (China)
http://www.chinadaily.com.cn.net/

Chosun Daily (Korea)
http://www.chosun.com

*Hong Kong Standard (Hong Kong,
China)*
http://online.hkstandard.com/

India Daily (India)
http://www.indiadaily.com/

Korea Times
http://www.koreatimes.co.kr/14_home
/199908/t40148.htm

Manila Bulletin (Philippines)
http://www.mb.com.ph/frntpage.asp

Myanmar Times (Myanmar/ Burma)
http://www.myanmar.com/myanmarti
mes/

*New Light of Myanmar (Myanmar/
Burma)*
http://www.myanmar.com/nlm/

New Straits Times (Malaysia)
http://www.nstpi.com.my/Current_Ne
ws/NST/nstindex

News Indonesia (Indonesia)
http://suratkabar.com/

People's Daily (China)
http://english.peopledaily.com.cn

Phnom Penh Post (Cambodia)
http://www.vais.net/~tapang/ppp/

Straits Times (Singapore)
http://straitstimes.asia1.com/

*South China Morning Post (Hong
Kong, China)*
http://www.scmp.com/

*Taipei Journal (formerly Free China
Journal, Taiwan)*
http://publish.gio.gov.tw/FCJ/fcj.html

The Hindu (India)
http://www.hinduonline.com

The Nation (Thailand)
http://www.nationmultimedia.com

The Star (Malaysia)
http://thestar.com.my/

The Times of India (India)
http://timesofindia.indiatimes.com

The Weekly Post (Japan)
http://www.weeklypost.com/

Vientiane Times (Lao PDR)
htpp://www.vientianetimes.com/Headl
ines.html

Other Resources and Materials

ACP-EU Courier
http://europa.eu.int/comm/developmen
t/publicat/courier/index_en.htm

*Carnegie Council on Ethics and
International Affairs (USA)*
http://www.carnegiecouncil.org
Encyclopaedia Britannica
http://www.Britannica.com

*Organization for Economic Co-
operation and Development (OECD)*
http://www.oecd.org

*United Nations Economic and Social
Commission for Asia and the Pacific*
http://unescap.org/

World Bank
http://www.worldbank.org/

Bibliography

Abad, M.C.
1996 'Re-engineering ASEAN', *Contemporary Southeast Asia*, 18.3: 237-53.

AEVG (Asia-Europe Vision Group)
1999 *For a Better Tomorrow: Asia-Europe Partnership in the 21st Century* (Korea: AEVG).

Ahmar, M.
2000 'Where is Pakistan Heading? Implications of the Coup d'Etat', *World Affairs*, 4.1: 62-82.

Algieri, Franco
1999 'The Coherence Dilemma of EU External Relations: The European Asia Policy', *Journal of the Asia-Pacific Economy*, 4.1: 81-99.

2000 'Asienpolitik', in Werner Weidenfeld and Wolfgang Wessels (eds.), *Jahrbuch der Europäischen Integration 1999/2000* (Institut für Europäische Politik, Europa Union Verlag GmbH, 2000): 215-20.

Anderson, Peter, Georg Wiessala and Christopher Williams (eds.)
2000 *New Europe in Transition* (London: Continuum).

Annan, Kofi
2000 'Globalisation Should Be a Positive Force for All', *The Independent*, Supplement: *Globalisation*, 12 December, p. 3.

Aspinwall, Mark
1999 'Teaching the European Union in China', *ECSA Review*, Spring: 16-17.

Augustine, St
2000 *The City of God* (trans. M. Dods; New York: The Modern Library).

Aung San Suu Kyi
1995 *Freedom from Fear* (London: Penguin Books).

1997 *The Voice of Hope: Conversations with Alan Clements, With Contributions by U Kyi Maung and U Tin U* (London: Penguin Books).

Avendon, John F.
1998 *In Exile from the Land of Snows: The Definitive Account of the Dalai Lama and Tibet since the Chinese Conquest* (Perennial [Harper Collins]).

Bartelson, Jens
2000 'Three Concepts of Globalisation', *International Sociology*, 15.2: 180-96.

Bauer, Edgar
1997 *Die Unberechenbare Weltmacht: China nach Deng Xiaoping* (Ullstein Tashenbuchverlag).

Bedini, Silvio A.
  2000   *The Pope's Elephant: An Elephant's Journey from Deep in India to the Heart of Rome* (New York: Penguin Books).
Beeson, Mark, and Kanishka Jayasuriya
  1998   'The Political Rationalities of Regionalism: APEC and the EU in Comparative Perspective', *The Pacific Review,* 11.3: 311-36.
Bell, Sandra
  2000   'A Survey of Engaged Buddhism in Britain', in Queen 2000: 397-422.
Benvenuti, Andrea
  1997–98   'Australian Responses to the Common Agricultural Policy, 1973–1993', *Australasian Journal of European Integration,* 1: 58-78.
Bodson, G.
  2000   *Cracking the Apocalypse Code* (Shaftesbury: Element).
Bonnet, Mercedes
  1999   'EU-ASEAN Relations', in Cosgrove-Sacks (ed.) 1999: 254-67.
Bourdet, Yves
  2001   'Laos in 2000', *Asian Survey* 41.1: 164-70.
Breazeale, Kennon (ed.)
  1999   'Thai Maritime Trade and the Ministry Responsible' in *From Japan to Arabia: Ayutthaya's Maritime Trade with Asia* (Bangkok: The Foundation for the Promotion of Social Sciences and Humanities Textbooks Project): 1-54.
Brenner, Rolf
  1992   'The European Community and the South Pacific', *The Courier*, 135: 54-55.
Bretherton, Charlotte, and John Vogler
  1999   *The European Union as a Global Actor* (London: Routledge).
Bridges, Brian
  1999   *Europe and the Challenge of the Asia Pacific: Change, Continuity and Crisis* (Cheltenham: Edward Elgar).
Brittan, Leon
  1999   'Europe/Asia Relations', *The Pacific Review,* 12.3: 491-98.
Buckley, Richard
  1993   *The Pacific Rim: Powerhouse of the 21st Century* (Understanding Global Issues; Cheltenham: European Schoolbooks Ltd).
  1998   *North and South Korea: The Last Ideological Frontier* (Understanding Global Issues; Cheltenham: European Schoolbooks Ltd).
  1999   *The New China: Joining the Wider World* (Understanding Global Issues; Cheltenham: European Schoolbooks Ltd).
Buruma, Ian
  2000   *God's Dust: A Modern Asian Journey* (London: Phoenix).
Busse, Nikolaus
  1991   'Constructivism and Southeast Asian Security', *The Pacific Review*, 1999, 12.1: 39-60.
Cacnio, Paul
  1996   'ASEM: Fostering Economic and Social Cooperation in Asia and Europe', *Bangkok Bank Monthly Review,* 37.3: 7-12.

CAEC (Council for Asia-Europe Cooperation)
1997 *The Rationale and Common Agenda for Asia-Europe Cooperation* (London: CAEC).

Camroux, David
2001 'The European Union Loses the Plot in Asia', *EURAsia Bulletin*, 5.10–11, October–November 2001 (Brussels: European Institute for Asian Studies, EIAS): 3-4.

Carnegie Council on Ethics and International Relations
1994–98 *Human Rights Dialogue* (11 vols.; New York; Carnegie Council on Ethics and International Relations).
2001 'The Successes and Failures of UN Intervention in East Timor' *Human Rights Dialogue*, Winter, 2.5: 12-13.

Cauquelin, Josiane, Paul Lim and Birgit Mayer-König
1998 *Asian Values: Encounter with Diversity* (Richmond: Curzon Publishers).

Chakravartty, Nikhil
1997 'Indian Democracy: Reflections and Challenges', *World Affairs*, 1.2: 80-90.

Chan, Joseph
1998 'Asian Values and Human Rights: An Alternative View' in Diamond and Plattner (eds.) 1998: 28-41.

Chandler, David P.
1999 *Brother Number One: A Political Biography of Pol Pot* (Boulder, CO: Westview Press).

Cheng, Li
2001 'China in 2000', *Asian Survey* 41.1: 71-90.

Chirativat, Suthiphand
1996 'ASEAN Economic Integration with the World through AFTA', *Journal of European Studies Chulalongkorn University,* 3 (Special Issue): 23-45.

Chirativat, Suthiphand, and Vera Erdmann-Kiefer
1998 'The First ASEM (Asia-Europe Meeting): Outcome and Perspectives', *Journal of European Studies, Journal Chulalongkorn University,* 1.1: 1-15.

Chirativat, Suthiphand, Carlo Filippini and Corrado Molteni (eds.)
1999 *ASEAN-EU Economic Relations: The Long-Term Potential Beyond the Recent Turmoil* (Conference Proceedings of the Chulalongkorn University European Studies Programme and Institute of Economic and Social Studies for East Asia; Milan: Bocconi University, EGEA).

Chirativat, Suthiphand, and Corrado Molteni (eds.)
2000 *EU-ASEAN Economic Relations: The Impact of the Asian Crisis on the European Economy and the Long-Term Potential* (Asia-Europe Studies Series, 1; Baden-Baden: Nomos).

Chirativat, Suthiphand, Franz Knipping, Poul Henrik Lassen and Chia Siow Yue
2001 *Asia-Europe on the Eve of the 21st Century* (Bangkok: Centre for European Studies at Chulalongkorn University/Institute of Southeast Asian Studies).

Christie, Kenneth, and Denny Roy (eds.)
2001 *The Politics of Human Rights in East Asia* (London: Pluto Press).

Commission of the European Communities

1976   *The Europe-Asia-Latin America Dialogue: Financial and Technical Co-operation 1976–1989* (Luxembourg: Office for Official Publications of the European Communities).

1982a   *Europe-Information: External Relations: The European Community and Australia* (55/82).

1982b   *Europe-Information: External Relations: The European Community and New Zealand* (56/82).

1984   *The European Community and Sri Lanka*, Europe Information, External Relations, No. 72/84, April, X/75/84-EN.

1986   *Europe-Information: External Relations: The EC and India* (Luxembourg: Office for Official Publications of the European Communities).

1987   *Europe-Information: External Relations: The EC and Nepal* (87/87, 159/X/87).

1988   *Draft Council Decision Approving the Conclusion by the Commission of the Agreement for Cooperation between the European Atomic Energy Community and the Government of Japan in the Field of Controlled Thermonuclear Fusion*, COM (1988) 603.

1989   *Amendments to the Proposal for a Council Regulation Relating to the Continued Import of New Zealand Butter into the UK on Special Terms*, COM (89) 441.

1991   *The Europe-Asia-Latin America Dialogue* (Luxembourg: Office for Official Publications of the European Communities).

1992   *Report from the Commission to the Council and Proposal for a Council Regulation Relating to the Continued Import of New Zealand Butter into the UK on Special Terms*, COM (92) 479.

1993a   *The Community and the Third World* (Europe on the Move Series; Luxembourg: Office for Official Publications of the European Communities).

1993b   *The External Relations of the European Community* (Europe on the Move Series; Luxembourg: Office for Official Publications of the European Communities).

1993c   *The European Union and Asia* (Europe on the Move Series; Luxembourg: Office for Official Publications of the European Communities).

1993d   *Special Rehabilitation Support Programme in Developing Countries*, COM (93) 204.

1994a   *Towards a New Asia Strategy*, COM (94) 314.

1994b   *European Commission Interactive Business Forum: Towards a New European Economic Strategy for Asia*, Summary of Proceedings (Brussels, 6 October 1994, in cooperation with the *Financial Times*).

1994c   *Stengthening the Mediterranean Policy of the European Union: Establishing a Euro-Mediterranean Partnership*, COM(94) 427.

1995a   *Europe and Japan: The Next Steps*, COM (1995) 73.

1995b   *A Long-Term Policy for China-Europe Relations*, COM (95) 279.

1995c   *A Level Playing Field for Direct Investment Worldwide*, COM (95) 42 fin.

1995d   *An Energy Policy for the European Union*, COM (95) 682.

1995e   *Europe: Partner of Asia. European Community Instruments for Economic Cooperation* (Luxembourg: Office for Official Publications of the European Communities).

1995f   *Preparation of the Associated Countries of Central and Eastern Europe for Integration into the Internal Market of the Union* (White Paper), COM (95) 163.

1995g   *Proposal for a Council Decision Concerning the Conclusion of the Co-operation Agreement between the European Community and the Socialist Republic of Vietnam*, COM (95) 305.

1996a   *Regarding the Asia-Europe Meeting (ASEM) to be held in Bangkok on 1-2 March 1996*, COM (96) 4.

1996b   *EU-India Enhanced Partnership*, COM (96) 275.

1996c   *Intensification of Dialogue and Co-operation with Asian Countries and Businesses on the Energy Sector*, COM (96) 308.

1996d   *Creating a New Dynamic in EU-ASEAN Relations*, COM (96) 314.

1996e   *Preparation and Coordination of the ASEM Follow-Up* (Luxembourg: Office for Official Publications of the European Communities).

1996f   *Investing in Asia's Dynamism. European Union Direct Investment in Asia* (Luxembourg: Office for Official Publications of the European Communities).

1996g   *The European Union and Asia- Background Report; Frontier-Free Europe Newsletter*, 4/1996: I/II (Luxembourg: Office for Official Publications of the European Communities).

1996h   *Investing in Asia's Dynamism. European Union Direct Investment in Asia* (Luxembourg: Office for Official Publications of the European Communities).

1996i   *Proposal for a Council Regulation Temporarily Withdrawing Access to Generalized Tariff Preferences for Industrial Goods from the Union of Myanmar*, COM (96) 711.

1997a   *Proposal to extend the Co-operation Agreement between the EU and the Association of Southeast Asian Nations (ASEAN) to the Socialist Republic of Vietnam*, COM (97) 2.

1997b   *Proposal for a Co-operation Agreement with Cambodia*, COM (97) 78.

1997c   *The European Union and Hong Kong: Beyond 1997*, COM (97) 171.

1997d   *Communication on a Europe-Asia Cooperation Strategy in the Field of Environment*, COM (97) 490.

1997e   *Perspectives and Priorities for the ASEM Process*, SEC (97) 1239.

1997f   *Commercial Policy and Relations with Education Programme (1996–1999)* (Luxembourg: Office for Official Publications of the European Communities).

1997g   *Alleviating Poverty: Twenty Years of European Community Support to Asia* (Luxembourg: Office for Official Publications of the European Communities).

1997h   *EU-Asia Relations: Higher Education* (Luxembourg: Office for Official Publications of the European Communities).

1998a   *Building a Comprehensive Partnership with China*, COM (98) 181.

1998b   European Union Policy towards the Republic of Korea, COM (98) 714.

1998c   *EU-ASEAN Relations: A Growing Partnership* (Luxembourg: Office for Official Publications of the European Communities).

1999a   *First Commission Report on Hong Kong*, COM (98) 796.

1999b   *Commission Working Document on Japan*, SEC (1999) 524.

1999c   *Proposal for a Council Decision Concerning the Conclusion of the Cooperation Agreement between the European Community and the People's Republic of Bangladesh*, COM (99) 155.

1999d   *Relations between the European Union and Macao: beyond 2000*, COM (1999) 484.

1999e   *PRASAC: Rural Development as a Priority* (Luxembourg: Office for Official Publications of the European Communities).

1999f   *European Union–China, Supporting China's Economic and Social Reforms* (Luxembourg: Office for Official Publications of the European Communities).

1999g   *First Annual Report by the European Commission on the Special Administrative Region of Hong Kong*, COM (98) 796.

1999h   *Proposal for a Council Regulation Concerning a Flight Ban and a Freeze of Funds in Respect of the Taliban in Afghanistan*, COM (1999) 662.

2000a   *Developing Closer Relations between Indonesia and the EU*, COM (2000) 50.

2000b   *Perspectives and Priorities for the ASEM Process (Asia-Europe Meeting) into the New Decade*, COM (2000) 241.

2000c   *Second Commission Report on Hong Kong*, COM (2000) 294.

2000d   *Accelerated Action Targeted at Major Communicable Diseases within the Context of Poverty Reduction*, COM (2000) 585 final.

2000e   *On the Implementation of Measures Intended to promote Observance of Human Rights and Democratic Principles in External Relations For 1996–1999*, COM (2000) 726.

2000f   *The European Union and the Kingdom of Cambodia* (Luxembourg: Office for Official Publications of the European Communities).

2000g   *The European Union and the Lao PDR.* (Luxembourg: Office for Official Publications of the European Communities).

2000h   *EU-Thai Economic Relations: Trade, Investment, Finance* (Luxembourg: Office for Official Publications of the European Communities).

2000i   *EU-Malaysia Relations: An Overview* (Luxembourg: Office for Official Publications of the European Communities).

2000j   *Developing Closer Relations between Indonesia and the European Union*, COM (2000) 50.

2000k   *The Response of the European Union to the Anti-Personnel Landmines Challenge* (Luxembourg: Office for Official Publications of the European Communities).

2000l   *The European Community's Development Policy*, COM (2000) 212.

2000m   *Report on the Implementation of the Communication 'Building a Comprehensive Partnership in China'*, COM (2000) 552.

2000n   *Proposal for a Council Regulation Prohibiting the Sale, Supply and Export to Burma/Myanmar of Equipment which Might Be Used for Internal Repression or Terrorism*, COM (2000) 299.

2000o   *Proposal for a Council Decision Concerning the Conclusion of the Protocol on the Extension of the Cooperation Agreement between the European Community and Brunei-Darussalam, Indonesia, Malaysia, the Philipines, Singapore, Thailand and Vietnam*, COM (2000) 423.

2000p   *Proposal for a Council Decision ... Amending the Agreement between the European Community and the Socialist Republic of Vietnam on Trade in Textile and Clothing Products*, COM (2000) 309.

2001a   *Third Commission Report on Hong Kong*, COM (2001) 431.

2001b   *First Commission Report on Macao*, COM (2001) 432.

2001c   *Communication from the Commission: Europe and Asia: A Strategic Framework for Enhanced Partnerships*, COM (2001) 469.

2001d   *Conflict Prevention and Preventative Action*, COM (2001) 211.

2001e   *The EU's Role in Promoting Human Rights and Democratisation in Third Countries*, COM (2001) 252.

2001f   *The Development of the External Service*, COM (2001) 381.

2001g   *Strengthening Cooperation with Third Countries in the Field of Higher Education*, COM (2001) 385.

2000h   *On Core Labour Standards*, COM (2001) 416.

2001i   *Programme for Action: Accelerated Action on HIV/AIDS, Malaria and Tuberculosis in the Context of Poverty Reduction*, COM (2001) 96.

2001j   *EU Strategy towards China: Implementation of the 1998 Communication and Future Steps for a more Effective EU Policy*, COM (2001) 265.

2001k   *Proposal for a Council Decision on the Conclusion of an Agreement between the European Community and Japan on Mutual Recognition in Relation to Conformity Assessment*, COM (2001) 25.

2001l   *Proposal for a Council Decision Concerning the Conclusion of the Agreement for Scientific and Technological Cooperation between the European Community and the Repulic of India*, COM (2001) 448.

1997–2001 *General Reports on the Activities of the European Union* (Luxembourg: Office for Official Publications of the European Communities).

Confucius
1993   *The Analects* (The World's Classics; Oxford: Oxford University Press).

Coogan, Michael D.
2001   *The Oxford History of the Biblical World* (Oxford: Oxford University Press).

Corn, Charles
1999   *The Scents of Eden: A History of the Spice Trade* (New York: Kodansha International).

Cosgrove-Sacks, Carol
1999   *The European Union and Developing Countries* (London: Macmillan).

Council of Ministers of the European Union
1971   Council Regulation (EEC) No 2785/76 of 16 November 1976 on the Conclusion of the Commercial Cooperation Agreement between the European Economic Community and the People's Republic of Bangladesh, *OJ* L 319/1, 19 November 1976.

1979a   Council Regulation (EEC) No. 2558/79 of 30 October 1979 Concerning the Conclusion of the Agreement between the European Economic Community and the People's Republic of Bangladesh on Trade in Textile Products, *OJ* L 298/38, 26 November 1979.

1979b   Council Regulation (EEC) No. 2561/79 of 30 October 1979 Concerning the Conclusion of the Agreement between the European Economic Community and the Islamic Republic of Pakistan on Trade in Textile

Products, *OJ* L 298/143, 26 November 1979.

1981   Council Regulation (EEC) No. 3246/81 of 26 October 1981 on the Conclusion of the Agreement for Commercial and Economic Cooperation between European Economic Community and India, *OJ* L 328/5, 16 November 1981.

1996a   Decisions Concerning the Conclusion of Cooperation Agreements with Vietnam and Nepal, *OJ* L 136, 1996 and *OJ* L 137, 1996.

1996b   Common Position on East Timor, *OJ* L 168, 1996.

1996c   Joint Action of 5 March 1996 adopted by the Council on the Basis of Article J.3 of the Treaty on European Union on Participation of the European Union in the Korean Peninsula Energy Development Organization (KEDO) (96/195/CFSP) No. L 63/1, 13 March 1996.

1996d   Council Decision of 20 May 1996 Concerning the Conclusion of the Co-operation Agreement between the European Community and the Kingdom of Nepal (96/354/EC), *OJ* L 137/14, 8 June 1996.

1999   Council Decision of 13 September 1999 on the Provisional Application of the Agreement between the European Community and the Kingdom of Nepal on Trade in Textile Products (2000/72/EC), *OJ* L 32/1, 7 February 2000.

Dae-Jung, Kim

1994   'Is Culture Destiny?', *Foreign Affairs,* 73.6: 189-94.

2000a   'Opening Address at the Third Asia-Europe Meeting' (Seoul: Media and PR Team, Office for the Third Asia-Europe Meeting).

2000b   'Closing Remarks at the Third Asia-Europe Meeting' (Seoul: Media and PR Team, Office for the Third Asia-Europe Meeting).

Daquila, Teofilo C.

1997   'Obstacles to Closer Trade and Investment Links: An ASEAN Viewpoint', in Tan and Chia Siow Yue (eds.) 1997: 103-34.

Davies, Norman

1996   *Europe: A History* (Oxford: Oxford University Press).

De Bartillat, Christian, and Alain Roba

2000   *Métamorphoses d'Europe: Trente siècles d'iconographie* (Brussels: Fondation Pout Une Civilisation Européenne, Editions Bartillat).

De Bary, W. Theodore

1998a   *Asian Values and Human Rights: A Confucian Communitarian Perspective* (Cambridge, MA: Harvard University Press).

1998b   'Confucianism and Human Rights in China', in Diamond and Plattner (eds.) 1998: 42-54.

De Bary, W. Theodore, and Weiming Tu (eds.)

1998   *Confucianism and Human Rights* (New York: Columbia University Press).

Dent, Christopher M.

1999   *The European Union and East Asia: An Economic Relationship* (London: Routledge).

Diamond, Larry, and Marc F. Plattner (eds.)

1998   *Democracy in East Asia* (Baltimore: The Johns Hopkins University Press).

Dimbleby, Jonathan
    1997   *The Last Governor: Chris Patten and the Handover of Hong Kong* (London: Little, Brown & Company).
Dinan, Desmond
    1999   *Ever Closer Union* (London: Macmillan, 2nd edn).
Dosch, Jörn
    2001   'The ASEAN-EU Relations: An Emerging Pillar of the New International Order?', in Chirathivat *et al.* (eds.) 2001: 57-71.
Drysdale, P., and D. Vines
    1998   *Europe, East Asia and APEC* (Cambridge: Cambridge University Press).
Duve, Freimut
    1998   'Universality of Human Rights-European Superiority or European Experience?', *World Affairs*, 2.4: 45-49.
Ebrey, Patricia
    2000   'The Chinese Family and the Spread of Confucian Values', in Gilbert Rosman, *The East Asian Region* (Preston: UCLAN): 42-58.
ECOSOC (Economic and Social Committee of the European Union)
    1989   'Opinion on the Relations between the European Community and the Newly Industrialising Countries of Southeast Asia' (Document CES 439/89).
Eglin, Michaela
    1997   'China's Entry into the WTO with Help from the EU', *International Affairs,* 73.3: 489-508.
EIAS (European Institute for Asian Studies)
    1996   *Understanding Asian Values* (Brussels: EIAS).
    2000   *EURASIA Bulletin* (Brussels: EIAS).
    2001   *EURASIA Bulletin* (Brussels: EIAS).
Elijah, Annmarie, Philomena Murray and Carolyn O'Brien
    2000   'Divergence and Convergence: The Development of European Union–Australia Relations' (Contemporary Europe Research Centre Working Paper series No. 3/2000; Melbourne: CERC).
EU Delegation to Indonesia
    2000   *The EU and Indonesia: Trade Relations* (Jakarta, PI09en, updated 27 June).
European Commission (see Commission of the European Communities)
European Parliament
    1992   *Resolution on Economic and Trade Relations between the European Community and ASEAN*, OJ C 125/269 (18.5.92 – A 3-0119/92).
    1996   'EU-ASEAN Relations: New Dynamic for EU Presence in Asia'*, EUR-OP NEWS*, 5.3: 2.
    1997   *Concerns over Hong Kong*, in *EUR-OP NEWS*, April 1997.
    2001   Committee on Foreign Affairs, Human Rights, Common Security and Defence Policy*: Report on the Commission Working Document: Perspectives and Priorities for the ASEM Process (Asia Europe Meeting) into the New Decade,* COM (2000) 241–C5-0505/2000–2000/2243 (COS), 31 May 2001, Final A5-0207/2001, RR\441407EN.doc, PE No.: 294.868.
Federal Government
    1994   *Concept on Asia*, 1994: 48-53 (*Inter Nationes*, ST 2-2001).

Fenby, Jonathan
    2000   *Dealing with the Dragon. A Year in the New Hong Kong* (New York: Arcade Publishing).

Ferdinand, Peter
    1995   'Economic and Diplomatic Interactions between the EU and China', in Richard Grant (ed.), *The European Union and China: A European Strategy for the Twenty-First Century* (London: Royal Institute for International Affairs, RIIA): 26-40.

Field, Heather
    1997   'Regional Integration in Europe Versus Globalisation and Closer Europe-Asia Relations', in Holland and Mikic (eds.) 1997: 29-45.
    1997–98 'Editorial', in *Australasian Journal of European Integration*, I: xi-xviii.

Filippini, Carlo
    2000   'The Impact of the Asian Crisis on the European Economy', in Chirativat, and Molteni (eds.) 2000: 9-34.

Fink, Christina
    2001   *Living Silence. Burma under Military Rule* (London: Zed Books).

Foreign and Commonwealth Office
    2000   *Focus International: Burma: 10 Years of Repression* (London: FCO).

Forster, Anthony
    1999   'The European Union in South-East Asia: Continuity and Change in Turbulent Times', *International Affairs*, 75.4: 743-58.
    2000   'Evaluating the EU-ASEM Relationship: A Negotiated Order Approach', *Journal of European Public Policy*, 7.5 (special issue): 787-805.

Franck, I.M. and D.M. Brownstone
    1984   *To The Ends of the Earth: The Great Travel and Trade Routes in Human History* (New York: Facts on File Publications).

Franz, Uli
    2000   *Im Schatten des Himmels* (Munich: Deutscher Taschenbuch Verlag, dtv).

Freeman, Nick
    2001   'The Rise and Fall of Foreign Direct Investment in Laos, 1988–2000', *Post-Communist Economies*, 13.1: 101-19.

Funabashi, Yoishi
    1993   'The Asianization of Asia', *Foreign Affairs*, 72.5: 75-85.

Fukasaku, Kiichiro, Fukunari Kimura and Urata Shujiro (eds.)
    1998   *Asia and Europe: Beyond Competing Regionalism* (Sussex Academic Press).

Galtung, J.
    1973   *The European Community: A Superpower in the Making* (Oslo: Universitetsforlaget).

Gasteyger, Curt
    1997   'The EU: Paper Tiger or Modern Power?', *World Affairs*, 1.4: 94-108.

Gilson, Julie
    2000   *Japan and the European Union* (London: Macmillan).

Glöckler, G.
    1999   'A 'Single Voice' for Europe's Single Currency? EMU and International Monetary Relations', *Current Politics and Economics of Europe*, 8.2: 187-206.

Godement, François
  1997   *The New Asian Renaissance: From Colonialism to the Post-Cold War* (London: Routledge).
  1999   *The Downsizing of Asia* (London: Routledge).
Gottschalk, Louis, and Donald Lach
  1954   *Europe and the Modern World Since 1870* (Chicago: Scott, Foresman and Company).
Grilli, Enzo R.
  1993   'EC and Asia: Growing Farther Apart', in *The EC and the Developing Countries* (Cambridge: Cambridge University Press): 271-95.
Gullick, J.M.
  1995   *Adventures and Encounters: Europeans in South-East Asia* (Oxford: Oxford University Press).
Guptara, Prabhu
  2001   'Age of Globalisation: Problems and Prospects', *World Affairs,* 4.4: 114-25.
Hänggi, Heiner
  1999   'ASEM and the Construction of the New Triad', *Journal of the Asia-Pacific Economy,* 4.1: 56-80.
Hainaut, Carol, and Pascal Kauffmann
  1999   'Where Asian Emerging Currencies Misaligned?', in Sang-Gon Lee and Pierre-Bruno Ruffini (eds.), *The Global Integration of Europe and East Asia* (Cheltenham: Edward Elgar): 149-67.
Haji-Ahmad, Zakaria, and Baladas Ghoshal
  1999   'The Political Future of ASEAN after the Asian Crisis', *International Affairs,* 75.4: 759-78.
Harris, Ian (ed.)
  1999   *Buddhism and Politics in Twentieth-Century Asia* (London: Pinter).
Harvey, Peter
  1990   *An Introduction to Buddhism: Teachings, History and Practices* (Cambridge: Cambridge University Press).
  2000   *An Introduction to Buddhist Ethics* (Cambidge: Cambridge University Press).
Hay, Denys
  1968   *Europe: The Emergence of an Idea* (Edinburgh: Edinburgh University Press).
Henkin, Louis
  1998   'Confucianism, Human Rights and "Cultural Relativism"', in De Bary and Tu 1998: 308-14.
Hernandez, Carolina
  1998   'Values and Civilisations', in Maull *et al.* (eds.) 1998: 32-34.
Herodotus
  1996   *The Histories* (trans. Aubrey de Sélincourt (London: Penguin Books).
Hershock, Peter D.
  2000   'Dramatic Intervention: Human Rights from a Buddhist Perspective', *Philosophy East and West*, 50.1: 9-33.
Hill, Christopher
  1993   'The Capabilities-Expectations Gap or Conceptualising Europe's

International Role', *Journal of Common Market Studies*, 31.3: 305-28.

Hill, Christopher, and Karen E. Smith (eds.)
    2000   *European Foreign Policy: Key Documents* (London: Routledge).

Holland, M.
    1995   'Bridging the Capability-Expectations Gap: A Case Study of the CFSP Joint Action on South Africa', *Journal of Common Market Studies*, 33.4: 555-72.

Holland, Martin, and Mia Mikic (eds.)
    1997   *European Union and Asia: Some Aspects of the Political and Economic Relations at the End of the Millennium* (Proceedings of the Third International Conference, EU Studies Association of New Zealand, 17–18 November 1997).

Hu, Weixing
    1996   'China and Asian Regionalism: Challenge and Policy Choice', *Journal of Contemporary China*, 5.11: 43-56.

Hunt-Perry, Patricia, and Lyn Fine
    2000   'All Buddhism Is Engaged: Thich Nhat Hanh and the Order of Interbeing', in Queen (ed.) 2000: 35-66.

Huntington, Samuel P.
    1993   'The Clash of Civilisations?', *Foreign Affairs*, 72.3: 22-49 (see also the response to this article, *Foreign Affairs* 72.4: 2-27 and Huntington's reply to his critics, *Foreign Affairs* 72.5: 186).
    1998   *The Clash of Civilisations and the Remaking of World Order* (London: Touchstone).

Hutchings, Graham
    2000   *Modern China: A Companion to a Rising Power* (London: Penguin Books).

Huxley, Tim
    2001   'Singapore in 2000', *Asian Survey* 41.1: 201-207.

Ibrahim, Anwar
    1996   *The Asian Renaissance* (Kuala Lumpur: Times Books International).

Innes-Miller, J.
    1969   *The Spice Trade of the Roman Empire 29 BC–AD 64* (Oxford: Clarendon Press).

International Commission of Jurists
    1992   *Countdown to 1997: Report of a Mission to Hong Kong* (Geneva: ICJ).

Jackson, Karl D.
    1999   *Asian Contagion: The Causes and Consequences of a Financial Crisis* (Boulder CO: Westview Press).

Jacobsen, Michael, and Ole Bruun (eds.)
    2000   *Human Rights and Asian Values* (Richmond: Curzon Press).

Jonghwan Ko
    2000a   'Why Not a Free Trade Agreement between Asia and Europe at the ASEM Level? (Paper for the 5th ECSA World Conference 'Enlarging the EU', Brussels, 14–15 December 2000) (unpublished at time of writing).
    2000b   'Should We Be Afraid of Trade Liberalisation between Europe and Asia through ASEM?: Analysis of its Impact using a CGE Model', in *Proceedings of the 3rd Seoul ASEM and Asia-Europe Relations, 29–30*

September 2000 (Seoul: Korean Society for Contemporary European Studies): 37-61.

Jordan, Bill
1998   'Jobs, Trade Union Rights, Markets and Democracy', *World Affairs*, 2.4: 50-59.

Kapur, H.
1990   *Distant Neighbours: China and Europe* (London: Pinter).

Kapur, J.C.
1999   'India. A Cosmic Vision For the Sixth Millennium', *World Affairs*, 3.4 (Special Supplement): 1-64.

Kausikan, Bilahari
1993   'Asia's Different Standard', *Foreign Policy*, No. 92 (autumn): 24-41.
1998   'The "Asian Values" Debate: A View from Singapore', in Diamond and Plattner (eds.) 1998: 17-27.

Kelly, David
1998   'The Chinese Search for Freedom as a Universal Value', in Kelly and Reid (eds.) 1998: 93-119.

Kelly, David, and Anthony Reid (eds.)
1998   *Asian Freedoms* (Cambridge: Cambridge University Press).

Keown, Damien V.
1995   'Are there "Human Rights" in Buddhism?' *Journal of Buddhist Ethics*, 2: 3-27.

Keown, Damien, Charles S. Prebish, and Wayne R. Husted (eds.)
1998   *Buddhism and Human Rights* (Richmond: Curzon Press).

Kim, Samuel S.
2001   'North Korea in 2000', *Asian Survey*, 41.1: 25-26.

Kirpalani, V.H. Manek, and Hannu Seristo
1998   'European Union and India: Potential for More Trade and Investment', *World Affairs*, 2.1: 88-98.

Krause, Joachim, Bernhard May and Ulrich Niemann (eds.)
1999   *Asia, Europe and the Challenges of Globalisation*, (Proceedings of the First Asia-Europe Foundation Summer School in Reutlingen (Germany), 12–24 July 1998; Berlin: Research Institute of the German Society/ Foreign Affairs).

Kremmer, C.
1997   *Stalking the Elephant Kings: In Search of Laos* (Honolulu: University of Hawaii Press).

Lach, Donald, F.
1994   *Asia in the Making of Europe*. I. *The Century of Discovery* (Books 1 and 2); II. *A Century of Wonder* (Books 1 to 3) (Chicago: University of Chicago Press).

Lach, Donald F., and Carol Flaumenhaft
1965   *Asia on the Eve of Europe's Expansion* (Englewood Cliffs, NJ: Prentice Hall).

Lach, Donald F., and Edwin J. Van Kley
1998   *Asia in the Making of Europe*. III. *A Century of Advance* (Books 1 to 4) (Chicago: University of Chicago Press).

Larner, John
　2001　　　*Marco Polo and the Discovery of the World* (New Haven: Yale University Press).

Lassen, Poul Henrik, with Suthiphand Chirativat
　1999　　　*European Studies in Asia* (Bangkok: Centre for European Studies, Chulalongkorn University).

Laursen, F.
　1991　　　'The European Community in the World Context: Civilian Power or Superpower?', *Futures,* (September): 747-59.

Lee, Chonngwha
　2000　　　'Trade and Investment Profiles in the ASEM Process: Issues and Prospects', in *Proceedings of the 3rd Seoul ASEM and Asia-Europe Relations, 29–30 September 2000* (Seoul: Korean Society for Contemporary European Studies): 37-61.

Leifer, Michael
　1999　　　'The ASEAN Peace Process: A Category Mistake', *The Pacific Review,* 12.1: 25-38.

Leong, Stephen
　1997　　　'ASEAN-EU Relations: The Political and Security Dimensions', *Journal of European Studies Chulalongkorn University*, 5.2: 17-25.

Lim, Paul
　1999a　　'Political Issues in EU-ASEAN Relations', *Panorama: Insights into Southeast Asian and European Affairs* 1/1999: 1-41 (Manila: Konrad-Adenauer Foundation).

　1999b　　'The Unfolding Asia-Europe Meeting (ASEM) Process: Issues for ASEM III', *Briefing Papers, European Institute for Asian Studies* (BP 99/04: 1-17, Brussels: EIAS).

　2000　　　'Beyond Economic Cooperation: Prospects for Mutual Social, Cultural and Educational Ties', in *Proceedings of the 3rd Seoul ASEM and Asia-Europe Relations, 29–30 September 2000* (Seoul: Korean Society for Contemporary European Studies): 109-33.

Lincoln, Edward J.
　1999　　　'Asian Countries and Globalization', in Krause *et al.* (eds.) 1999: 115-26.

Lloyd, P.J., and L.S. Williams (eds.)
　1998　　　*International Trade and Migration in the APEC Region* (Oxford: Oxford University Press).

Losserre, Philippe, and Hellmut Schütte
　1999　　　*Strategies for Asia-Pacific: Beyond the Crisis* (Basingstoke: Macmillan).

Low, Linda
　1996　　　'Recent Developments on APEC: Perspectives and Implications for ASEAN-EU Economic Cooperation', *Journal of European Studies, Chulalongkorn University*, 3, Special Issue: 73-98.

　1998　　　*The Political Economy of a City-State: Government-made Singapore* (Oxford: Oxford University Press).

Maclay, Carolyn
　1996　　　'How Thailand Pulled off the Perfect Meetings Coup' (Bangkok: Government of Thailand).

Mahani Zainal Abidin
    1999   'The Significance of the Economic and Currency Crisis on ASEAN-EU Trade and Investment Relationship', in Chirativat *et al.* (eds.) 1999: 47-75.

Mahbubani, Kishore
    1992   'The West and the Rest', *The National Interest*, summer (Washington DC: National Affairs Inc.).
    1993   'Dangers of Decadence: What the Rest Can Teach the West', *Foreign Affairs*, 72.4: 10-14.
    1995   'The Pacific Way', *Foreign Affairs,* 74.1: 100-11.
    1998a   'The Pacific Way', in *Asia Rising or Falling: A Foreign Affairs Reader* (Council on Foreign Relations): 87.
    1998b   *Can Asians Think?* (Kuala Lumpur: Times Books International).

Mallet, Victor
    1999   *The Trouble with Tigers: The Rise and Fall of Southeast Asia* (London: Harper Collins).

Malouf, David
    1993   *Remembering Babylon* (London: Chatto & Windus Ltd).

Manning, Robert A., and Paula Stern
    1994   'The Myth of the Pacific Community', *Foreign Affairs,* 73.6: 79-93.

Marbett, Ian
    1998   'Buddhism and Freedom', in Kelly and Reid (eds.) 1998: 19-36.

Mason, Colin
    2000   *A Short History of Asia* (London: Macmillan).

Mathou, Thierry
    2001   'Bhutan in 2000', *Asian Survey* 41.1: 131-37.

Maull, Hanns, with Gerald Segal and Jusuf Wanandi (eds.):
    1998   *Europe and the Asia Pacific* (London: Routledge).

McCormick, John
    1999   *Understanding the European Union* (London: Macmillan).

McMahon, Joseph A.
    1998   'ASEAN and the Asia-Europe Meeting: Strengthening the European Union's Relationship with South-East Asia', *European Foreign Affairs Review,* 3: 233-51.

Media and Public Relations Team Office for the Third Asia-Europe Meeting
    2000a   *ASEM Roundtable on Globalization.*
    2000b   *Initiative to Address the Digital Divide.*
    2000c   *New Initiative* (DUO, ASEM Fellowship Programme).
    2000d   *Seoul Declaration for Peace on the Korean Peninsula* (Seoul: Media and Public Relations Team Office for the Third Asia-Europe Meeting).

Milner, Anthony, and Mary Quilty (eds.)
    1996   *Australia in Asia: Communities of Thought* (Melbourne: Oxford University Press).

Milton, Giles
    1999   *Nathaniel's Nutmeg* (London: Hodder & Stoughton).
    2001   *The Riddle and the Knight: In Search of Sir John Mandeville* (London: Sceptre; Hodder & Stoughton).

Ministry for Foreign Affairs, Sweden
   1999   *Our Future with Asia: Proposal for a Swedish Asia Strategy* (The Asia
             Strategy Project; Stockholm: Regeringskansliet; original title: *Framtid
             med Asien. Förslag till en svensk Asienstrategi*).
Muntharbhorn, Vitit
   1998   *ASEM Summitry. The Asia-Europe Meeting (ASEM) 1996 and Beyond*
             (Bangkok: Child Rights, Asianet and the Faculty of Law, Chulalongkorn
             University).
Murray, P.
   2000   *Challenge Europe Online Journal*, 21 November. http://www.theepc.be/
             Challenge_Europe/text/memo.asp?ID=187).
Nagai-Berthrong, John H., and Evelyn Nagai-Berthrong
   2000   *Confucianism: A Short Introduction* (Oxford: Oneworld Publications).
Nakamura Hajime and P.P.Wiener
   1984   *Ways of Thinking of Eastern Peoples: India, China, Tibet, Japan* (repr.;
             Honolulu: University of Hawaii Press [1962]).
Narine, Shaun
   1999   'ASEAN into the Twenty-First Century: Problems and Prospects', *The
             Pacific Review,* 12.3: 357-80.
Nugent, Neill
   1999   *The Government and Politics of the European Union* (London,
             Macmillan, 4th edn).
Nuttall, Sarah
   1997   'Nationalism, Literature and Identity in South Africa and Australia',
             Australian Studies 12.2, winter: 58-68.
Nuyen, Tuan
   1999   'Chung Yung and the Greek Conception of Justice', *Journal of Chinese
             Philosophy* , 26.2: 187-202.
O'Brian, Nicholas
   2001   'ASEM: Moving from an Economic to a Political Dialogue?' (European
             Institute for Asian Studies, Briefing Paper 01/02, September, Brussels).
Osborne, Milton
   1997   *Southeast Asia: An Introductory History* (St Leonards, New South Wales:
             Allen & Unwin, 7th edn).
   2000   *The Mekong: Turbulent Past, Uncertain Future* (St Leonards, New South
             Wales: Allen & Unwin).
Pagden, Anthony
   2001   *Peoples and Empires: A Short History of European Migration, Explora-
             tion and Conquest, from Greece to the Present* (New York: The Modern
             Library).
Pattugalan, Gina
   1999   'The European Union in Southeast Asia: Trends, Shifts and Issues', in
             Panorama: Insights into Southeast Asian and European Affairs 1/1999:
             43-65 (Manila: Konrad-Adenauer Foundation).
Patten, Chris
   1998   *East and West* (London: Macmillan).
   2000   External Relations: Demands, Constraints and Priorities, a 'non-paper' of
             10 June 2000, source: http://www.radicalparty.org/monitor/patten-e.html

Pelkmans, Jacques (ed.)
1996   'Understanding Values in Asia', in *Europe-Asia Forum, Venice, 18–19 January 1996* (Reference Paper, Working Group 4, European Institute for South and Southeast Asian Studies, Brussels).

Pelkmans, Jacques, and Hiroko Shinkai (eds.)
1997   *ASEM: How Promising a Partnership?* (Occasional Paper, No. 2, European Institute for Asian Studies, Brussels).
1998   *APEC and Europe* (Occasional Paper, No. 3, European Institute for Asian Studies, Brussels).

Pertierra, Raul
1998   'The Market' in Asian Values', in Cauquelin *et al.* (eds.) 1998: 118-38.

Petchsiri, Apirat
1987   *Eastern Importation of Western Criminal Law* (Publications of the Comparative Criminal Law Project, 17; Littleton, CO: Fred B. Rothman & Co.).

Pfetsch, Frank R.
2000   'The Politics of Regional Integration: Europe and Asia Compared', in *Proceedings of the 3rd Seoul ASEM and Asia-Europe Relations, 29–30 September 2000* (Seoul: Korean Society of Contemporary European Studies): 160-76.

Phatharodom, Vimolvan
1998   'EU and ASEAN in the 1990s: A New Era of Relationship', *Journal of European Studies Chulalongkorn University*, 6.2: 59-83.

Piening, Christopher
1997   *Global Europe* (Boulder, CO: Lynne Rienner).

Pisani, Elisabeth
1996   'Asia Going too Fast for Eurocrats', *Asia Times*, 11 December.

Pou-Serradell, Victor
1996   'The Asia-Europe Meeting (ASEM): A Historical Turning Point in Relations Between the Two Regions', *European Foreign Affairs Review*, 2: 185-210.

Preston, P.W., with Julie Gilson
2001   *The European Union and East Asia Inter-Regional Linkages in a Changing Global System* (Cheltenham: Edward Elgar).

Prodi, Romano
2000   *Europe As I See It* (Oxford: Blackwell; Polity Press).

Queen, Christopher S. (ed.)
2000   *Engaged Buddhism in the West* (Boston: Wisdom Publications).

Ramdas, L., M. Ahmar and Y. Samad
2001   'South Asia: A Search for Solutions', *World Affairs*, 4.4: 26-42.

Ramstetter, Eric D.
2000   'Survey of Recent Developments', *Bulletin of Indonesian Economic Studies* 36:3: 3-45.

Ravenhill, John
1998   'The European Union and Asia-Pacific Security', in Holland and Mikic (eds.) 1998: 11-17.
2000   'APEC Adrift: Implications for Economic Regionalism in Asia and the Pacific', *The Pacific Review*, 13.2: 319-33.

Reid, Anthony
    1998   'Merdeka: The Concept of Freedom in Indonesia', in Kelly and Reid
                (eds.) 1998: 141-60.
Ribes, Jean-Paul
    2000   *Die Flucht des lebenden Buddha. Der 17. Karmapa und die Zukunft
                Tibets* (Munich: Ullstein).
Richards, Gareth A., and Colin Kirkpatrick
    1999   'Reorienting Interregional Cooperation in the Global Political Economy:
                Europe's East Asian Policy', *Journal of Common Market Studies,* 37.4:
                683-710.
Royal Thai Government
    1996a   Asia-Europe Meeting, Bangkok, 1–2 March 1996: *PM Banharn Silpa-
                Archa's Opening Address* (Bangkok: Ministry of Foreign Affairs): 11-19.
    1996b   Asia-Europe Meeting, Bangkok, 1–2 March 1996: *The Asia-EU Dialogue*
                (Bangkok: Ministry of Foreign Affairs): 1-13.
    1996c   Asia-Europe Meeting, Bangkok, 1–2 March 1996: *Asia-Europe Meeting:
                Dynamic Partners in the 21st Century* (Bangkok: Ministry of Foreign
                Affairs): 1-6.
    1996d   Asia-Europe Meeting, Bangkok, 1–2 March 1996: *The Rationale for the
                ASEM* (Bangkok: Ministry of Foreign Affairs): 28-33.
Rüland, Jürgen
    1996   *The Asia-Europe Meeting (ASEM): Towards a New Euro-Asian
                Relationship* (Rostock).
    1997   'Asian Values and Liberal Democracy: A European Perspective', *Journal
                of European Studies Chulalongkorn University*, 5.2: 71-88.
    2001   'The EU as an Inter-Regional Actor: The Asia-Europe Meeting', in
                Chirathivat *et al.* (eds.) 2001: 43-53.
Sabhasri, Chayodom
    1999   'Euro and Asia', *Journal of European Studies Chulalongkorn University,*
                7.1: 34-51.
Said, Edward
    1978   *Orientalism* (London: Penguin Books).
Sakwa, Richard, and Anne Stevens (eds.)
    2000   *Contemporary Europe* (Basingstoke: Macmillan).
Santer, Jacques
    1996   'European Union and Japan: Common Interests and Shared Challenges'
                European Access No. 6 (December): 8-11.
Saravanamuttu, Paikiasothy
    2000   'Sri Lanka in 1999', *Asian Survey*, 40.1: 219-25.
Schiavone, Giuseppe
    1989   'Western Europe and South-East Asia: Partners in a Pacific Age?', in
                Giuseppe Schiavone (ed.) *Western Europe and South-East Asia. Co-
                operation or Competition* (London: Macmillan).
    2000   'Regional Integration Arrangements in Europe and Asia: An Attempt At
                A Comparative Survey', in *Proceedings of the 3rd Seoul ASEM and Asia-
                Europe Relations, 29–30 September 2000* (Seoul: Korean Society for
                Contemporary European Studies): 199-214.

Segal, Gerald
 1993 *The Fate of Hong Kong* (London: Simon and Schuster).
 1997 'From Tiger to Poodle?', *Times Higher Education Supplement*, 20 June
     1997: 17-18.
 1999 *Towards Recovery in Pacific Asia* (London: Routledge).
Sesser, Stan
 1994 *The Lands of Charm and Cruelty* (New York: Vintage; Random House).
Severino, Rodolfo C. Jr
 1999a 'ASEAN and the Growth of Regional Cooperation in Southeast Asia'
     World Affairs 3.3: 14-22.
 1999b 'No Alternative to Regionalism', in *Panorama: Insights into Southeast
     Asian and European Affairs* 1/1999: 67-78 (Manila: Konrad-Adenauer
     Foundation).
Sewell, John W.
 1998 'Challenges of Globalization', *Human Rights Dialogue,* 11/98: 7-8 (New
     York: Carnegie Council on Ethics and International Affairs).
Shambaugh, David
 1996 *China and Europe, 1949–1995* (University of London, Research Notes
     and Studies No. 11/ 1996; London: School of Oriental and African
     Studies, SOAS).
Sheridan, Greg
 2000 *Asian Values, Western Dreams* (London: Allen and Unwin).
Singh, Jaswant
 2000 'India in a Changing World', *World Affairs,* 4.2: 14-20.
Singh, Manmohan
 1962 'India and the European Common Market', *Journal of Common Market
     Studies,* 1.3: 263-77.
Snitwongse, Kusuma
 1996 'Integrating Southeast Asia through an Expanded ASEAN', *Journal of
     European Studies Chulalongkorn University*, 3, Special Issue: 11-21.
So, Alvin S.
 2000 'Hong Kong's Problematic Democratic Transition', *The Journal of Asian
     Studies*, 59.2, May: 359-81.
Spence, Jonathan
 1998 *The Chan's Great Continent: China in Western Minds* (London: Penguin
     Books).
Spencer, Jonathan
 2000 *A Sinhala Village in a Time of Trouble* (Oxford: Oxford University
     Press).
Stubbs, Richard
 2000 'Signing on to Liberalization: AFTA and the Politics of Regional
     Economic Cooperation', *The Pacific Review,* 13.2: 297-318.
Sundaram, G
 1997 *India and the EU* (New Dehli: Allied Publishers Ltd).
Tan, Joseph L.H., and Chia Siow Yue (eds.)
 1997 *ASEAN and EU: Forging New Linkages and Strategic Alliances* (Paris:
     OECD Development Centre; Singapore: Institute of Southeast Asian
     Studies).

Tang, Jiaxuan
    2000   'China in a Changing World', *World Affairs*, 4.3: 14-30.
Thanh-Dam, Truong
    1998   ' "Asian" Values and the Heart of Understanding: A Buddhist View', in Cauquelin *et al.* (eds.) 1998: 43-69.
Thio Li-ann
    1997   'Human Rights and Asian Values: At the Periphery of ASEAN-EU Relations?', *European Studies Journal Chulalongkorn University*, 5.2: 27-70.
Thongswasdi, Tarnthong (ed.)
    1993   'Thailand and the European Community, New Dimensions of Inter-dependence', *Journal of European Studies, Chulalongkorn University, 1, Special Issue* (Bangkok: CUESP).
Tingsabadh, Charit
    1996   'What ASEAN Might Learn from EU Environmental Management', *Journal of European Studies, Chulalongkorn University*, 3, Special Issue: 137-41.
    1999   'Notes on ASEAN-EU Cooperation on Environmental Issues', in Chirativat *et al.* (eds.) 1999: 181-87.
Tsang, Steve
    1997   *Hong Kong: An Appointment with China* (London: I.B. Tauris).
Ul-Haq, Obaid
    1999   'ASEAN: Search for Regional Security in Southeast Asia', *World Affairs*, 3.3: 24-39.
Vande Walle, Willy
    1998   'The Encounter Between Europe and Asia in Pre-colonial Times', in Cauquelin *et al.* (eds.) 1998: 164-200.
Vandenborre, Joost
    1999   'India and the EU', in Cosgrove-Sacks (ed.) 1999: 268-83.
Vijapur, Abdulrahim P.
    1993   'The Islamic Concept of Human Rights and the International Bill of Rights: The Dilemma of Muslim States', in *Turkish Yearbook of Human Rights* 15 (Ankara).
    1998   'Diversity of Concepts of Human Rights', *World Affairs*, 2.4: 22-35.
Vijapur, P.A., Zhu Muzhi, Freimut Duve and Bill Jordan
    1998   'Perspectives on Human Rights', *World Affairs*, 2.4: 22-59.
Wang, Annie
    2001   *Lili: A Novel of Tiananmen* (New York: Pantheon).
Wang, Gungwu
    2001   'Europe's Heritage in Asia', in Chirathivat *et al.* (eds.) 2001: 17-27.
Weber, Eugen
    1999   *Apocalypses* (London: Hutchinson).
Weber, Maria
    1998   'China in Transition: The Changing Economic Scene', *World Affairs,* 2.1: 74-86.
Weggel, Oskar
    1994   *Die Asiaten* (Munich: dtv-Deutscher Taschenbuch-Verlag).

Weiss, Meredith L.
2000   'The 1999 Malaysian General Elections', *Asian Survey*, 40.3: 413-35.
Wiessala, Georg
1998   'Studies in European Integration on the Eve of the Millennium', *World Affairs*, 2.4: 124-36.
1999   'An Emerging Relationship? The European Union's New Asia Strategy', *World Affairs*, 3.1: 96-112.
2001   'The European Union, Human Rights and "Asian values"', *Journal of European Studies, Chulalongkorn University*, 9.1, January–June: 19-35.
Wilson, K. and J. van der Dussen (eds.)
1993   *The History of the Idea of Europe* (London: Routledge).
Wyatt, David K.
1984   *Thailand: A Short History* (New Haven: Yale University Press).
Xiao, Zhi Yue
1993   *The EC and China* (London: Butterworths).
Xu, Gang
1999   'The Aesthetic in Confucianism Examined from Three Viewpoints', *Journal of Chinese Philosophy,* 26.4: 425-44.
Yeo, Lay Hwee
2000   'ASEM: Looking Back, Looking Forward', *Contemporary Southeast Asia*, 22.1: 113-44.
Yahuda, Michael
1999   'China's Foreign Relations: The Long March Future Uncertain', *The China Quarterly,* 159, September: 650-59.
Zakaria, Fareed
1994   '"Culture is Destiny" A Conversation with Lee Kuan Yew', *Foreign Affairs,* 73.2: 109-26.
Zhu, Muzhi
1998   'A Knot to Be Untied: Differences on Human Rights between China and the West', *World Affairs*, 2.4: 36-44.

General Index

Index of Authors

UNIVERSITY ASSOCIATION FOR CONTEMPORARY EUROPEAN STUDIES
UACES Secretariat, King's College London, Strand, London WC2R 2LS, UK
Tel: +44 (0)20 7240 0206   Fax: +44 (0)20 7836 2350   Email: admin@uaces.org
www.uaces.org

UACES

University Association for Contemporary European Studies

The Association
- Brings together academics involved in researching Europe with representatives of government, industry and the media who are active in European affairs
- Primary organisation for British academics researching the European Union
- Over 600 individual and corporate members from Dept such as Politics, Law, Economics & European Studies, plus over 150 Graduate Students who join as Associate Members

Membership Benefits
- Individual Members eligible for special highly reduced fee for The Journal of Common Market Studies (JCMS)
- Regular Newsletter - events and developments of relevance to members
- Conferences - variety of themes, modestly priced, further reductions for members
- Publications, including the new series *Contemporary European Studies*, launched in 1998
- Research Network, and research conference
- Through the European Community Studies Association (ECSA), access to a larger world wide network
- Information Documentation & Resources eg: The Register of Courses in European Studies and the Register of Research into European Integration

Current Cost of Membership per annum
☞ Individual Members: £25.00   ☞ Associate (Student): £10.00   ☞ Corporate Members: £50.00

APPLICATION FOR MEMBERSHIP OF UACES
Please complete the appropriate details and return the entire form to the address above.

Last Name: _____ First Name: _____ Title (eg Mr): ___

Institution: _____

Faculty / Dept: _____

Institution Address: _____

_____

Work Tel No: _____ Work Fax No: _____

Home Tel No: _____ Home Fax No: _____

E-mail: _____

Address for correspondence if different: _____

_____

Where did you hear about UACES? _____

Signature and Date: _____

PTO TO COMPLETE PAYMENT DETAILS

PAYMENT DETERMS

PAYMENT DETAILS

☛ ## TO PAY BY CHEQUE*

I wish to pay my membership subscription by cheque. Please make cheques payable to UACES, not King's College.

Please find enclosed a cheque (in pounds sterling) for:
❏ £25 (Individual)   ❏ £10 (Associate - Student)   ❏ £50 (Corporate)

* Please Note: we are no longer able to accept Eurocheques

☛ ## TO PAY BY CREDIT/DEBIT CARD

I wish to pay my membership subscription by (mark appropriate box):
❏ Visa   ❏ Mastercard   ❏ Eurocard   ❏ Switch   ❏ Solo

I authorise you to debit my Account with the amount of (mark appropriate box):
❏ £25 (Individual)   ❏ £10 (Associate - Student)   ❏ £50 (Corporate)

Signature of cardholder: _____   Date: _____

My Card Number is: ☐☐☐☐ ☐☐☐☐ ☐☐☐☐ ☐☐☐☐ ☐☐☐☐

Cardholder's Name and Initials*:_____   Cardholder's Title* (eg Mr): _____
*As shown on the card

Expiry Date: ☐☐☐☐   Start Date (if present*): ☐☐☐☐   Issue No. (if present*): ☐
*Usually for Switch and Solo cards

Cardholder's address and postcode (if different from overleaf):
_____

☛ ## TO PAY BY STANDING ORDER* (UK Bank only)
*This option not available for Corporate or Associate (Student) members

Please complete the details below and return to UACES. We will process the membership application and then forward this authority to your bank. This authority is not a Direct Debit authority (ie we cannot take money out of your bank account without your permission).

To (insert your Bank Name) _____   at (insert your bank address)

_____

_____ (insert Post Code) _____, UK.

Please pay to Lloyds Bank, Pall Mall Branch, 8-10 Waterloo Place, London SW1Y 4BE, UK, in favour of UACES, Account No. 3781242, Sort-Code 30-00-08, on the (insert date, eg 1st) _____ day of (insert month, eg June) _____ , the sum of £25 (TWENTY FIVE POUNDS) and the same sum on the same date each year until countermanded.

Signature: _____   Date: _____
Name: _____
Address: _____
Account No.: _____   Sort-code: _____